Most Catholic priests would probably be disinclined to pay much notice to a work that was heavily dependent upon statistical data unless they themselves were statisticians or sociologists. Msgr. Rossetti's work, *Why Priests Are Happy*, should be the exception. This careful analysis of the attitudes, experiences, and factors that go into making priests happy is a wonderful example of how the sciences and the candid survey of priest respondents reveal the reasons why the Catholic priesthood remains among the happiest vocations to be studied—in spite of the challenges that we face in the current climate in today's society. It is refreshing and enlightening at the same time.

Most Rev. Wilton D. Gregory
Archbishop of Atlanta

This will be an important study for priests and all those involved in their formation and care.

Rev. Benedict J. Groeschel, C.F.R.
Author of *I Am With You Always*

At last some good news about priests! Rossetti's encouraging book not only draws on his own experience, but also on solid data to tell us that the vast majority of priests are happy men who love their jobs. This "very human portrait of very human men," while not ignoring some of the problems priests face, recognizes the spirituality that has a "direct and profound effect on their lives." A must-read for the laity, seminarians, priests, and especially bishops.

Cokie Roberts
Journalist and Author

Msgr. Stephen Rossetti's careful research dispels the myth that the priesthood is an unhappy and lonely life, demonstrating that the overwhelming majority of priests experience high levels of joy and satisfaction in their vocation. *Why Priests Are Happy* offers useful and sage advice to ensure the health and wellness of our present and future priests and provides an invaluable tool for those responsible for their formation. Indeed, all the faithful would benefit from reading it!

Msgr. Robert Panke
President
National Conference of Diocesan Vocation Directors

Msgr. Rossetti's book is a splendid synthesis of theory and practice. With elegance of style and economy of words, he presents the most authoritative account of the lived experience of priesthood since the groundbreaking work *The Catholic Priest in the United States: Psychological Investigations*. He presents the compelling evidence that priests are happy and well-adjusted because they like who they are, they like what they do, and they know whose they are. This book corrects the fallacy that priests are unhappy with the truth that can only come from painstaking research. As a seminary rector, I suggest this is a must-read for seminary formators and vocation directors.

Melvin C. Blanchette, S.S.
Rector
Theological College of the Catholic University of America

At long last, there exists a highly scientific and large-scale study from a well-respected expert on the challenges of the American priesthood that reveals a "secret" joy in the celibate priestly vocation of today! Msgr. Rossetti's scientific study confirms a current high level of priestly satisfaction, happiness, and psychological health in the Catholic priesthood precisely at a time when just the opposite is often perceived. At the same time, he sets forth a series of most helpful recommendations to strengthen the priesthood of our time.

Msgr. Peter J. Vaghi
Author of *The Commandments We Keep*

Why PRIESTS *are* HAPPY

A STUDY of the PSYCHOLOGICAL and SPIRITUAL HEALTH of PRIESTS

STEPHEN J. ROSSETTI

ave maria press AMP notre dame, indiana

Nihil Obstat: Rev. Darr F. Schoenhofen
Imprimatur: Most Rev. Robert J. Cunningham
          Bishop of the Diocese of Syracuse
          Given at Syracuse on February 1, 2011

Founded in 1865, Ave Maria Press is a ministry of the United States Province of Holy Cross.

www.avemariapress.com

ISBN-10 1-59471-274-3   ISBN-13 978-1-59471-274-6

Cover image © Fred de Noyette/Godong/Corbis.

Cover and text design by John R. Carson.

Printed and bound in the United States of America.

Library of Congress Cataloging-in-Publication Data
Rossetti, Stephen J., 1951-
  Why priests are happy : a study of the psychological and spiritual health of priests / Stephen J. Rossetti.
     p. cm.
  Includes bibliographical references (p.   ).
  ISBN-13: 978-1-59471-274-6 (pbk.)
  ISBN-10: 1-59471-274-3 (pbk.)
  1. Priests--Psychology. 2. Mental health--Religious aspects--Catholic Church. 3. Happiness--Religious aspects--Catholic Church. 4. Priests--Religious life. 5. Priesthood--Catholic Church. I. Title.
  BX1912.7.R67 2011
  253'.2088282090511--dc23
                          2011018170

With Gratitude to James V. Kimsey
Founding Chairman, America Online
for his personal interest in the welfare of our priests and his generous
support that made this research possible.

* * *

In Remembrance of Dean R. Hoge, PhD
Professor Emeritus, Catholic University of America
for a lifetime of research dedicated to helping the Church understand
and improve the lives of its clergy and people.

But it is necessary here below to understand properly the secret of the unfathomable joy which dwells in Jesus and which is special to Him. It is especially the Gospel of Saint John that lifts the veil. . . . If Jesus radiates such peace, such assurance, such happiness, such availability, it is by reason of the inexpressible love by which He knows that He is loved by His Father.

—Pope Paul VI, *Gaudete in Domino*

Contents

Illustrations

Figures

Tables

Foreword

I n their twenty-first-century form, scandals both reveal and conceal. They cast needed light on ugly secrets and often kick-start a process of reform, but they also obscure other important truths about the individuals or institutions whose reputations now lie in ruins. Politicians with a long record of public service, for instance, come to be remembered almost entirely for a sleazy encounter in an airport bathroom. Companies that helped build the global economy become defined by an oil spill, or by ill-advised loans. Athletes who once lifted the nation's spirits are written off as juicers and frauds.

A scandal, in other words, concentrates attention upon the least attractive aspect of whomever or whatever stands at its epicenter, exiling any other storyline to the shadows.

That, certainly, has been the trajectory of the sexual abuse crisis which has gripped the Catholic Church for the last decade. Revelations brought forward by victims, reporters, litigators and reformers forced the Church to confront an internal cancer, one which officialdom long sought to ignore, and, when that failed, to disguise. Yet the scandals have also created a terribly one-sided public narrative about the Catholic Church, and perhaps especially its priesthood. In the wake of the crisis, the conventional wisdom is that Catholicism is imploding—its priests demoralized, its bishops embattled and corrupt, its laity either jumping ship or simply going through the motions out of inertia. The overall impression is of an institution in decline, slouching toward oblivion.

No one, of course, should minimize the devastating impact of the sexual abuse crisis, nor the staggering number of people who have been deeply, in some cases irreversibly, scarred. Yet alongside and underneath the heartache, the embers still smolder of what has always drawn people to the Church. There's still extraordinary faith, energy, hope, and humor coursing through the Catholic bloodstream, even if all that usually flies below the media radar screen. In a word, there is tremendous residual health in the Church. For those who know the Church from the inside out, the untold story is that in most places and at most times, being

Catholic is still inspiring and uplifting, not to mention often a hell of a lot of fun.

Monsignor Stephen Rossetti offers a powerful contribution toward a more balanced appraisal of the state of the Catholic soul in this unique empirical study of American priests. By now, the Catholic priesthood is probably the most dissected and commented-upon occupational category in the country, yet Rossetti moves the conversation forward by doing something no one else ever seems to try: asking the priests themselves what they think.

At the big picture level, and contrary to what most people would presume, Rossetti's data show that priests in the United States are, by and large, remarkably content. They're far happier in their work than the typical American, less likely to be depressed or to suffer "burn-out," and largely at peace with the demands of the priestly life, including the requirement of lifelong celibacy.

Rossetti debunks a whole series of stereotypes:

- Although many observers assume that relationships between bishops and priests have been fatally ruptured, three-quarters of priests in the United States say they have a good relationship with their bishop and approve of his leadership.
- Many people presume that the sexual abuse crisis was caused in part by the celibacy requirement, assuming that it must breed an unhealthy degree of repression. In truth, Rossetti finds, a positive view of celibacy is strongly correlated with the psychological health of priests; the more content they are with celibacy, the better adjusted they're likely to be.
- In contrast to assumptions that priests are often lonely and struggle to form healthy friendships, Rossetti's data show that most priests have strong relationships both with other priests and with laity. In fact, the strength of a priest's human friendships turns out to be among the best predictors of the quality of his spiritual life.

Since these findings so flatly contradict the assumptions in the cultural air these days, one hopes they might prompt some soul-searching. The obvious question they beg is the following: What is it about Catholicism that fosters such striking happiness among its clergy, despite all the ways in which the Church, and in particular the priesthood, have taken a beating? (It is largely a self-inflicted beating, to be sure, but a beating nonetheless.)

The reminder of underlying Catholic health is probably the main take-away for the outside world. *Ad intra*, the great gift of Rossetti's book is that by clearing away the debris of myth and public prejudice, he helps the Church focus on the very real challenges facing the priesthood.

For instance, Rossetti's data confirms that newly ordained priests these days are at special risk. They're often terribly overworked, pushed into positions of leadership and administrative responsibility much more quickly than earlier generations of priests, and they're often forced to tackle those challenges largely on their own. They've embraced celibacy in a culture that tells them such a choice is at best odd, at worst inhuman or a smokescreen for sexual abnormality. Further, a strikingly larger share of these new priests comes from broken and dysfunctional family backgrounds. All that means newly ordained priests need some tender loving care from their bishops and their brothers in the priesthood, and it also implies that Catholics in the pews might do well to cut them a bit of a break.

On a related note, Rossetti confirms something about these younger priests which has been amply documented both empirically and anecdotally: They tend to be more conservative, or "evangelical," than the Vatican II generation which came before them. In itself, that doesn't create a challenge the Church hasn't seen before: just as the Vatican II cohort sometimes struggles to relate to more conservative parishioners and priests, the rising generation in the priesthood (and, for that matter, the episcopacy) sometimes runs afoul of the Church's liberal wing.

These tensions, however, are unfolding at a time when American Catholics are increasingly inclined to smuggle their political allegiances into the Church, seeing Catholic life as a terrain upon which interest-group battles are fought. Special efforts are required to promote a deeper spirituality of communion in the Church, a pastoral project in which all generations in the priesthood, and all the different tribes that dot the Catholic landscape, must be involved. (As a corollary, it won't do simply to demand that younger priests "lighten up." Everybody has to give a little; the Catholic Church is simply too big and too complex for anyone, ever, to live completely in the Church of his or her dreams.)

Perhaps the most jarring finding in Rossetti's data is this: Only 42 percent of American priests trust the Church to treat them fairly if accused of misconduct. That "credibility gap" points to arguably the central defect in how Catholic officialdom, both in the United States and in Rome, has responded to the sexual abuse crisis. The Church, in some ways, has lurched from a system that covered up crimes by priests to one which presumes them guilty until proven innocent. Procedures now too often fail to protect priests against false allegations, and sometimes neglect their right to due process. One could argue, and many analysts have, that the same underlying pattern runs through both imbalances—prioritizing the interests of the institution over the right to justice of the individuals who inhabit it. Over time, restoring a measure of balance to these procedures is a challenge to which Church leadership must return.

Rossetti ends with a series of recommendations to seminary and formation personnel, to bishops, and to priests. I earnestly hope that each group reads his guidance carefully. My only quibble is that Rossetti does not address another constituency that's arguably even more crucial for Catholic fortunes—the rest of us, i.e., the People of God.

If I were to offer a recommendation to rank and file Catholics based on Rossetti's data, it would boil down to this. The priests of this country obviously love serving you and ministering to you, because otherwise there's no way to explain why they're basically happy, in the teeth of a culture which constantly tells them they're not supposed to be. They love you; try to love them back.

John L. Allen Jr.

Acknowledgments

With heartfelt gratitude to John J. Convey, PhD, of the Catholic University of America for his generous and expert assistance with statistical aspects of this study. Many thanks to Daniel K. Lapsley, PhD, of the University of Notre Dame and again to Dr. Convey for their professional reviews of the manuscript. I am indebted to Colin Rhoades, research associate, who provided a great deal of technical assistance, particularly in the developmental stages of this research project. My thanks to Bishop Edward Burns who kindly assisted with the formation-related questions in the 2009 survey. There were a number of readers of the manuscript who were invaluable in providing important feedback: Msgr. Edward J. Arsenault; Rev. Melvin C. Blanchette, PhD; Msgr. Kevin W. Irwin, S.T.D.; Rev. Shawn McKnight; Msgr. Robert J. Panke; and Rev. David L. Toups, S.T.D. I am especially grateful to Msgr. Arsenault and staff of Saint Luke Institute for their ongoing support that made this research project possible. Many thanks to my editor Bob Hamma and all the kind people at Ave Maria Press who published my previous works and who believed in the importance of this study.

Introduction

Not long ago, I was called by a television producer who wanted to put together a television special investigating priesthood and depression. I asked him what the angle of the story would be, and he replied, "We want to investigate why so many priests are depressed." I responded, "Well, we have some priests who are, in fact, depressed. But I am not sure that the rate of depression in the priesthood is any higher, or any lower, than the general population." Since I never heard another word about it, I presume he eventually decided not to produce the program. But I found it interesting that he simply assumed that priests have a special problem with depression. It is likely that, after reading mountains of media stories on child sexual abuse in the priesthood, he presumed that priests must be depressed.

Similarly, I was in New Zealand giving a workshop, and one of the young priests pulled me aside. He told me that two young men in his hometown were seriously considering becoming priests. They shared their desire with other adults in the community, who were horrified at the idea and talked them out of it. These well-intentioned adults told them that priesthood was a sad and lonely existence. They did not want to see them enter such a negative and unsatisfying life.

Stories like these are legion today. In the wake of the child abuse crisis that appears to be encircling the globe, celibate priesthood is often assumed to be a sad and lonely life that attracts psychologically unhealthy men. Its seminary system and subsequent lifestyle are presumed to have a further deleterious effect on the health of the psyche. We read many stories and listen to individuals pointing to celibacy, seminaries, and priestly lifestyle as serious contributing causes to priestly pathology.

Elders in our society can remember a day, not so very long ago, when priesthood was thought to be a life almost devoid of human weakness. I well remember the first year of my priesthood when a little girl walked up to me and asked, in the presence of her mother and my older pastor who was eating breakfast, "Do priests go to the bathroom?" The mother turned red, and the pastor choked on his toast.

One can still see old movies portraying the seeming angelic life of priesthood like *The Bells of St. Mary's* (1945) and *Going My Way* (1944), with Bing Crosby playing the lead character of Fr. O'Malley. Both movies received a variety of Academy Awards and nominations including best actor and best picture. *The Bells of St. Mary's*, adjusting for inflation, is one of the largest grossing movies of all time, and *Going My Way* was the highest grossing picture of its year. With his velvet voice, Bing Crosby's Fr. O'Malley was an image of an idyllic priesthood.

Obviously, there has been a dramatic shift in the public image of priesthood in these sixty-five years. The image of priesthood has gone from angelic saint to despicable sinner.

In the end, these extreme public images do a disservice to the Church and to the priesthood. Most priests are neither angelic saints nor disturbed pedophiles. The image of the celibate priest remains, for the average person, something hard to comprehend. The priest works long hours for little pay. He spends his days serving the spiritual needs of others. He does so without the comfort of a wife or the natural joys of a family. And he serves a Church that, to the modern secular mind, seems antiquated and, to some, full of ancient superstitions that they profess to have grown beyond. The priest remains a mystery to society and one upon whom people are naturally given to project their own presumptions and misconceptions.

In the midst of such misunderstandings, the need for solid research and objective study is all the more important. It was St. Thomas Aquinas himself, the Angelic Doctor, who said, "Any truth, no matter by whom it is spoken, is from the Holy Spirit." This study is an attempt to break through the myth and the mystery to investigate a few basic truths about the priesthood. We begin this more balanced look at the priesthood through statistical research into its psychological and spiritual state. How well, or unwell, are our priests? Are they depressed, as the one television producer presumed?

The best place to investigate this reality is with the priests themselves. Instead of presuming what they must be like, based upon our own prejudices, we ought to go to the priests themselves. Instead of telling them how they are thinking and feeling, we ought to ask them directly. This book is a step in that direction. Two large-scale studies of priests were accomplished, the first in 2003 to 2004 using 1,242 priests (hereafter referred to as the 2004 study), and the second from 2008 to 2009 surveying 2,482 priests (hereafter referred to as the 2009 study).

These surveys allow us not only to take the psychological and spiritual temperature of our priests; they also allow us to investigate the likely factors that promote or detract from their health and wellness. Using the latest advanced statistical techniques in PASW 18 (Predictive Analytics SoftWare, SPSS), we were able to develop statistical models that predict much of what goes into making a healthy or unhealthy priest, psychologically and spiritually.

These models are important for screening, seminary formation, and the ongoing formation of our priests. Any individual responsible for priestly formation and indeed any priest himself will want to look at the findings in this unique study and apply them to his own life and ministry. They present an opportunity to enhance the wellness and welfare of the priesthood in general and for the individual priest in particular.

In the aggregation of these data, what emerges is a portrait of the priesthood today that often edifies, at times surprises, occasionally disappoints, and sometimes mystifies.

Ultimately, what surfaces is a very human portrait of some very human men. And yet they are imbued with a spirituality that has a direct and profound effect on their lives. *Priests are clearly, and really not surprisingly, normal men. And yet they are not. There is something more to their lives that sets them apart.* In this study we will often witness their humanity, and we will also see clear signs of their spiritual uniqueness.

This is perhaps their best witness and their best homily. What sets priests apart, and yet connects them to us all, gives witness to the truth of their message. The living witness of Christians has always been the scriptures most often read.

Thesis

1

Summary of Findings

This book primarily presents the findings of survey research completed in 2009 of 2,482 priests from twenty-three dioceses around the United States. It is supplemented by a previous research study completed in 2004 of 1,242 priests from sixteen dioceses. The focus of the studies was the psychological and spiritual health of Catholic priests in the United States.

One of the unique elements is that this large-scale study compared priests to norm samples of the general population using standardized psychological testing. In addition, using modern statistical techniques, this research was able to investigate statistically the elements that make a happy priest, what makes a priest think of leaving priesthood, and what are important parts of a priest's spiritual life.

Physical Health and Self-Care

A short section of the study was devoted to the physical health and self-care of priests. The findings showed that while most priests are good about taking the necessary time off for recreation and rejuvenation, more than a few do not. Moreover, there are a number who do not exercise and have health-related issues such as diabetes. Like their lay counterparts, a large percentage of priests is overweight or obese.

Similarly, a significant percentage deals with stress in unhealthy ways, such as eating and/or drinking excessively.

Even though priests are similar to lay males in society in terms of self-care, this does not mitigate the serious health implications of deficient physical self-care. For the physical welfare of our priests, beginning with their seminary formation, renewed emphasis on physical self-care such as diet, exercise, and regular physicals is needed. In addition, helping seminarians and priests cope with stress in more positive ways might prevent them from falling into more dysfunctional ways of dealing with the very real stresses of priestly life.

The Psychological Wellness of Priests

One of the central findings of the study was that the psychological health of priests tested as similar, indeed slightly better, than the psychological health of the laity. On standardized tests measuring such elements as depression, anxiety, and general psychological health, priests scored slightly better than their lay counterparts. Moreover, priests reported high rates of close friendships both with other priests and with laity. *Occasional intimations in the public forum that Catholic priests are either deficient in chaste intimate relationships or psychologically deficient were not borne out by these results. Priests held up very well in comparison to others.*

Similarly, a smaller percentage of priests versus their lay counterparts scored in a range suggestive of their having clinical syndromes. Nevertheless, priests hold a position of public leadership and public trust. So, having even a relatively small number of priests with psychological problems is a source of distress for some laity and a challenge for the Church as a whole. Just as one healthy priest can positively influence a large number of people, so can one unhealthy priest negatively influence a similarly large number of people.

Of all priests, younger priests reported the relatively highest level of coming from dysfunctional families as well as the relatively highest levels of childhood mental health problems. The current challenge of candidates with significant histories of childhood dysfunction coming forward to apply for priesthood has been witnessed to me many times by screening and formation personnel in today's Church. The findings in this study confirm that experience.

Given the increasing dysfunction of society with its breakdown of the nuclear family, this finding is understandable. Thus, it is not surprising that the youngest priests had higher current levels of anxiety and depression on the mental health test compared to the oldest of priests. Childhood dysfunction places a person at greater risk for having psychological problems in adulthood. *These, too, argue in favor of continuing efforts to screen rigorously candidates for the priesthood as well as making healing resources readily available for those in formation and in the early years of priesthood.*

Indeed, priests are not reticent to access voluntarily mental health services when needed. Almost half self-reported to have done so. This is one factor likely contributing to the better-than-average scores of the priest sample on the psychological tests.

There was a spike in the percentage of priests in their middle years experiencing childhood sexual problems. These priests were at greater risk of having sexual problems as adults. This could be one factor in explaining the spike in incidents of child sexual abuse by Catholic clergy in the 1970s and early 1980s reported by the John Jay College of Criminal Justice. The John Jay College conducted the "Nature and Scope" study of child sexual abuse in the priesthood for the US Bishops and its follow-up study on the "Causes and Context." The studies also found similar cohorts of priests who had elevated rates of child abuse perpetration around the same time frame.[1]

The John Jay study also suggested that the culture of the 1960s might have been a factor in the spike in incidents of abuse within the priesthood. Fortunately, these abuse rates are now dropping precipitously, probably due to a new culture of child abuse prevention in the society and in the Church. The US Bishops have instituted an increasingly comprehensive child-safe environment program that highlights increased education and awareness, greater vigilance, rapid civil reporting, and ongoing follow-up. Also, there is a more aggressive screening of candidates who present sexual problems. Some vocation directors have recently spoken to me privately of their successful attempts to do just that.

The findings in this book and those of the John Jay studies suggest that part of the original problem may have been taking in sexually unsuitable candidates who, when situated in a permissive societal and church environment that did not condemn and punish child sexual abuse, were at significant risk for abusive behavior. If substantiated, this strongly argues in favor of rigorous screening of candidates for the priesthood, especially in the area of their psychosexual history and overall psychosexual health. Candidates with seriously disturbed psychosexual histories ought not to be admitted as candidates for the priesthood. Moreover, it strongly argues in favor of the Church and society continuing their efforts in creating a child-safe environment.

Burnout and Priesthood

Like their better scores on standardized psychological tests, when given a standard burnout measure, priests in this large sample of 2,482 actually scored much less burned out than the laity. Thus, one cannot say that priests, as a group, are suffering from high rates of burnout. In fact, the opposite is true.

Nevertheless, priests were very concerned with their rising workload and a large percentage feels overwhelmed with it. Despite the fact that a large percentage of priests feels overwhelmed with their workload, their burnout scores were significantly lower than other norm samples of laity. How can we explain this seeming contradiction?

Burnout is not a measure of simply being burdened with too much work. While many priests are working very long hours on a regular basis, most are not becoming emotionally hardened and emotionally depleted. Rather, they feel a high sense of accomplishment and fulfillment.

Burnout is not a measure of how much work one has to do, but rather one's level of emotional exhaustion, depersonalization, and sense of personal accomplishment as a result of the workload. Despite being overwhelmed with work, priests are finding much satisfaction, nourishment, and self-fulfillment in their vocations. As a result, their burnout levels are lower than the general society.

Nevertheless, there was a small percentage that tested with high rates of burnout. Again, given the visibility and leadership positions of most priests, having only a few priests who are significantly burned out can create a serious problem not only for the priests themselves, but for the hundreds, perhaps thousands, of people whom they serve and for the diocese as a whole. *Diocesan leadership ought to find ways to identify and assist those priests who are burned out or, more important, on the road to burnout.* While excessive workloads do not automatically lead to burnout, common sense suggests that excessive working can make some people vulnerable to debilitated states, such as physical problems and/or burnout. As workload and stresses on priests continue to increase, these issues must become increasingly important to the Church.

Surprisingly, the ordination cohorts of priests among the most burned out on this inventory were the youngest priests, those ordained fewer than twenty years. One might have initially surmised that burnout scores would be low among the newly ordained and gradually increasing into middle age. However, this was not the case. The youngest priests scored as high if not higher than priests in their middle years.

In retrospect, this finding is not so surprising when one recognizes the challenges younger clergy face of adjusting to a celibate priestly lifestyle in a secular culture, increasing workload, fewer younger priests, and taking on significant responsibilities, such as being a pastor, at a very early age.

Moreover, the youngest priests reported higher levels of coming from a dysfunctional family and having childhood mental health problems. These positively correlated with higher burnout scores as an adult. In fact, having childhood mental health problems and coming from dysfunctional families were much stronger predictors of burnout scores than such typically cited factors as not taking time off every week or taking an annual vacation. When a man comes into priesthood with a dysfunctional background, he is more vulnerable to having problems as an adult, including becoming burned out.

Helping younger priests to manage their sometimes too busy lives and their adjustment to and mature integration of priesthood ought to be a focus of attention. This is especially critical for those younger priests who bring with them psychic wounds from childhood that have not been fully healed. Under the stress of a demanding priestly ministry, these may erupt into serious problems.

Happiness and Priesthood

A central finding of this study is the extraordinarily high rates of priestly happiness and satisfaction. The findings are strong, replicable, and consistent: priests, as a group, are very happy men. They like priesthood. They are committed to it. They find much satisfaction in their lives and ministries. In fact, the satisfaction rates of priests are among the highest of any way of life or vocation in the United States.

On standardized measures of happiness as well as direct survey responses, priests reported some of the highest satisfaction rates of any vocation/work in the country. These findings are consistently supported by other surveys and research studies. The undeniable truth is that the large majority of priests are very happy in their vocation and ministries. Priesthood time and again measures as one of the most satisfying and happiest of callings.

Given the sometimes negative portrayal of priesthood in the media and rumors to the contrary, the very high levels of happiness of our priests are counterintuitive to many, and one of the best-kept secrets in the United States. The happiness of priesthood ought to be made publicly known and kept a secret no longer.

While priestly happiness and morale rates are generally consistent over time, there was apparently a slight dip in morale in the wake of the sexual abuse crisis. But this dip appears to be fading. The public excoriation of the Church and priesthood during this time was painful for all priests, and to some extent, it continues. The fact that morale did not dip further is remarkable.

But when priests were asked about the morale of other priests, the results indicated that they perceived their brothers as having a lower morale than when they were asked about themselves. Every priest is acutely aware of the challenge and suffering of these days. Every priest has his own experiences of public humiliations and embarrassments. The priestly perception of a lower morale than actually is the case may be tied to this acute awareness of these sufferings and other challenges of priests today.[2]

But as one priest commented on his survey, "They're at their best under fire." One could argue that the crisis has actually strengthened priests and the priesthood. The recent slight but noticeable uptick in vocations in the United States is seemingly counterintuitive and may be yet another sign that the Church grows most when it suffers. As another priest wrote on his survey, concerning priestly morale, "It is no longer based on superficialities; it has had to go deeper."

Factors Contributing to Priestly Happiness

Another unique contribution of this study was its building of a statistical equation that predicted important constitutive elements of priestly happiness. What makes a happy priest? There were fourteen factors *14* found to be significant and accounting for almost half of what makes a happy priest.

The strongest predictor of priestly happiness was the priest's own sense of inner peace. Thus, priestly happiness is first and foremost affected by what the man himself brings to the priesthood. A man who is happy inside is likely to be a happy priest.

It was instructive to observe how important *spiritual* variables were for priestly happiness. Such realities as one's relationship to God, view of celibacy, religious obedience, and spiritual practices, such as spiritual reading, prayer, and reception of the Sacrament of Penance, all contributed directly and positively to the happiness of a priest. *Many priests wrote on their survey about the importance and satisfaction of celebrating the Eucharist and the other sacraments.* As Dean Hoge found in his 2001 survey of American priests, researching the sources of priestly satisfaction, "Clearly in first place is 'joy of administering the sacraments and presiding over liturgy.'"[3]

These findings highlight the interpenetration of spiritual and psychological realities. *They also highlight the fact that priesthood is a spiritual life. To be a happy priest necessarily includes having a strong relationship to God and daily nurturing that relationship with typical priestly spiritual practices.*

Nevertheless, it would be a mistake to overlook psychological realities. Priesthood is a challenging and demanding vocation. Priests who came from dysfunctional backgrounds, had childhood mental health problems, anger problems, sexual conflicts, narcissistic traits, and other mental health challenges were less likely to be happy men. We overlook these factors to the detriment of the individual and of the priesthood at large.

It was interesting how important a priest's sense of his own commitment to celibacy was for his happiness. More than viewing celibacy simply as a necessary part of one's priesthood, when a priest integrates his celibacy as a calling from God that has been a personal grace despite its challenges, he is much more likely to be a happy priest.

Also, a priest's relationship to his bishop was critical. A priest who reported a good relationship to his bishop was much more likely to be a happy priest. The relationship between priest and bishop is a deep theological reality. Catholic theology speaks of the bishop as father, brother, friend, and coworker to his priests.[4] Fortunately, the findings showed that the relationship between bishops and priests is strong. Over three-fourths of priests reported having a good relationship with their individual bishops and approved of their leadership.

As Pope John Paul II noted, the priest is a "man of communion." Thus, priesthood is necessarily a relational life. It requires certain important psychological strengths, including the ability to build and sustain solid relationships with others. Building such relationships with God and others, including priests and laity, is a constitutive element of priestly life and spirituality. Relationships are essential to building a happy and effective priesthood.

One of the themes that emerged from just about every section in this study is that priests who live their priestly lives and spirituality with integrity are likely to be happier priests. If one were to list integral aspects of the life and spirituality of a priest, they would be significant elements for what makes a happy priest.

Those Thinking of Leaving Priesthood

The study investigated those who were thinking of leaving the priesthood. The percentage of priests considering leaving is low and has been declining over recent years. Given the very high satisfaction rates reported by priests, this is expected. The group that is most at risk for considering leaving is younger priests, especially those ordained less than twenty years. As a group, they may need increased support and assistance.

Some of the strongest predictors of priests thinking of leaving are *psychological* variables including measures of burnout and psychopathology. Priests who score higher on burnout measures and measures of depression and anxiety are more likely to think of leaving priesthood. This highlights the need for extra vigilance in assisting priests who show early signs of burnout and also priests who exhibit symptoms of anxiety and depression.

Similarly, a childhood history of psychological problems and seriously dysfunctional backgrounds are also predictors of a priest considering leaving priesthood. These research findings offer particular caution when considering applicants for the priesthood with seriously dysfunctional childhoods. They may not have the capacity to live decades in a stressful and demanding priestly ministry.

Nevertheless, spiritual values cannot be overlooked. Such variables as relationship to God, one's bishop, and Mary plus spiritual practices such as private prayer and receiving the Sacrament of Penance, were all significantly and negatively correlated with a priest thinking of leaving. As a priest's spiritual life deteriorates, or was never properly formed in the first place, he is increasingly at risk for leaving the priesthood. This research demonstrated the importance of a priest's spiritual life for his well-being and happiness. Here we see what happens if he is not living a spiritual life sufficient to nourish his priesthood. He will very likely consider leaving the priesthood.

Thus, when a priest is thinking of leaving the priesthood, he is advised to look more deeply at his life and priesthood. His desire to leave may not simply be dissatisfaction with celibacy or another particular aspect of priesthood. For example, a burned-out, depressed priest will consider leaving the priesthood. Also, priests who carry a significant amount of childhood psychological "baggage" are likewise at risk for leaving. When a priest thinks of leaving, it is likely a complex dynamic and may include underlying psychological challenges that first need to be addressed. Obviously, marriage or other such individual "fixes" do not address such problems. *A "crisis of celibacy" may be a symptom rather than a cause.*

Before a priest decides to leave priesthood, he should take a good look at his inner psychological and spiritual life. He ought to check to see if the source of his dissatisfaction is actually within, just as the first source of a priest's satisfaction was found, in an earlier chapter, to be within as well.

The Spiritual Lives of Priests

A strong source of priestly joy is the dynamic spiritual relationship priests have with God. Almost unanimously, they reported feeling a sense of closeness to God, that God loves them personally. They feel a joy from God and that their relationship to God is nourishing for them. *Since the correlation between their relationship to God and their personal happiness was so high, it is more than likely that this strong relationship to God is a major source of happiness for priests.*

The research findings here confirmed previous studies that found a positive correlation between one's spiritual life and one's mental health and well-being. *Again, given the strong spiritual lives of priests, this is likely another reason for their enhanced mental health scores and their strong sense of satisfaction and well-being.*

Another statistical equation was constructed that found thirteen factors that were strongly predictive of a priest's relationship to God. What helps to build a strong relationship to God for our priests? A very interesting finding is that the composite variable Close Friends was the strongest predictor of one's Relationship to God. This gives statistical support to the New Testament teaching of the importance of loving God and neighbor. Love of neighbor is strongly predictive of love of God. The findings of this study suggest that if one wishes to be closer to God, one might start with improving one's relationships with others.

The research confirmed the importance of a number of traditional aspects to the spiritual lives of priests such as devotion to Mary, theological and spiritual reading, private prayer, Sacrament of Penance, Liturgy of the Hours, obedience to religious authority, and attending priest gatherings. All of these common elements of priestly spirituality correlated significantly with a priest's relationship to God. *In addition, one of the most common comments made by priests was the centrality of the Eucharist and other sacraments in their lives.* Once again, the research confirms the importance of living one's priestly life with a full integrity, embracing priesthood as it is meant to be lived. Throughout this study, it continues to surface that when a priest lives his life with integrity, he is a happier and more fulfilled priest.

In particular, it is interesting how a devotion to Mary so strongly predicted a priest's relationship to God. In the wake of the Second Vatican Council, there were places in which this traditional devotion was downplayed. However, rather than detracting from one's relationship to God, the statistics here suggest the opposite is true. As one's devotion to Mary increases, one's reported relationship to God improves. In fact, the strong majority of priests in this survey professed a personal devotion to Mary and affirmed that she is an important part of their lives. There is probably more of a devotion to her in the priesthood currently than is publicly known.

Also, it is instructive that the relationships with one's mother and father are important predictors of one's relationship to God. Relationship with mother was more highly predictive, but both were statistically significant. This suggests that parents teach their children about God and faith in many ways, not the least being in the quality of their own relationship with their children. When mother and father both develop a good relationship with their children, this itself is formative of their children's future relationship to God.

It might be useful also to highlight the importance for priests of attending priest gatherings. Its correlation with a priest's Relationship with God was strong. For a priest to connect and be part of the presbyterate is not something peripheral to the priesthood. The priest is ordained into a community, and an essential part of his spiritual life is this sacramental bond he shares with his bishop and brother priests. Nurturing these relationships nurtures his own priesthood and contributes significantly to his overall spiritual life.

Throughout the study, despite the overall very positive findings of the study for the priesthood, areas of needed attention surfaced. For example, while the large majority of priests were diligent in their spiritual practices, there remained a minority who were not. For example, some (11%) did not receive the Sacrament of Penance even yearly. Some (19%) were engaged in only a minimum of daily private prayer, less than fifteen minutes. Only 58% said they prayed most or all of the Liturgy of the Hours daily. Some did not regularly go to priest gatherings (20%), and a few (9%) rarely went on an annual retreat. It would be unreasonable to expect 100% in such matters where human beings are involved, but a high percentage is a goal for which the presbyterate as a whole ought to strive. The findings of this study suggest that making improvement in this goal would be a grace for the entire priesthood and for the individual priests themselves.

Priests and Prayer

A separate chapter of the study was devoted to the private prayer lives of priests. The chapter demonstrated the broad positive effects of prayer in a priest's life. As the priest's time in private prayer increased, he was less emotionally exhausted, less depressed, less lonely, less likely to be obese, better able to deal with stress, had an increased sense of inner peace, reported being happier as a priest, and had a stronger relationship to God.

Spending time in private prayer also correlated positively with a number of beneficial results. Private prayer time positively related to better mental health scores, decreased burnout scores especially emotional exhaustion, increased priestly happiness, and a reported stronger relationship to God. As prayer time increased, these variables largely improved in an arithmetic line upward. This suggests that as a priest's time in private prayer increases, each of these variables will likely steadily increase.

The study continued to affirm the direct connection between psychological and spiritual health. In this case, as one's spiritual practices are stronger, there is a likely concomitant increase in psychological health.

Conversely, those who stopped praying privately were more prone to burnout and thinking of leaving the priesthood. They reported much lower happiness rates as priests.

Some of the more interesting findings concerned obesity and loneliness. As their time in daily private prayer increased, priests were less likely to be obese and they were less likely to report feeling lonely. While correlation does not prove causation, private prayer was correlated with a number of factors that would help to explain these results.

The improvements in these variables continued up to spending one hour daily in private prayer. Beyond this point, the survey did not examine.

Young Priests, Old Priests, and Those in the Middle

The study compared younger priests to those in the middle and to the oldest of priests (pre–Vatican II priests). It has been speculated that our youngest priests resemble pre–Vatican II priests or their "grandfathers" in the priesthood regarding their theological stance. In many traditional aspects of priesthood this is true.

The U-shaped curves in this study, with the youngest and oldest priests looking similar, were consistent and remarkable. For example, the youngest priests looked like their "grandfathers" in priesthood in support for a number of traditional priestly values such as devotion to Mary, use of private prayer and the Sacrament of Penance, view of celibacy, relationship to the bishop, and valuing religious obedience.

For all cohorts of priests, the large majority reported personally experiencing celibacy in a positive way, despite its challenges. The idea that celibacy is an onerous burden, which most priests would willingly discard if given the chance, is not accurate. Nevertheless, there is a minority, but a significant number, who do experience celibacy in a negative way, and these individuals might benefit from additional support and assistance.

The support for mandatory celibacy among priests appears to be rising. One of the important reasons for this is its very strong support among the newly ordained. These young priests more closely resemble their "grandfathers" in the priesthood in support for mandatory celibacy, and the newest ordained actually support it even more strongly. As one young priest wrote on his survey, "Celibacy impresses on me what my vocation is." If these current trends continue, mandatory celibacy is likely to decrease, if not largely disappear, as a "hot button" issue among priests in this country.

There appear to be some priests in the middle years who are feeling "left behind." As one priest wrote on his survey, "I feel as if I live in a bubble of time that is passing, and that the future leadership of the Church is moving retrograde to my orientation and formation." While the larger trends cannot, and arguably should not, be altered, it would be important that the concerns of these "middle priests" be heard and that they feel as fully incorporated into the current presbyterate as possible. The good of the unity of the presbyterate calls for it. While all priests invariably feel more or less included in the Church given passing trends and leadership changes, the unity of the presbyterate ought to be one of the enduring foundations of Church stability. Whether a priest feels in or out ought not to deter him from counting himself, and being counted by others, fully and completely as one of the brothers in the priesthood.

In this study as a whole, there was an emerging trend of priests becoming slightly even more positive toward all aspects of priesthood and Church from 2004 to 2009. This could be due, in part, to increasing distance from the trauma of the 2002 public sex abuse scandals, but also due to the new cohort of a younger, more positive group of priests.

Like all priestly cohorts, the "New Priests" are also men of their time, appropriately so, and thus they are different. They are sometimes called "Evangelical Priests" because of their evangelical fervor and their professing a clear and separate identity as Catholics and as priests. This fervor for evangelization is arguably needed in our secular world. They might indeed be the right priests to engage in the new evangelization called for by Pope Benedict XVI. They profess to be proud to be priests today and strongly claim to encourage other men to become priests. They strongly hold and give witness to their Catholic identity.

Nevertheless, like all priestly cohorts before them, they too need good formation as seminarians and strong ongoing formation and support as young priests. Despite being theologically similar to their "grandfathers" in the priesthood, they are not simply returning to a previous age. They, like all cohorts of priests, are men of their time. In their case, their laudable evangelical fervor must also be tempered with pastoral sensitivity and compassion. They need older priests to teach them how to become compassionate shepherds of souls.

Dolon 19

Moreover, previous sections of the study have shown that our youngest priests come at a greater rate from dysfunctional backgrounds with childhood mental health problems. Thus, in their first years of priesthood, these priests have higher rates of depression, anxiety, and burnout. They also need the mentoring and assistance of older priests to learn how to survive and thrive in a lifetime of demanding service.

Our new priests are entering a demanding and challenging vocation in a Church and a world that are much different than the ones their "grandfathers" entered. These new priests will need their strong prayer life, their firm adherence to Catholic identity and values, and the help of their older brothers in the priesthood to do the Lord's work faithfully and gracefully.

The "Secret" Joy of Priesthood

Not too long ago, one newspaper reported, "In the wake of one scandal after another, the image of the genial, saintly cleric has given way to that of a lonely, dispirited figure living an unhealthy life that breeds sexual deviation."[5] The facts in this study dispel such erroneous presumptions. Just the opposite is true.

Priesthood consistently measures as perhaps the most fulfilling and satisfying vocation of any. Priests reported levels of happiness that are remarkably high and consistent across many studies. Moreover, priests, by and large, are not lonely. They live in an intimate communion of relationships with other priests and laity. Nor are their lives unhealthy; they are much less burned out, more satisfied, and less psychologically impaired than their lay counterparts.

Most importantly, all of these "secrets" of priesthood must be considered secondary to the greatest "secret" of a priest's life and the source of his joy. Again and again, these findings highlighted the centrality of the priest's spiritual life for his inner peace, well-being, and personal joy. For this reason, a quotation from Paul VI was chosen as the epigraph for this work:

> But it is necessary here below to understand properly
> the secret of the unfathomable joy which dwells in Jesus

and which is special to Him. It is especially the Gospel of Saint John that lifts the veil. . . . If Jesus radiates such peace, such assurance, such happiness, such availability, it is by reason of the inexpressible love by which He knows that He is loved by His Father. (*Gaudete in Domino*)

This love remains the bedrock and treasure of our priests' lives and explains much of the astounding findings contained in these pages.

2

Two Statistical Surveys: The Sample and the Method

The 2004 Survey

Two separate surveys of priests were accomplished. The first written survey of three pages was accomplished by 1,242 priests from 2003 to 2004, herein named the 2004 study. This was distributed shortly after the 2002 child sexual abuse crisis in the United States. This crisis profoundly affected the priests of this country. One could not pick a time to take priests' psychological and spiritual "temperature" that was more replete with turmoil and distress. We will see some of the effects of this crisis in their responses, and, at the same time, some of the results will be all the more surprising.

The priests surveyed in the 2004 study came from sixteen dioceses across the United States, including the Northeast, Southeast, Midwest, West, Southwest, Northwest, and West Coast. The first nine dioceses were chosen because I was at their annual convocations for all priests, secular and religious, serving in the diocese. The surveys were handed out in advance of the presentations. The next seven dioceses volunteered to be part of the study, in order to receive feedback on the state of their priesthood. The surveys were mailed out by these seven dioceses to every priest under its jurisdiction, religious and secular. The surveys for all participants were anonymous and confidential.

The sixteen dioceses included in the study were spread out across the United States. While maintaining their confidentiality, two were larger archdioceses, most were middle-sized dioceses, and a few were smaller, rural dioceses. Some were especially hard hit by the 2002 sexual abuse crisis while others less so. It should be noted that this was not a random sample but rather an opportunity sample. Nevertheless, the dioceses included were not atypical and, overall, I believe them to be representative of dioceses in the United States.

Table 2.1 gives us a breakdown of the sample based upon years ordained. We see the sample relatively evenly distributed across ordination cohorts.

The mean response rate was 64.9%. Diocesan priests numbered 1,054 and religious priests were 188 for a total of 1,242 respondents. While a mean response rate of 64.9% for a survey is excellent, caution should be exercised since 35.1% did not respond. There is nothing that one can say with certainty about those who did not respond except to say they did not respond. As with any survey, it is helpful to compare the results of this study with other studies to see if there are similar findings. This confirmation will give further credence to my results. Such comparisons are given in several places in this book.

Table 2.1. 2004 sample by years ordained

Number of years as a priest	Frequency	Percent	Valid percent
Valid			
1–9	201	16.2	16.2
10–19	216	17.4	17.4
20–29	264	21.3	21.3
30–39	282	22.7	22.7
40–49	200	16.1	16.1
50 and above	78	6.3	6.3
Total	1241	99.9	100.0
Missing	1	.1	
Total	1242	100.0	

However, given the large sample size, its being spread across the United States, and the strong response rate, the 2004 survey should have some important things to say about the state of the priesthood in the United States, especially during that difficult time.

The survey items were either Likert scales (strongly disagree, disagree, unsure, agree, strongly agree) or fill-in-the-blank questions. They covered a variety of topics such as morale, satisfaction, spiritual practices, and time-off habits (see Appendix 1 for a complete copy of the written survey).

The 2009 Survey

The second survey was longer and larger. There were 2,482 priests surveyed from twenty-three dioceses around the United States in 2008 to 2009, named here the 2009 survey. Dioceses around the country, through their vicar for clergy offices, were given a chance to volunteer to be a part of the study, and twenty-three requested to be included. Only two of the dioceses in the 2004 sample were repeated in the 2009 sample.

Once again, this was not a random sample. However, the dioceses surveyed were spread across the United States from East Coast to West Coast and from North to South. There was no major region of the continental United States that was omitted. Again, there were several larger dioceses including five archdioceses, and some small rural dioceses, with most being moderate-sized dioceses from different states around the country. Again, the dioceses included are not atypical of those around the United States, and I believe they are largely representative of all the dioceses. The individual participants were assured of and given anonymity and confidentiality. The participating dioceses were also afforded confidentiality.

The written six-page surveys were mailed out by the respective dioceses largely either via the postal service or electronic email; most dioceses mailed reminders to all. The mean response rate was 57%. They included 2,145 diocesan priests and 337 religious priests serving in these dioceses. Once again, the 57% response rate is excellent, but it is not 100%; 43% failed to respond presumably for a variety of reasons. Thus, as with any survey research, caution is always advised when interpreting the findings, and it is important to look for similar research that may or may not support one's findings. When possible, such similar research will be cited in this book.

This larger 2009 survey also used Likert scales plus yes/no questions. It included standard psychological tests, satisfaction scales, childhood and developmental experiences, spiritual practices, attitudes toward a number of current issues in priesthood, and the like (see Appendix 2 for the complete survey).

The 2009 sample by years ordained is found in table 2.2.

The sample is fairly well distributed over the entire range of ordination cohorts from the youngest group, 0–10 years ordained, to the oldest, more than 50 years ordained. There were fourteen priests in the sample who did not indicate how many years they had been ordained.

This second survey in 2009 forms the core of this book since it is the larger, more recent, and more comprehensive of the two studies. Findings from the first 2004 survey were used in this report as verification of the findings of the second 2009 study and to add additional information not covered in the second survey. All of the statistics cited in this book are from the 2009 study unless otherwise noted.

Table 2.2. 2009 sample by years ordained

Number of years as a priest	Frequency	Percent	Valid percent
Valid			
0–10	356	14.3	14.4
11–20	330	13.3	13.4
21–30	372	15.0	15.1
31–40	565	22.8	22.9
41–50	511	20.6	20.7
More than 50	334	13.5	13.5
Total	2468	99.4	100.0
Missing	14	.6	
Total	2482	100.0	

The Method

The statistical package used, as noted previously, was the PASW 18 (Predictive Analytics SoftWare, SPSS). In the 2009 study, a principal components analysis and factor analyses were performed on the survey items. The factor analyses used two different extraction methods: maximum likelihood and principal axis. These analyses were done so that individual survey items could be combined to form stronger composite variables. When several items that load strongly on one factor are combined, the resulting composite variable is much more likely to measure what it purports to measure and to do so with greater psychometric accuracy. Factor analyses were done separately on the Likert scaled questions and the yes/no questions, since it is advisable not to combine such differently scored items into a single variable.

Items were combined into composite variables based upon these factor analyses and researcher judgment based upon their theological and psychological face validity of fitting together. For example, the two items: "I have a good relationship with my bishop," and "I support my bishop's leadership," both loaded highly on the same factor and obviously fit together as well. They were combined to form a new variable named Relationship to Bishop. For a list of the new composite variables, see Appendix 3.

A variety of statistical comparison techniques were used, based upon the type of data and the desired output. Pearson's r correlations were computed to determine if two continuous variables were related. ANOVAs or analyses of variance were computed when comparing means of several groups while a T test compared the means of only two groups. If an ANOVA was found to be significant, the conservative Scheffe post-hoc test was usually computed to see which specific group means were significantly different. (The Scheffe was used since the sample sizes were not identical.)

When trying to understand what variables predict an important dependent variable, a multiple regression (MR) equation was used. For example, a number of variables were regressed on the composite variable Priestly Happiness to determine some of the important variables that are part of a happy priesthood.

A significant factor influencing the results of the multiple regression equations was multicollinearity. That is, many of the dependent variables entered into the multiple regression equation were highly correlated with each other. Thus, as the first few variables are entered into the *MR* equation, other variables will find the strength and significance of their contribution to be diminished since part of the variance the latter variable would be contributing has already been accounted for by a previously entered variable. Thus, when interpreting the *MR* results, one should take into account this strongly interrelated set of variables or multicollinearity. This will be noted in key areas in the book.

For those not acquainted with statistical techniques, I attempted to write the book in a more easily accessible style. The results should be readily understood without needing to delve into the statistical underpinnings. For those acquainted with statistical techniques, the book should give enough specifics so that these readers can understand how the conclusions were statistically supported as well as providing other statistical nuances.

Survey instruments in general have obvious limitations. Participation is never 100%. One cannot know with certainty why some chose not to participate. But it is likely they did so for a wide variety of reasons, depending upon the individual. It is always possible that the actual sample available is not completely representative of the whole. Nonetheless, the relatively large size of the sample compared to the numbers of priests in the Catholic Church in the United States, the wide variety of dioceses sampled across all regions of the United States, and the rather high response rate compared to comparable social science research, suggest that the data should reveal important information about priests in the United States.

Written surveys also are limited in the depth of the data that they communicate. They do not tell us deeper reasons why respondents chose to answer a particular question in one way rather than another. For example, if one priest says that his morale is good, this might mean something very different to a second priest using the same word, good, to describe his morale. They might mean two different things using the same answer.

Similarly, care should be taken when interpreting correlations in social science research. It is important to distinguish the difference between correlation and causation. For example, whenever my mother, a nervous flyer, is flying in an airliner and the plane starts to take off, she holds her breath and grips the armrest with a death-grip. Every time she has done this, the plane has successfully taken off. Therefore one might erroneously conclude that holding one's breath and gripping the armrest tightly ensures a successful takeoff. The correlation is a perfect 1.0. When told this, my brother, an airline pilot, commented, "I find it much more helpful to pull back on the yoke." Correlation does not prove causation (but it should be added that correlation is a necessary condition for causation).

Our experience and our psychological and theological background will be necessary to help us understand the meaning of the correlations in this study. Of course, the data presented herein are open to other interpretations, such as the reader might have.

Despite such limitations, these surveys can begin to give us some concrete, objective, and quantifiable measurement about the wellness and attitudes of Catholic priests today. Moreover, because the 2009 sample of priests was given standardized psychological tests, we can actually compare the responses of our priests to those of a sample of the general population throughout the United States. This will be one of the first times a large-scale study of American priests has statistically compared priests to the general population of Americans using quantitative norms. Are priests less or more psychologically well than their lay counterparts? Are they less or more happy in their work? Are they truly more depressed than others, as the TV producer assumed?

These are the types of questions this study can begin to answer with some confidence. Hopefully, this will move us one step beyond relying only on individual judgment, which is easily contaminated by one's preconceived notions, personal biases, and psychic projections. Our first goal will be to let the numbers speak for themselves and to listen intently to their message. Then we can begin to build a more accurate portrait of the Catholic priest today.

3

Physical Health and Self-Care

Time Off

While the focus of this study was on psychological and spiritual health, a few questions were asked on both surveys regarding physical health and self-care. For example, in the 2009 survey, priests were asked about taking time off. As we see in table 3.1, 77% take a weekly day off almost all the time or usually and 86.6% take an annual vacation almost all the time or usually.

A composite variable called Time Off was formed of these two variables and correlated with the other variables (see Appendix 3). Time Off correlated mostly strongly with three variables: (1) the composite variable Close Friends, (2) the BSI-18 SOM scale (the somatization scale of

Table 3.1. Weekly day off and annual vacation

	Almost all the time (%)	Usually (%)	Sometimes (%)	Rarely (%)	Almost never (%)
"I take a day off per week"	53.4	23.6	12.8	6.5	3.7
"I take an annual vacation"	67.8	18.8	8.1	2.9	2.3

the Brief Symptom Inventory 18), and (3) the Maslach Burnout Inventory scale Personal Accomplishment.[1]

Thus, those who did not take time off were less likely to have close friends (r=.19, p<.001). This makes sense since those who do not take time off do not have time to cultivate and maintain friendships. Overworking tends to isolate people from important social and personal supports. Conversely, it is likely that those without close friends are less likely to be motivated to take a day off to spend it with friends. It can become a reinforcing downward spiral: overworking leads to fewer friendships which then gives less of a reason to take time off, and so forth.

Also, Time Off was negatively correlated with the BSI-18 SOM scale (r= -.11, p<.001). Since the correlation was negative, as one variable increases, the other decreases. Those who did not take time off were more likely to report having somatic problems possibly related to psychological difficulties such as faintness, dizziness, trouble catching one's breath, chest pains, nausea, numbness or tingling, or body weakness. Without proper rest, the body is more likely to react and develop negative physical symptoms.

Similarly, Time Off was positively correlated with the Personal Accomplishment scale of the Maslach Burnout Inventory (r=.11, p<.001). Those who took less time off were less likely to feel a sense of personal accomplishment! They are less likely to feel they are making a difference in people's lives, less likely to feel energetic, and less likely to feel they are accomplishing worthwhile things. Working without a break does not necessarily result in feeling successful. Some may actually feel driven to work harder and harder and paradoxically feeling increasingly less effective. And conversely, those who have a diminished sense of accomplishment may feel driven to work harder and not take the necessary time off.

There were no significant differences among ordination cohorts of priests regarding taking time off, either a day off per week or an annual vacation. The different ordination age groups of priests were statistically the same.

The results suggest that those who do not take time off tend to be more emotionally isolated, suffer more psychosomatic problems, and paradoxically feel less successful in their work. Taking regular time off gives a priest a chance to reenergize and to step back and take a healthier view of his ministry. It allows time to connect with friends. Time off is good for the body as well, giving it a chance to relax and to let go of the daily stresses.

Fortunately, most priests, about three-fourths, do regularly take time off. But a good one-fourth regularly do not. Given the possible negative consequences, the latter might be encouraged to reflect upon their balance of work and rest.

Weight and Exercise

The 2009 survey asked priests if they engage in physical exercise (see table 3.2).

Thus, 58.3% of priests say that they exercise on a regular basis, either agreeing or strongly agreeing, and sadly about 24.2% do not, that is, about one-fourth of priests.

When we look at priests' Body Mass Index (BMI)[2], which is a standard measure relating height to weight, the 2009 results are in table 3.3.

These are obviously not good results. Fully 29.7% of priests are actually labeled by the BMI as being obese. The mean BMI for the entire sample of 2,482 priests is 28.5, which is in the upper range of being overweight. In 2002, the Center for Disease Control and Prevention (CDC) reported the average BMI for males and females in the United States was 28.[3] Similarly, about one-third of Americans are considered to be obese, which is slightly higher than the figure for priests in our sample, which was 29.7%.[4] So, our priest sample, while too many being very overweight, was typical of adult American males.

Table 3.2. Regular exercise

	Strongly agree (%)	Agree (%)	Neutral (%)	Disagree (%)	Strongly disagree (%)
"I exercise on a regular basis"	21.5	36.8	17.4	20.5	3.7

Table 3.3. Body mass index

	Underweight (%)	Normal weight (%)	Overweight (%)	Obese (%)	Morbidly obese (%)
Body mass index (BMI)	.4	23.8	46.0	26.3	3.4

It ought to be noted that priests were asked if obesity was a problem for them, and only 21.8% agreed versus the 29.7% that actually tested as obese. Therefore, we have 7.9% of priests whom the BMI labels as obese but did not indicate an awareness of it.

Nevertheless, as is well known, obesity tends to shorten one's life through increased blood pressure and cholesterol, and a greater incidence of diabetes. This increases the risk of heart disease, stroke, and other related illnesses.

Similarly, 14.8% of priests said they currently suffer from diabetes. There were 186 priests, or 7.5% of the total sample who were both obese and had diabetes. We have a large percentage of priests who are overweight to the point of being obese, many of whom are not exercising, and a significant percentage have diabetes as well.

Moreover, 24.4% of the entire sample admitted they have unhealthy ways of coping with stress through excessive food or alcohol consumption. When asked when their last medical checkup was, 9.3% report that it had been three years or longer since their last exam.

Obesity and Unhealthy Coping

Based on the factor analyses, a composite variable called Obesity and Unhealthy Coping was constructed using the following three survey items: "I exercise on a regular basis"; "Obesity is a problem for me"; and "I have some unhealthy ways of coping with stress (such as excessive food or alcohol)" (Appendix 3). Correlations were computed with the other composite variables with interesting results (Appendix 4).

Obesity and Unhealthy Coping correlated most strongly with the variables Lonely and Unappreciated (r=.32, p<.001), Inner Peace (r= -.32, p<.001), Anger Problems (r=.26, p<.001), and Dysfunctional

Childhood (r=.25, p<.001). Also, a correlation was run with the BSI-18 GSI (Brief Symptom Inventory 18, Global Severity Index) and the resulting r=.26, p<.001. Thus, those who have unhealthy ways of coping with stress, do not exercise, and are overweight are more likely to feel lonely and unappreciated, lack inner peace and self-esteem, have anger problems, and come from dysfunctional childhoods.

For those priests struggling with obesity and unhealthy responses to stress, these results suggest that it is possible that, for some, these are behavioral manifestations of underlying residual childhood psychological problems. As I have sometimes said upon the conclusion of an assessment week in our psychological treatment program where I ministered, "This priest is eating his problems." That is, he is suffering from a variety of psychological problems and his way of dealing with them is excessive eating.

To deal with the problems of obesity in the priesthood, and I suspect in the general population, some individuals will benefit simply from a healthy regimen of diet and exercise. But for others, their obesity is likely a symptom of inner problems that need to be addressed in a suitable setting.

Obesity and Prayer

An interesting finding that surfaced in this study is the correlation between private prayer and obesity. The two items, the BMI and the survey item asking about one's time in private prayer, have a statistically significant, negative correlation: r= -.12 with p<.001. Figure 3.1 visually demonstrates the point.

Again, we are reminded that correlation does not mean causation. Spending time in private prayer does not directly cause one to lose weight (unless, of course, this means one spends less time eating!). However, the results give one pause. For example, priests who do not pray daily have a mean BMI value in the obese range (30 or above). On the other hand, priests who pray more than sixty minutes a day had an average BMI in the overweight range; their mean value was a full three points lower. The ANOVA indicated a statistically significant difference between these groups with F=10.039, p<.001.

Some further correlations might help us make sense of this finding. For example, the survey item on time spent in private prayer is negatively correlated with the survey item "I have some unhealthy ways of coping with stress (such as excessive food or alcohol)" with $r= -.20$, $p<.001$. Thus, those who pray are more likely able to deal with stress better, rather than through excessive eating or drinking.

Similarly, those who engaged in daily private prayer were less likely to be depressed as measured by the BSI-18 DEP scale ($r= -.12$, $p<.001$). Some people who are depressed find themselves eating more in response to their depression, while others eat less. For those whose depression is manifested in eating more, private prayer may have a positive effect. Again, this is a correlation and not causation. It is also possible that depressed people are less likely to pray. The true relationship is probably a mutually interactive one with prayer helping to ameliorate depression and depression reducing one's proclivity to pray.

As we shall see in this study, the benefits of prayer are manifold. One of the benefits of prayer appears to be an ability to deal better with

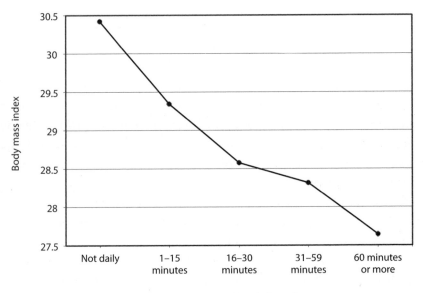

"I pray privately each day . . ."

Figure 3.1. "I pray privately each day . . ." and body mass index

stress. Prayer is also connected to a reduction in depression. Some react to depression by trying to "medicate" it through eating. These dynamics can help to explain the significant correlation between private prayer and the BMI. Priests who do not pray privately are more likely to be obese, and those who engage in a daily regimen of substantive time in prayer are likely to have a lower Body Mass Index. Prayer is good for your physical health as well.

Summary

In former days in the United States, there were often several priests in a rectory that had a housekeeper and a cook. Thus, the priests were fed healthy meals at regular hours. Now, with many priests living alone and sometimes in individual houses, many fend for themselves at mealtime. Not surprisingly, some neglect their physical well-being by rushing through meals at odd hours and eating fast foods.

Similarly, a large percentage of American priests, like their adult male counterparts, is overweight and lacks exercise. While Catholic priests are typical of their adult male counterparts in the United States, this is still not good news. Many American males are obese, are at risk for cardiovascular diseases, and are in danger of foreshortened lives.

Moreover, because of increasing workload and decreasing numbers of priests, some are already feeling pressured to skip their days off and annual vacations. This is particularly true with the increasing difficulty of finding a replacement priest to cover Sunday Masses. The pressure for priests' vacations is to take off a few days during the week and return for the weekend. However, there is no substitute for a good annual two-week vacation with a weekend off in the middle. Can dioceses maintain a list of possible replacement priests to cover for pastors' annual vacations?

The Catholic Church in the United States would do well to institute programs to ensure that priests maintain a proper weight, exercise regularly, eat healthy foods, have regular medical checkups, and take the proper time off. Teaching healthy ways of dealing with stress that do not include overeating and excessive alcohol consumption would be helpful, certainly for at least one quarter of our priests. But for some, their obesity and difficulties dealing with stress are symptomatic of personal problems that need attention. These might benefit from a direct and concentrated healing regimen.

It will be difficult to change the health habits of busy Catholic priests. Innovative programs will be needed. For example, some dioceses are providing free, brief medical examinations by local healthcare professionals during the mornings of the annual priest convocations. Thus, the priests can have a physical exam in the morning right at the convocation site before their day starts. These and other kinds of creative programs will be important to maintain the physical health of our priests.

In the days ahead, with fewer priests and greater pastoral responsibilities, the challenge of maintaining a healthy lifestyle will only become greater. Concentrated and focused efforts to maintain and improve the physical health of our priests will not only be good for the priests themselves, but important for the Church as a whole.

4

The Psychological Wellness of Priests

Some Previous Studies

As noted in the introduction, there is much misinformation, speculation, and projection about how psychologically well or sick Catholic priests are. Our Christian theology tells us that the human condition is subject to the ravages of weakness and sin. As St. Paul wrote, "We know that the law is spiritual; but I am carnal, sold into slavery to sin. What I do, I do not understand. For I do not do what I want, but I do what I hate" (Rom 7:15–16). All of humanity is subject to sin, and this truth is attested to in all corners of the globe and down through every century. So it is not news that we would find human weakness in our priests as well, given they are subject to the same fallen humanity. Rather, the question is: "How psychologically disturbed or healthy are they compared to others?"

Thus the first question is one of comparison. If priests are consistently more disturbed than their lay counterparts, then the Catholic Church must begin to look at recruitment, training, and lifestyle. Perhaps the Church is recruiting disturbed men to be priests; more than a few have assumed such in their public writings. Some have speculated that the celibate religious lifestyle attracts sexually dysfunctional individuals. Others have intimated that priesthood, with its celibate lifestyle that includes access to minors, attracts an inordinate percentage of child molesters. Others assume that priestly life, including celibacy and living under a religious authority, fosters unhealthy living. They have variously hinted that priests are less mature, more narcissistic, sexually underdeveloped, and the like.

So if priests are more disturbed than the general population, then the Church has to ask: "What are we doing wrong?" and "How can we fix it?" But if they are actually healthier, the first question ought to be: "What are we doing right?" Is there something about priestly life that actually contributes to health? Or maybe there is no difference at all, psychologically speaking, between priests and laymen. This in itself would be an important finding.

Perhaps the most oft-quoted study of priestly psychological wellness is the 1972 Kennedy and Heckler study, "The Catholic Priest in the United States: Psychological Investigations." The clinical researchers extensively interviewed 271 priests and made personal clinical judgments about their level of psychological maturity. They judged that approximately 8% (23) were maldeveloped; 66% (179) were underdeveloped; 18% (50) were developing; and 7% (19) were developed. These numbers have been much trumpeted in recent articles and media reports to support the notion that priests are seriously psychologically dysfunctional and thus especially prone to sexual deviance.

However, such interpretations are not faithful to the report itself. Kennedy and Heckler themselves summarized their results with the sentence: "The priests of the United States are ordinary men."[1] Also, they did not compare their priest sample with any statistical norms of the general population, so their reflections are merely their own clinical judgments. Nonetheless, they found that "American priests are bright and good men who do not as a group suffer from major psychological problems."[2] And, although there were no general statistical norms, the study concluded, "Priests probably stand up psychologically, according to any overall judgment, as well as any other professional group."[3]

What they did note was that the public expectations of priests were very high, and thus their results, while supporting the common "fallen" humanity of priests and their lay counterparts, could be particularly devastating to some people. This has become all too evident in the clergy sexual misconduct scandals, especially when it involves the abuse of a minor. The sexual abuse of a minor is rightly one of the most despised of all crimes, but when a priest is the perpetrator, it understandably carries even greater emotional outrage and condemnation.

Thomas Nestor in his 1993 clinical study of priestly wellness compared 104 Chicago priests to 101 laymen, also from Chicago. Nestor was critical of Kennedy and Heckler's study for not using a control group and standardized testing, thus relying on their own clinical observations and assessments. Nestor wrote, "The likelihood of bias, inconsistency, and expectancy effects increases substantially when such an assessment modality is utilized."[4]

Nestor compared his sample of priests to the lay control sample and found that the priests actually did "well in interpersonal relationships," and he suggested that "Kennedy and Heckler may have been subject to experimenter bias."[5] Nestor recognized, "There is a general presumption that priests . . . are deficient in interpersonal relationships. The results of the present study contradict that notion."[6] Comparing priests to the laymen in his study on such tests as the Miller Social Intimacy Scale, the Symptom Checklist-90 (SCL-90), and the Satisfaction with Life Scale (SWLS), he concluded, "Priests in this study were more intimate, more satisfied with their vocations, and better adjusted than their male peers."[7]

Similarly the National Opinion Research Center study of 1971, as reported in a National Federation of Priests' Counsels review, also found similar results. "The researchers report there is no evidence to suggest Catholic priests are any more or less deficient in emotional maturity when compared to both married and unmarried men of similar ages and education." They based their findings on their study of 5,155 priests using the norms of the Personal Orientation Inventory.[8]

Current Study

The 2,482 priests in my 2009 study were given a standardized test called the Brief Symptom Inventory 18 (BSI-18). With 18 individual items, it was developed as a "highly sensitive screen for psychiatric disorders and psychological integration."[9] Our population of Catholic priests was compared to the BSI-18 community norm sample of 605 adult males. This is a nonclinical sample of males taken from the general community, similar to our sample of priests. Thus, the BSI-18 is particularly appropriate in our priest study precisely because it can be used with nonclinical samples and has norms for males.

The BSI-18 has four scales. The first scale is Somatization (SOM), which measures the presence of distress caused by bodily dysfunction. These dysfunctions are often present in somatized versions of anxiety and depression, and thus they can be an indicator of underlying psychological distress. For example, the symptoms may include faintness or dizziness, pains in the heart or chest, nausea or upset stomach, trouble getting one's breath, numbness or tingling in parts of the body, and feeling weak in parts of the body.

The second scale is Depression (DEP) and looks for core symptoms of clinical depression such as feeling lonely, feeling blue, feeling no interest in things, feelings of worthlessness, feeling hopeless about the future, and thoughts of ending one's life.

The third scale is Anxiety (ANX), which looks for the presence of symptoms most often associated with anxiety, including nervousness or shakiness inside, feeling tense or keyed up, suddenly scared for no reason, spells of terror or panic, feeling so restless one cannot sit still, and feeling fearful.

The Global Severity Index (GSI) is a summary of the previous three scales, which Leonard Derogatis, the author of the instrument, describes as "the single best indicator of the respondent's overall emotional adjustment or psychopathologic status."[10] The results for the BSI-18 are noted in table 4.1.

Table 4.1. BSI-18 pathology results

	Priests' median	Priests' mean	General male population
BSI somatization scale	48	48.89	50
BSI depression scale	45	48.95	50
BSI anxiety scale	47	47.48	50
BSI global severity index	48	49.11	50

Note: BSI scales are calibrated as T-scores. Thus the mean for the sample group of males is 50 with a standard deviation of 10. The priest sample median and mean responses were calculated by determining the T-score for each respondent and then, for the median, finding the middle T-score and, for the mean, adding up all the T-scores and dividing by the number of valid cases.

As the chart demonstrates, on all four measures of psychological health, the mean scores of the sample of priests are modestly lower than the norm sample of males. Thus the results suggest that priests, as a group, are slightly healthier and a bit less psychologically distressed than the general population of males. The mean scores between the priests and the norm sample were statistically compared using a one-sample T test, and the differences were all statistically significant ($p<.001$). Therefore, the chances that this is a random finding are less than one in one thousand, and thus highly reliable.

T-scores of 45, 47, 48, and 49 are in the 31st, 38th, 42nd, and 46th percentile, respectively, with a score of 50 putting the person in the mean or 50th percentile. Thus, one could say that the mean priest score was slightly lower or "better" than the general population of males. Directly put, they score slightly psychologically healthier than their peers.

Derogatis noted, "Close to 80% of the psychiatric disorders that occur in community and medical populations are anxiety and depressive disorders with depression representing the most prevalent disorder in primary care."[11] Thus, using these scales should be good overall predictors of general mental health.

Nestor gave his sample of priests the SCL–90R, a similar test by Derogatis that also screens for psychopathology. This test is quite a bit longer, with ninety items measuring a broader range of psychopathology. There is a summary scale, also called the Global Severity Index (GSI). Again we see that, in Nestor's study, the priests scored less distressed than the general population. His mean score for the priests on the SCL–90R GSI was 34.187. His control group of adult males' mean score on the GSI was considerably higher at 48.602.[12] Finally, it should be noted that the SCL-90R also uses T-scores; thus the norms are set at 50 with 10 points being one standard deviation. Therefore, the priests' scores were markedly better than the general population in Nestor's study, over one standard deviation below.

Priests and Human Intimacy

Kennedy and Heckler said that priests, like their male lay counterparts, have difficulty with human intimacy, that is, close personal relationships. This was their clinical judgment based upon their subjective personal interviews. However, when priests were given objective psychological tests in Nestor's study, this judgment was not borne out. Nestor gave his sample of priests and the lay control group the Miller Social Intimacy Scale. His research results showed that "priests were more likely to enter into close relationships than their male peers. The priests experienced significantly higher levels of intimacy in their relationships than other men."[13]

This finding is supported by my 2009 study. A large percentage of the priests sampled reported having close personal relationships in which they share their problems and feelings. For example, 90.9% of the 2,482 priests agreed or strongly agreed that they "get emotional support from others"; 93.0% said they have "good lay friends who are an emotional support"; 87.6% said they have close priest friends; and 83.2% said they share "problems and feelings with close friends." Thus, a high percentage of priests reports having solid, close personal relationships both with other priests and with laity.

These close relationships no doubt contribute to the positive mental health of the priests. This is supported by the Pearson's *r* correlations reported in table 4.2. Each of these four questions regarding the presence of friendships was positively correlated with mental health. Thus, the BSI-18 GSI scale, as well as each of the individual pathology scales measuring anxiety, depression, and somatization, dropped significantly (thus there was a negative correlation) as the priests reported stronger friendships. In short, priests with good relationships tended to be healthier men.

While the sizes of the correlations were not large, they were modest and significant. These four questions, plus two other questions about past relationships ("Growing up I had close friends" and "During the seminary, I made some close friends") were combined into one larger variable labeled Close Friends (see Appendix 3). When this composite variable was correlated with the BSI GSI (Global Severity Index), the results were as expected. The correlation was significant ($p<.001$) with a slightly larger correlation, $r= -.22$, further statistically confirming the positive influence of relationships on mental health.

As we shall see later in the study, there are other factors that even more powerfully influence the mental health of our priests. Nevertheless, the presence of strong human relationships, which priests overwhelmingly report, positively contributes to their psychological well-being and helps us to understand why the general mental health of priests is as good as the study reported.

Priesthood and Sexual Problems

Do our priests suffer from sexual problems, including sexual pathology? Obviously, a few of them do. But again our first question is: How

Table 4.2. Correlations of BSI scales with emotional support and friendships

	BSI GSI	BSI ANX	BSI DEP	BSI SOM*
"I get emotional support from others"	-.18	-.13	-.22	-.08
"I have good lay friends . . ."	-.15	-.12	-.17	-.05
"I currently have close priest friends"	-.15	-.10	-.15	-.07
"I share my problems and feelings with close friends"	-.15	-.10	-.16	-.09

*All of the above correlations were statistically significant at $p<.001$.

do priests compare with their lay counterparts? Are these problems specifically related to the priesthood? More directly, do priests have sexual problems because they are men or because they are priests?

If they have sexual problems because they are priests, then the Catholic Church needs to do some soul-searching regarding its screening, formation, and lifestyles of its priests. But if the presence of sexual problems occurs because priests are men, then the assumption that there is something uniquely dysfunctional about the priesthood and the Church is not supported.

Nevertheless it must be added that even one highly visible person, like a priest, with considerable authority and responsibility with a sexual problem, while statistically not important, is hugely important to many people. This is true especially for those who may be negatively affected, even directly harmed, by his actions. But to implement more effective solutions so that the Church can eradicate such scandalous problems to the greatest extent possible, we must first know where the locus of the problems lies. We cannot solve a problem if we do not know its pathogenesis.

Obviously, the presence of such sexual difficulties is something difficult to research, especially in a survey. However, the presence of higher levels of healthy intimacy and overall mental health in priests initially suggests a lower level of sexual dysfunction. It would be unlikely for priests as a group to have higher levels of healthy intimacy and mental health and then have lower levels of sexual health.

In the area of child sexual abuse, there are some initial numbers available. The John Jay College of Criminal Justice reported in 2004, with unique access to confidential Catholic Church data, that 4% of Catholic priests had been accused of perpetrating child sexual abuse.[14] Thomas Plante, PhD, in *Psychology Today* noted: "*The 4% figure is lower than school teachers (at 5%) during the same time frame and perhaps as much as half of the numbers of the general population of men.*"[15]

Similarly, psychologist Richard Cross analyzed a report by Anglican Clergy of Australia. Using their statistical abuse data, he estimated the abuse rate of Anglican clergy from 3.0 to 4.4%. He thus concluded that the abuse rate reported in the John Jay study for celibate Catholic clergy of 4.0% was approximately the same and therefore that celibacy is unlikely to be a factor.[16] I would add that catholicity is unlikely to be a factor as well.

One case of child sexual abuse is unacceptable for any organization, especially an organization dedicated to preaching the Good News of Jesus who had a special love of children. Nevertheless, it is important to note that the rate of child sexual abuse in Catholic clergy appears to be less than other populations, given the very limited data we currently have. Much more research and data are needed. But it is important to note how rampant child sexual abuse is in our society in general. It ought to be a source of shame and outrage for us all. If we find many cases in the Catholic Church, it is because we find many cases everywhere in our society. Truly, it is a devastating societal epidemic.

Priests as Victims of Sexual Abuse

While public accounts have focused on priests as perpetrators of child sexual abuse, this survey had a unique opportunity to ask priests about themselves being victims of child sexual abuse. This 2009 survey found that 8.7% of the priests sampled said they were "sexually abused before the age of eighteen." This is more than twice the rate of priest perpetration of abuse and should be an important consideration for the Church.

Dr. Plante wrote, "Research states that 17% of American women and 12% of American men were sexually violated when they were children by an adult."[17] Plante's figure of 12% for American males being sexually abused as children is a conservative estimate. Other sources report even higher rates of offense. For example, the National Center for Victims of Crime summarized the data saying that one in four girls are sexually abused and one in six boys. Thus, the victimization rate for priests, at 8.7%, is markedly below the rate for males in the general society.

Mental health problems, including an increased risk of abuse perpetration, are well-documented effects of victimization. This is another factor that supports the finding of the higher mean mental health rate findings for priests. Since the percentage of priests who are victims of abuse is lower than the general male population, then the well-documented mental health challenges in its wake should be diminished in the Catholic presbyterate as well. For example, the John Jay study found that "Priests who had themselves been victims of abuse were twice as likely to have a history of difficulties with alcohol, illegal drugs, or both."[18] Similarly, in my study, those priests who reported having been sexually abused as minors also reported modest but significantly higher levels of depression, anxiety, and somatization on the BSI-18.[19] This gives us perhaps another reason why the mental health scores of the priests sampled were slightly better than the general population—there were fewer priests who were victims of child sexual abuse.

Nevertheless, 8.7% of clergy themselves having suffered from childhood sexual abuse is a significant number and should be cause for reflection by the Church. It is sad that the public perception of the Catholic Church is that it has been a roadblock to dealing with child sexual abuse. Even from a statistical perspective, given that so many of its priests are themselves victims of abuse, not to mention Christian moral and ethical imperatives, the Catholic Church should be at the forefront, strongly promoting the rights and healing of victims of abuse. In the last few years, we have seen a remarkable strengthening in the Church's understanding and dealing with this issue. The pope himself has been personally engaged in this and has repeatedly addressed this important issue in the public forum using strong language and regularly stressing the importance of victims' rights. Dealing effectively with child sexual abuse will remain an important issue not only *ad extra*, but also *ad intra*.

Looking at possible differences in priestly victimization rates among different ordination cohorts is likely to be important in charting trends. If there are differences in ordination cohorts, then this will affect the mental health of the presbyterate, and possibly future perpetration rates of sexual misconduct as well. Indeed, there were statistical differences for Years Ordained and victimization rates (Pearson Chi-Square: χ^2=11.372, p=.044). The results are in table 4.3.

The mean results per ordination cohort are graphed in figure 4.1.[20]

Being abused as a child is a risk factor for subsequently becoming an abuser (although it must be quickly noted that the vast majority of victims do *not* become abusers). For example, at Saint Luke Institute it was found that one third of priest abusers treated at the Institute themselves had been sexually abused as minors with another third being subjected to other kinds of maltreatment and abusive childhoods. Similarly, the

Table 4.3. Years ordained and "I was sexually abused before the age of eighteen"

| | "I was sexually abused before the age of eighteen" | | |
	No (%)	Yes (%)	Total
Number of years as priest			
0–10	92.42	7.58	356
11–20	91.21	8.79	330
21–30 1979 – 1988	88.98	11.02	372
31–40	91.50	8.50	565
41–50 1969 – 1968	89.63	10.37	511
More than 50	95.21	4.79	334
Total	91.33	8.67	2468

National Center for Victims of Crime reported a study by Vanderbilt in 1992 estimating that 40% of abusers themselves were abused as children.[21]

The John Jay study found that a disproportionate percentage of priest-child sexual abusers was ordained between 1950 and 1979, especially 1960–1969, the latter accounting for 25.3% of all alleged priest abusers in their study. At the time of my study, this latter John Jay group would have been ordained 41–50 years.[22] The graph for my study (fig. 4.1) shows there were higher victimization rates for priests ordained 21–30 years and again for those ordained 41–50 years, with lower victimization rates for the oldest and most newly ordained priests.

Therefore, for the group ordained 41–50 years, the John Jay study found that this group had the very highest rate of accusations of child sexual abuse of any ordination group, and my study found that they had slightly elevated rates of being abused as children. The victimization rates for younger priests, those ordained less than 10 years, appear to be dropping slightly, which may be one factor that is influencing the dropping rates of abuse by the clergy in recent years. While the decline for the newly ordained in table 4.3 is not yet statistically significant at the .05 level, visual inspection of the numbers show that 11% of priests ordained 21–30 years report being sexually abused as minors versus only 7.6% of priests ordained 0–10 years, representing a 31% decrease.

While there are many factors that result in abuse, it may be that there was a group of priests more at risk for abusing minors since they themselves were sexually abused as children at a higher rate. The difference is

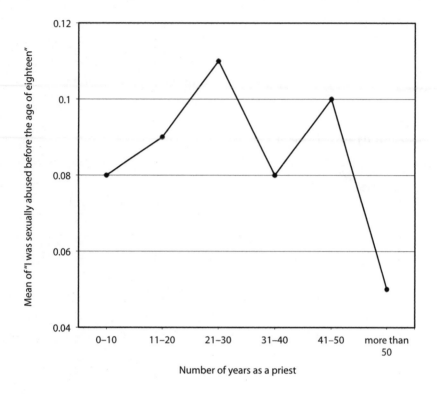

Figure 4.1. Years ordained and "I was sexually abused before the age of eighteen"

not enormous and thus cannot account for the total decline in new cases of abuse, but it may be one factor.

Priests with Sexual Difficulties in Childhood

Moreover, we see a similar and even larger spike in those age cohorts growing up with sexual problems. See figure 4.2. The survey item was, "Growing up, I had difficulty coming to grips with my sexuality." Again, the youngest and the oldest priests do not report the same level of sexual problems growing up as do those priests in the middle years. The difference was statistically significant (ANOVA results: $F=17.091$, $p<.001$).[23]

This difference is strong and noteworthy. For example, 20.5% of priests ordained 0–10 years agreed or strongly agreed that they had sexual difficulties growing up. A much larger 37.7% of priests ordained 31–40 years agreed/strongly agreed. This is almost double the rate of the newer priests. Priests in their middle years reported a much larger rate of sexual difficulties in their developing years than did the newer or older priests. It is to be expected that those men who had more sexual problems as minors are more likely to have sexual problems as adults.

Again, it is important to note that the John Jay study found that cohorts of priests ordained in the 1950s, 1960s, and 1970s had the highest rates of the perpetration of child sexual abuse, which dropped markedly before and after that time. If we take both of the graphs together ("I was sexually abused before the age of eighteen" and "Growing up, I had difficulty coming to grips with my sexuality"), then it appears that the priests ordained between 21 and 50 years—that is, ordained between 1960 and 1989—experienced higher levels of sexual problems in childhood than those priests ordained before or after them. These problems

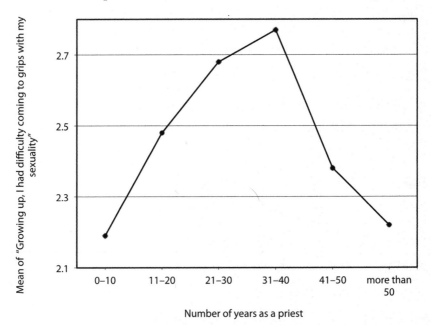

Figure 4.2. Years ordained and "Growing up, I had difficulty coming to grips with my sexuality"

took the form of either child sexual abuse itself and/or growing up with sexual problems.

The John Jay study demonstrated that there is clearly a statistical increase in reported incidents of child sexual abuse among Catholic clergy in cohorts of priests ordained 1950–1979 time frame.[24] While not exactly overlapping with my two graphs, much of it does overlap. I found that priests during this time frame generally reported higher rates of childhood sexual difficulties and/or themselves being sexually victimized. These are obviously risk factors for becoming future abusers.

The second John Jay study, The Causes and Context of Sexual Abuse of Minors by Catholic Priests in the United States, 1950–2010, also noted that the sexual abuse of minors by priests peaked in the late 1970s and early 1980s. While they indicate it was a complex phenomenon, they suggest that the "sexual liberation" and similar social changes of the 1960s and 1970s were important factors influencing the spike in cases of abuse.[25]

As a clinician and researcher, I must admit that I have been skeptical when individuals blame the increased incidents of priest perpetration of child sexual abuse on the sexual climate of the 1960s. Child sexual abuse is everywhere and has been going on as long as history records; it is not a new phenomenon. Nevertheless, the social context clearly helps to promote or deter crimes of all stripes, including child abuse. For example, the current climate in society and church that has promoted child safety and condemned and punished child abuse is clearly having a positive effect. So, culture can affect crime rates, positively and negatively.

It may be that the spike in priest-perpetration of child sexual abuse that peaked in the late 1970s and early 1980s was a combination of both factors: some priests themselves growing up with sexual difficulties and then being surrounded by a societal environment more conducive to sexual expression and not yet condemning of child sexual abuse, which fostered higher levels of abuse. From a psychological perspective this makes sense: it takes both a person psychically predisposed to problems and then being in an environment that permits, perhaps even exacerbates, the underlying vulnerability which most likely results in pathology being manifested.

In response, one might ask why the priests in the 21–30 year group did not perpetrate higher levels of abuse since they themselves also had higher levels of childhood sexual problems. But recall that it takes both a predisposition to such problems and being placed in an environment conducive to acting out of their problems. Beginning in 1985, the leadership of the Catholic Church progressively began to respond more directly and effectively to the phenomenon of child sexual abuse as did the general society. Church leadership especially began to institute strong programs designed for the education and prevention of abuse before it occurred. The surrounding culture was changing, including a gradual diminution of the "sexual revolution" that began in the 1960s. The changing cultures in the Church and society both likely affected declining rates of abuse.

It is encouraging and important to note that more newly ordained priests are not reporting these same higher levels of sexual difficulties growing up and that crime of child sexual abuse is more aggressively condemned and punished. Child sexual abuse has rightly become one of the most despised crimes of our time. The Catholic Church in the United States has mandated extensive educational and prevention efforts among priests, laity, and children to deter future acts of child sexual abuse. With the underlying sexual vulnerability of priests appearing to decrease and the social environment changing, John Jay's findings of a marked decline in child sexual abuse among US Catholic clergy is understandable.

These data suggest that it continues to be critically important to screen out candidates for the priesthood with significant sexual problems in childhood. While it must be noted that most victims of child sexual abuse do not go on to become perpetrators, a traumatic sexual history of any kind should be dealt with directly and sufficiently before a candidate is considered for entrance into priestly formation. Candidates reporting any kind of significant sexual problem in childhood should be extensively screened and, if accepted, closely monitored during the formation period.

I am happy to report that, being involved in the screening of candidates for the priesthood over the past seventeen years, I have seen a marked increase in direct screening for sexual pathology. It should be added that it is, indeed, a difficult and a sensitive issue to screen candidates for sexual problems. Standardized psychological tests such as the Minnesota Multiphasic Personality Inventory (MMPI) and personality inventories are not sufficient, nor are they meant to screen for sexual pathology. Currently, many mental health professionals who screen candidates are using clinical interviews with an in-depth psychosexual history as the most effective means of psychosexual screening.

Overall, I think it clear that, in some places, the previous screening standards for priesthood, especially in the area of sexuality, were too low. The Church at all levels has paid a heavy price for that, as have countless children and their families. The bar is being raised, particularly in the area of sexual health, and it needed to be raised. These changes are already having strong positive and measurable results.

Years Ordained and Overall Mental Health

The previous discussion focused specifically on the sexual health and healthy intimacy of priests. Regarding Years Ordained and general mental health, one might expect that younger priests would be comparatively healthier because of enhanced psychological screening and attention to psychological wellness. However, comparing the respondents' BSI-18 scores by numbers of years ordained did not show an improvement in general mental health scores for the young.

In fact, just the opposite was true. The older priests, those ordained over 40 years, reported being markedly less depressed and anxious than their younger colleagues. The results were statistically significant (for BSI-18 Anxiety $F=7.029$ with $p<.001$; for BSI-18 Depression $F=4.035$ with $p=.001$). As shown in figures 4.3 and 4.4, depression and anxiety scores for priests ordained 41 years or more were significantly less than those priests ordained 40 years or less.[26] It appears that our older priests are aging gracefully. However, it is not surprising that they scored higher on the BSI Somatization scale, given the well-known physical problems of aging.

To explain the difference, one might first hypothesize that older priests are more comfortable with themselves, especially as they grow close to retirement.[27] Thus, their levels of anxiety and depression would likely decrease. However, there was another important factor that surfaced in analyzing the data. This latter factor may be offsetting the increased intensive psychological screening of candidates for the priesthood and thus resulting in higher levels of depression and anxiety among younger priests.

A composite variable called Dysfunctional Childhood was computed after the factor analysis showed that these items statistically loaded together on a single factor (see Appendix 3). There were six individual survey questions that were combined: "I grew up in a dysfunctional family"; "I was emotionally abused as a child"; "Growing up, I had a good relationship with my mother" (coded in reverse); "Growing up, I had a good relationship with my father" (coded in reverse); "I was physically abused as a child"; and "A member of my immediate family has suffered from psychological problems."

Figure 4.5 shows the overall scores on the composite variable Dysfunctional Childhood for different ordination cohorts.[28]

While younger priests reported having fewer sexual problems in childhood and lower victimization rates of childhood sexual abuse, their

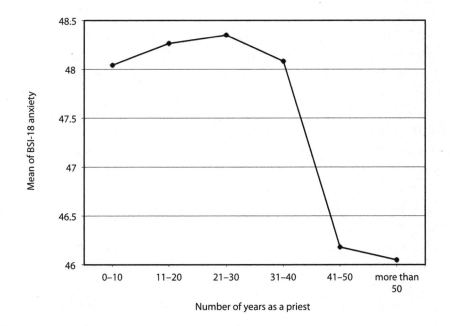

Figure 4.3. Years ordained and BSI-18 anxiety

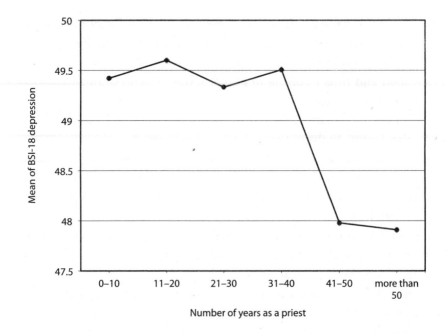

Figure 4.4. Years ordained and BSI-18 depression

overall levels of anxiety and depression were higher than older priests. Figure 4.5 may help to explain it. Younger priests reported higher rates of growing up in a dysfunctional family and experiencing a dysfunctional childhood. The results were statistically significant (ANOVA results were F=36.309, p<.001). For example, 20.5% of newly ordained priests (0–10 years) reported growing up in a dysfunctional family compared to only 6.9% of priests ordained over 50 years. This is a large increase of roughly 300%!

Similarly there was a statistically significant difference in priests reporting growing up with Childhood Mental Health Problems (F=13.098, p<.001). See figure 4.6. This is another composite variable composed of three individual items: "Growing up, I suffered from depression"; "Growing up, I saw a mental health professional for some difficulties"; and "Growing up, I suffered from anxiety." Again, it was the youngest priests who reported greater mental health problems in childhood.

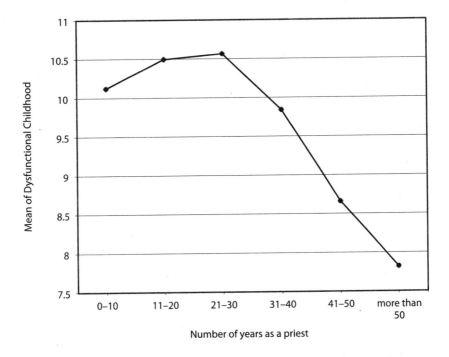

Figure 4.5. Years ordained and Dysfunctional Childhood

Moreover, there is a sharp rise in the percentage of priests with divorced parents. In table 4.4, the percentage steadily rises from 1.4% (priests ordained over 50 years) to 9.8% of priests ordained 10 years or less.

When comparing the variable of Divorced Parents with the composite variables of Childhood Mental Health Problems and Dysfunctional Childhood, the ANOVA shows that those priests whose parents are divorced are significantly more likely to report having Childhood Mental Health Problems ($F=8.237$, $p=.004$) and much more likely to report coming from a Dysfunctional Childhood ($F=143.086$, $p<.001$). The composite variables of Childhood Mental Health Problems and Dysfunctional Childhood correlate positively and significantly to each other and to the four BSI-18 pathology scales, as noted in table 4.5.

This statistically supports the notion that coming from a dysfunctional family, including having divorced parents and having childhood mental problems, makes it more likely that the individual will have

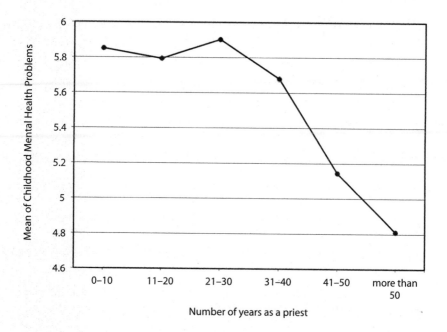

Figure 4.6. Years ordained and Childhood Mental Health Problems

psychological problems as an adult, in this case, as a priest. (However, it should be noted that the overall percentage of priests who have divorced parents is still only 4.8%. Given the fact that divorce is so widespread in US society, this must be a relatively low percentage compared to the general population.) Similarly, with the higher incidence of younger priests reporting coming from dysfunctional backgrounds, their experiencing of psychological symptoms as priests was concomitantly higher.

This is certainly no surprise to anyone doing priestly screening and formation work today. It is commonly believed that some candidates for the priesthood come from and are significantly affected by a society suffering from a breakdown of the nuclear family and concomitant psychological dysfunction. This is something that formators of priests continue to struggle with: how do we deal with the dysfunctional backgrounds of some young people today, including those knocking on the door to enter the priesthood?

Table 4.4. Years ordained and Divorced Parents

Number of years as a priest	Divorced parents (divorced/total)	Percent
0–10	35/356	9.8
11–20	30/330	9.1
21–30	25/372	6.7
31–40	20/565	3.5
41–50	7/510	1.4
More than 50	2/334	1.4
Total*	120/2481	4.8

* One priest with divorced parents did not indicate his number of years ordained, thus the total number of priests with divorced parents is one more than the sum of the individual year cohorts.

Another Measure: IPIP Neuroticism Scale

The respondents in the 2009 survey were also given the ten-item IPIP neuroticism scale.[29] The International Personality Item Pool or IPIP is a publicly available five-factor personality inventory. Our respondents were given only the neuroticism (or emotional stability) scale, which included the following items: "I often feel blue"; "I rarely get irritated"; "I dislike myself"; "I seldom feel blue"; "I am often down in the dumps"; "I feel comfortable with myself"; "I have frequent mood swings"; "I am not easily bothered by things"; "I panic easily"; "I am very pleased with myself." As the statements suggest, the scale measures symptoms related to anxiety, depression, self-esteem, and other symptoms of emotional health.

While the basic test has no published norms per se, Tom Buchanan administered eight of these items to 991 males (leaving out "I rarely get irritated" and "I am very pleased with myself" for psychometric reasons of factor loadings). These males voluntarily sought out a personality inventory and completed the inventory online. Their mean score was computed to be $M=21.57$ with a $SD=6.76$.[30] The mean score for my 2009 sample of priests using the same items ($n=2467$ with 15 missing

Table 4.5. Correlations of Dysfunctional Childhood, Childhood Mental Health Problems, and BSI-18 scales

	Childhood Mental Health Problems	BSI-18 SOM	BSI-18 DEP	BSI-18 ANX	BSI-18 GSI
Dysfunctional Childhood					
Pearson correlation	.590**	.132**	.273**	.286**	.281**
Sig. (2-tailed)	.000	.000	.000	.000	.000
n	2477	2481	2479	2481	2477
Childhood Mental Health Problems					
Pearson correlation	1	.223**	.380**	.419**	.415**
Sig. (2-tailed)		.000	.000	.000	.000
n	2477	2476	2474	2476	2472

**Correlation is statistically significant.

responses) was $M=19.04$ and $SD=3.59$. The difference in means is statistically significant ($p<.001$).

While this is not a rigorously derived set of norms, the results are similar to the previous findings of this study and a modest confirmation of the previous results. The priest sample again reports being significantly less neurotic than a comparable sample of male laity.

BSI-18 "Caseness"

For the BSI-18 Derogatis gave a cutoff guideline for "caseness," that is, for the likely presence of a clinical syndrome. He recommended using two criteria: (1) if the GSI T-score is 63 or greater, or (2) if any two of the three scales' T-scores are 63 or greater. A T-score of 63 is the 90th percentile for the sample population. Thus, if any priest has a T-score of 63, he is in the upper 10% of American males in psychopathology.

There were 143 priests with a T-score of 63 or above on the GSI scale. In addition, Derogatis said that "caseness" should also be applied to those individuals whose GSI scores were less than 63 if any two of the three scales were 63 or higher. There were 13 individuals who fell into this second category. Overall, there were 156 priests out of the total sample of 2,482 or 6.3% who fell into the category of "caseness" or who likely had the presence of a psychopathological syndrome (table 4.6). This is markedly below the 10% of the male community sample. Again, this suggests that the overall pathology rate of priests is modestly lower than the general population of males.

However, 6.3% of priests with significant psychological problems can be a serious problem for the Church, given their level of responsibility and visibility. And, depending upon the manner in which this psychopathology is manifested, the effects can be devastating. Thus, while the finding that priests are psychologically healthier than their lay counterparts is good news, this should not be cause for relaxing our efforts to do all possible to ensure that each priest is as high functioning as possible and free from potentially devastating, even scandalous, psychopathology.

Psychological Screening of Candidates for the Priesthood

The results of the 2009 study emphasize the need to have comprehensive psychological screening for candidates for the priesthood, with high standards for admittance. Virtually every diocese in the United States today already has some kind of psychological screening of candidates for the priesthood. This study strongly supports the presence of such screening, including direct screening for psychosexual health.

Some guidelines for the use of psychological services have been provided by the Vatican's Congregation for Catholic Education in its "Guidelines for the Use of Psychology in the Admission and Formation of Candidates for the Priesthood." This 2008 document recognized the

Table 4.6. Number of priests with "caseness" on the BSI-18

	BSI GSI ≥63	DEP & ANX ≥63	SOM & DEP ≥63	SOM & ANX ≥63	Total	Percent
Caseness	143	7	3	3	156	6.3

need for psychological assessment when it noted: "To arrive at a correct evaluation of the candidate's personality, the expert can have recourse to both interviews and tests" (#5) and the "Church has the right to verify the suitability of future priests, including by means of recourse to medical and psychological science. In fact, it belongs to the bishop or competent superior not only to examine the suitability of the candidate, but also to establish that he is suitable" (#11). Nevertheless, the document rightly cautions that psychological consultation can never take the place of the formators' role in judging the suitability of candidates, which includes not only psychological suitability but also spiritual and pastoral considerations as well.

Currently, when significant psychological trauma in childhood surfaces during this initial screening, some candidates are rejected outright. Others, who are less distressed but still suffering from significant trauma, are requested to engage in a healing regimen before reapplying for admittance as a candidate. The least distressed may require some modest psychological assistance during their time of formation, for which most seminaries have already made some provision. The Vatican document expressed openness to referring seminarians for consultation with mental health professionals when needed and accepted by the seminarian (#12–#13).

Thus, it is commonplace in many seminaries today to have ready access to psychological services for seminarians when needed. The data in this study support the need for such services. While the seminary is not considered the place for major remedial psychological work, it is realistic to think that a wounded society will inevitably produce some wounded young people, a few of whom will end up in the seminary. Most American seminaries are paying increased attention to "human formation" issues. Again, this study supports the need for this "human formation" and perhaps ways for the seminaries to consider augmenting this area of increasing need.

It was Pope John Paul II himself in his pivotal Apostolic Exhortation on the formation of priests, *Pastores Dabo Vobis*, who emphasized the importance of human formation. He called it the "foundation" of priestly formation: "The whole work of priestly formation would be deprived of its necessary foundation if it lacked a suitable human formation" (#43). Later, using strong language in a talk to bishops, he warned the bishops of their sacred responsibility:

> It is my duty therefore to recommend a renewed atten-
> tiveness in the selection of vocations for the seminary,
> with the use of all available means for coming to an
> adequate knowledge of the candidates, above all, from
> the moral and affective point of view. Let no bishop feel
> excluded from this duty of conscience for which he will
> have to render an account directly to God. It would be
> deplorable that . . . he would ordain young men who
> are immature or exhibit clear signs of affective disorders,
> who, as is sadly known, could cause serious confusion in
> the consciousness of the faithful with obvious harm for
> the whole Church.[31]

The mental health of priests in general appears to be slightly better than their male counterparts in society. In retrospect, this should not be completely surprising. Candidates for the priesthood are screened in several ways. First, starting decades ago, many priests in the United States went through psychological screening in their application process for the priesthood. For example, in 1979 I went through a full day's evaluation with a licensed psychologist, including standardized testing, projective testing, and a clinical interview, as a normal part of the process of application for the priesthood required of all applicants. It was mandatory for my diocese as well as for any applicants for the national Catholic seminary that I attended. It was standard practice, even as early as the late 1970s, for many dioceses and religious orders to engage the assistance of a mental health professional to screen applicants for the priesthood. And, not surprisingly, some with significant pathology were screened out.

Moreover, seminarians undergo a multi-year formation process. During this process, some voluntarily opt out, but others are deemed unsuitable for various reasons, including mental instability. Thus, future priests undergo screening on many different levels, a process that their lay counterparts generally do not undergo. Therefore, while not 100% effective, it would not be unreasonable to expect that this process would screen out the more obvious mental health problems. This accounts for the rarity of major mental health issues in the priesthood such as schizophrenia and bipolar I disorders. While these occasionally do occur, they are isolated cases and often are unusual, late onset syndromes.

"Then why do we have priests with problems?" it might be asked. The answer is twofold: (1) screening processes are not infallible, and they are especially limited for disorders that are hidden or can be hidden by a seminarian; (2) some disorders can manifest themselves or become more serious as the years pass or may be manifest only in particular settings or under some kinds of stress. There is no "silver bullet" in psychological screening. A case in point, one of my fellow seminarians eventually became one of the first widely publicized cases of priest-child sexual abuse. While we lived and studied with him every day, years later when he appeared on the television screen and eventually went to prison, we were as shocked as anyone else that this happened. While our screening has had some positive effects, it is not nor will it ever be 100% effective.

Mental Health Assistance for Priests

There is another reason why the mental health of priests might be slightly better than the general population. This is the ready availability and use of mental health resources for priests. The 2009 survey asked if, during their priesthood, priests have voluntarily sought out a counselor. A relatively large 46.3% (n=1148) said yes. This suggests that many priests are not hesitant about seeking some professional assistance if they feel the need.

This finding indicates priests' openness to looking at personal mental health issues and a willingness and humility to ask for help. It is well documented, for example, that mental health services can successfully lower levels of depression and anxiety, as well as successfully treat other disorders. Given the stresses on the very public and interpersonally intense ministry of our priests, this is a positive finding and may also help to explain the better scores of priests on the BSI-18.

At other times, bishops or religious superiors will personally ask priests to seek assistance. When queried if they had been asked to see a counselor by their diocese or order, 9.1% (n=226) said yes. Together, 155 priests fell into both categories of voluntarily seeing a counselor and being asked to see one, so a total of 1,219 or 49.1% of priests had seen a counselor during their priesthood. The great majority were in outpatient care, presumably for less significant personal challenges, while 8.8% indicated that they went through a residential care program, which likely involved more serious problems.

As someone who has spent many years providing both residential and outpatient care for clergy, I have witnessed the often powerful healings that can take place in such settings. It was my experience and the experience of many of my colleagues that priests are, by and large, great clients with which to work. They are usually hard-working and intelligent. They bring a level of faith and trust to therapy, which is important. Their faith opens them up to a deep level of divine healing. Plus the presence of their Christian spirituality brings a depth of healing to which the science of psychology has only begun to be aware.

The openness and rather frequent use of mental health services by priests is remarkable. It does not mean that they are necessarily suffering from a serious dysfunction, but may simply want a more objective professional to help them during a challenging period. It also indicates that priests are serious about their psychological health and see it as important in their ministerial lives. Their bishops and major superiors agree. With 9.1% of priests being asked to see a counselor by a superior, it is clear that they will intervene when necessary and recommend a priest for counseling if indicated.

Those in the helping professions, such as psychologists, social workers, nurses, and other caregivers, often speak of the importance of support and care for their own professionals. My own experience of health care professionals is that they, as a group, will usually engage the help of another professional if they feel a need. Indeed, those giving care should themselves be open to receiving care when needed. These interpersonally intense lifestyles can often present and precipitate personal challenges that are best processed with the help of others. The ready presence of mental health support can be a significant help to the mental health and welfare of all professionals.

Mental Health of Religious versus Diocesan Priests

I investigated the mental health of sample subgroups, as measured by the BSI-18. There were no statistical differences between religious priests ($n=337$) and diocesan priests ($n=2145$). Both groups' scores on the four wellness scales were statistically equivalent. An ANOVA was computed with $p=.066$ for the BSI-18 Somatization scale, $p=.679$ for the BSI-18 Depression scale, $p=.706$ for BSI-18 Anxiety scale, and $p=.467$ for BSI-18 Global Severity Index scale. Thus, none of the mean differences were large enough for the probability of error to reach the desired threshold of .05 or less. Therefore, we cannot posit a significant difference between the mental health of religious versus diocesan priests based on this survey.

Summary

The results of this 2009 survey suggest that the psychological health of Catholic priests in the United States is slightly better than that of their lay male counterparts. They scored better on measures of anxiety, depression, somatization, and thus the overall severity index as well as on other indicators of mental health. The differences were modest but statistically significant. The Nestor study, which also used standardized psychological tests, found similar results. To judge the overall mental health of the priesthood, I think it would be unwise to rely on studies that do not use normed samples but rely only on personal judgment. Particularly in the case of priests, given the intense transferential emotions people often project onto the priesthood, such judgments are highly subject to personal bias.

Priests' better mental health scores are not completely surprising considering the initial psychological screening that most candidates for the priesthood in the United States have undergone for almost thirty years. In addition, they are monitored during a multi-year formation process, and some are dismissed due to a lack of mental suitability. Still other seminarians are sent for counseling when indicated. In addition, almost half of the priests in the United States have been in some sort of professional counseling during their priesthood. All of these factors contribute to the overall mental health of priesthood. As this book progresses, there will be other factors noted that will also contribute to the psychic health of American priests, including spiritual factors.

There were some especially challenging findings of this study. A spike in priests in their middle years reported having a childhood history of sexual difficulties. These priests reported either a childhood history of being sexually abused or sexual difficulties growing up. Many of these priests were formed or were young priests in the 1960s and 1970s. The John Jay study found a spike in perpetration rates of child sexual abuse by priests in a similar, though not exactly overlapping, time frame. The John Jay study suggested that it had something to do with the "sexual liberation" of the 1960s. While the surrounding culture is important in either promoting or inhibiting crime, my data also suggest that it may have something to do with the underlying sexual vulnerabilities in this cohort of priests themselves.

Fortunately, the situation is improving. The culture in society and church have vociferously condemned and punished the sexual abuse of minors. Also, candidates for the priesthood initially appear to have a history of fewer sexual difficulties. I am personally aware of many dioceses that have begun to screen directly for the presence of psychosexual problems in candidates for the priesthood, as difficult as they are to uncover. I am also personally aware of some candidates who were found to have very serious sexual problems and were not allowed to continue on toward priesthood. Some major future scandals were obviously avoided in these cases. So, psychosexual screening that has begun is likely having a few but very important positive results. And the Church's and society's markedly stronger response to the tragedy of child sexual abuse has also contributed to a significant decrease of new incidents of child sexual abuse in the Church and in US society as a whole. These positive trends should give us cause, not to relax our efforts, but to continue in the same direction of increasing our vigilance and the safeguarding of minors.

It is very possible that screening for sexual difficulties in candidates for the priesthood may have been insufficient during an extended period of time in the past for which victims, families, and the Church have all suffered. It also suggests the need for continued improvement in the screening of candidates, particularly in terms of psychosexual health.

Another important finding in this chapter is the higher incidence of general anxiety and depression in younger priests. While apparently having lower levels of sexual pathology in the wake of enhanced sexual screening and societal changes, they tested as demonstrating higher levels of general anxiety and depression. How to account for this trend? Older priests may have lower levels of anxiety and depression probably partly due to the greater emotional integration of priests as they age and approach retirement. But the younger priests also reported coming from dysfunctional backgrounds at a much higher rate than the older priests. This is of significant concern. Younger priests are much more likely to come from divorced families and more likely to experience childhood emotional problems. This is not news to many seminary formators. Our candidates for the priesthood come from a dysfunctional society with the breakdown of the nuclear family. This study found a significant positive correlation between reporting growing up with a dysfunctional childhood or having childhood mental health problems and later reporting symptoms of depression and anxiety.

As we shall see in the next chapter, coming from a dysfunctional background with greater inner psychic liabilities will make successful functioning in the demanding ministry of a priest more difficult. It will make a successful transition into priesthood more difficult. The pressure on formators to produce sufficient numbers of priests is strong, although we are all aware of the dangers of ordaining a man who cannot live priesthood with integrity. The particular challenges of our often dysfunctional society pose difficulties for those who screen and form our candidates today. But this process must begin with sufficiently high standards for accepting candidates and an equally strong human formation program that includes consultation with mental health professionals when indicated.

Despite these challenges, the mental health of priests as a group is strong. Their desire and capacity for healthy, chaste intimacy is also strong. They are men who are in a variety of life-giving, chaste, human relationships with other priests and with laity. While there are, and always will be, a few priests with serious psychological problems, the findings in this study suggest that priesthood itself is not the cause. If it were, the rates of pathology would necessarily be higher.

Of course, for some, priesthood is not the proper life or calling. And, if they are in priesthood by mistaken judgment, as is rarely but sometimes the case, dysfunction and even scandal can result. Given the great responsibility and high visibility of the priesthood, the few misplaced individuals sadly can cause great harm to others and can garner much public notoriety.

However, the large majority appear to be living priesthood well and is prospering on many levels, including psychologically. John Paul II called human formation the "foundation" of a priest's formation. To protect the public, especially our children, continuing to improve the mental health of our priests as part of their human formation must remain an important element of the foundation of priestly formation and a priority for the years ahead.

5

Burnout and the Priesthood

The 2,482 priest respondents in the 2009 survey were also given a leading measure of burnout: the Maslach Burnout Inventory.[1] The inventory is divided into three subscales: Emotional Exhaustion (EE), Depersonalization (DP), and Personal Accomplishment (PA). Burnout is defined and measured in the Maslach Inventory by these three factors using a total of twenty-two items. When people are burned out, they typically are emotionally exhausted and depleted; they can become emotionally hardened and impersonal, especially to those to whom they minister; and they feel like their work is accomplishing little and that they are not fully competent or effective.

Given the increasing demands on priests and the sometimes intensive nature of their work, there are many who speculate that priests are experiencing high levels of burnout. As a clinician, I am personally aware of individuals who fit into the category of being "burned out." But the question remains: how is the priesthood as a whole doing with burnout? Given the fewer numbers of priests, their increasing workload, and the very real stresses in their lives, it is only reasonable to wonder if priests are burning out. More than a few have speculated that they are.

To answer this question, I compared the mean scores of the entire sample of priests with the norm samples of laity provided by Christina Maslach et al. in the *Maslach Burnout Inventory Manual*.[2] I also compared the mean scores of priests below the age of seventy to ensure that retired priests did not skew the results. The results are in table 5.1.

Table 5.1. Maslach burnout inventory scores

	Emotional exhaustion	Depersonalization	Personal accomplishment
Priests (*n=2460*)	13.57	4.07	37.62
Priests under age 70 (*n=1747*)	15.53	3.95	37.89
Total Maslach sample (*n=11,067*)	20.99	8.73	34.58
Social services (*n=1538*)	21.35	7.46	32.75
Medicine (*n=1104*)	22.19	7.12	36.53
Males (*n=2247*)	19.86	7.43	36.29

Source: Christina Maslach et al., *Maslach Burnout Inventory Manual*, third edition (Mountain View, CA: CPP Inc., 1996), 8.

The findings are clear and remarkable. Contrary to speculation, regardless of which Maslach sample is used (the entire sample or subsamples of those working in medicine, social service occupations, or males in general), priests score much lower on Emotional Exhaustion, much lower on Depersonalization, and much higher on Personal Accomplishment. These are all positive findings. Higher scores on Personal Accomplishment are desirable, and it means that priests are more likely to see their ministries as fruitful and themselves as being efficacious. The lower scores for priests on Emotional Exhaustion and Depersonalization are also positive because it means that priests are less likely to feel emotionally depleted, emotionally hardened, and distant from the people whom they serve. The differences were all statistically significant ($p<.001$).

Thus, priests as a group score much better on the Maslach Burnout Inventory than the general population or compared to those in medicine, social services, or males in general. This is true even when possibly retired priests, those over age seventy, were taken out of the sample. Priests as a group are less emotionally exhausted, less depersonalized, and have a greater sense of personal accomplishment than the general population or subgroups of males, people in medicine, or in social services.

Those with a High Degree of Burnout

Despite these positive findings, this does not mean that there are no burned-out priests. Maslach et al. indicated that those with scores in the upper third of Emotional Exhaustion and Depersonalization and the lower third of Personal Accomplishment are considered to have a "high degree of burnout."[3] Using this criterion, thirty-six of the priests in our sample are considered to have a "high degree of burnout" or 1.5% (of 2,460 with twenty-two missing cases) when compared to Maslach's overall sample. If the "social services" sample norms are used, then thirty-five of the priests are considered to have a high degree of burnout. If the norms for medicine are used, then fifty-seven priests or 2.3% are considered to have a high degree of burnout. This is indeed a small percentage. Regardless of which norm sample is used, a small percentage of priests, 2.3% or less, is considered to have a high degree of burnout.

If we were to investigate each scale separately and compare them with our priest sample, investigating how many priests measured in the upper third of each scale, then the results in table 5.2 would apply.

In each of the three subscales measuring burnout, there were markedly fewer priests in the upper third of the overall sample (i.e., $EE{\geq}27$, $DP{\geq}13$, $PA{\leq}31$). Thus, priests were less emotionally depleted, less emotionally hardened, and had a greater sense of personal accomplishment than the overall norm sample.

Nevertheless, for those of us concerned with the mental health of priests, it still means that about 2.3% of our priests are likely experiencing a high level of burnout on all three scales and are in need of personal assistance.

This suggests the question: do we, as a Church, have a way of finding out which priests are seriously burned out and providing assistance to

Table 5.2. Priests scoring in the upper one-third of the Maslach norm sample

	Emotional exhaustion	Depersonalization	Personal accomplishment
Priests (n=2460)	268 or 10.9%	136 or 5.5%	459 or 18.7%
Maslach sample	33%	33%	33%

them? Currently, the Church usually relies on either the priest himself coming forward or the diocesan vicar for clergy or similar person in authority identifying the problem.

Similarly, once a person with burnout is identified, the obvious remedies include some time off and/or personal psychotherapy. However, with the decreased numbers of priests, it is increasingly difficult for a priest to get a sabbatical. This kind of constructive time away is an important preventative measure for those on the road to becoming burned out as well as a needed help to those who are already in a burned-out state.

Faced with fifty years of priestly service almost exclusively as a pastor of a parish, some priests will need to have other options for ministry and/or time away to reenergize and to be renewed. Others will need some kind of direct healing regimen to deal with underlying factors contributing to their burnout. While the temptation in this time of reduced numbers is just the opposite, that is, to feel one cannot afford to send priests away for care and/or renewal, we cannot afford not to take care of the priests that we do have.

Years Ordained and Burnout Scores

Given the significant differences between younger and older priests on previous statistical measures in the last chapter, it would make sense to check if there are any differences among ordination cohorts on levels of burnout. One might typically hypothesize that midlife priests would be the most burned out given their stage in life, workload, and longevity in the ministry. For example, I casually asked several fellow priests to guess which ordination cohorts would be most burned out. Invariably, they responded, "Middle-aged priests." This makes sense.

However, the priests who showed the highest levels of burnout on the three scales were the youngest priests. See figures 5.1, 5.2, and 5.3.

As can be visually seen from the charts, priests ordained twenty years or less had relatively higher mean averages of Emotional Exhaustion and Depersonalization and lower mean averages of Personal Accomplishment (except for the priests ordained over fifty years, presumably retired). Overall, the differences between the younger cohorts of priests

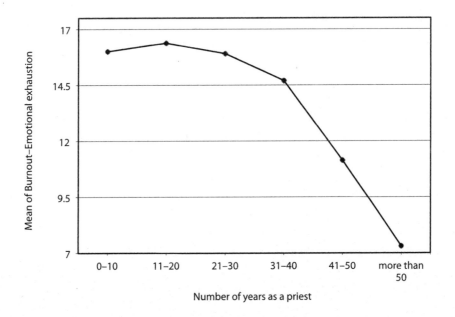

Figure 5.1. Years ordained and Burnout-Emotional exhaustion

were not large, so they should not be overestimated. However, the over-all ANOVAs were statistically significant on all three scales: Emotional Exhaustion (F=54.934, p<.001); Depersonalization (F=25.007, p<.001); Personal Accomplishment (F=3.965, p=.001).[4] We recall that the greater the emotional exhaustion and depersonalization and the lower the sense of personal accomplishment, the higher the level of burnout.

How can it be that the newest priests, the ones with the least amount of time in ministry, tend to score as burned out as the middle-aged priests, if not slightly more so? Moreover, it is usually priests in their late forties and fifties with the greatest leadership and pastoral responsibilities. Shouldn't we expect priests with more responsibility and more years in ministry to score higher on measures of burnout?

However, we recall in the last chapter that it was the youngest priests who had the highest levels of anxiety and depression, as measured by the BSI-18 (cf. figures 4.3 and 4.4). Also, it was the youngest priests who had the highest levels of growing up in dysfunctional families. As noted previously, they are coming from a society of broken families and sometimes with psychological problems in childhood. Thus, they are

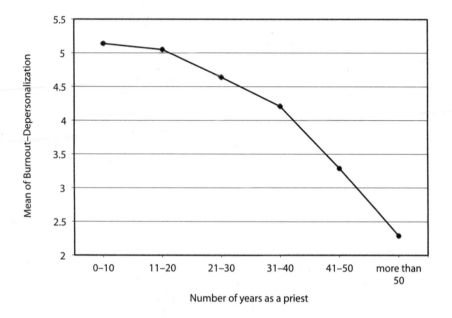

Figure 5.2. Years ordained and Burnout-Depersonalization

bringing with them a greater vulnerability to burning out. Indeed, when a Pearson's *r* correlation was computed on the composite variable Dysfunctional Childhood with the three burnout scales, all were statistically significant correlations.

We can see in table 5.3 that the higher the levels of childhood mental health problems and the greater the dysfunctional childhood, the greater the emotional exhaustion and depersonalization plus the lower the level of personal accomplishment as a priest. Given the fact that younger priests report greater dysfunctional childhoods and more mental health problems in childhood, they are thus more vulnerable to burnout.

Moreover, such factors as childhood dysfunction and mental health problems were much more important in predicting burnout than such typically cited factors as taking time off. While the correlations between the composite variable Time Off and the three burnout scales were significant, they were modest and considerably less than the childhood mental health and dysfunction factors. While those who took time off were slightly less likely to experience emotional exhaustion and depersonalization, and they were more likely to have a sense of personal

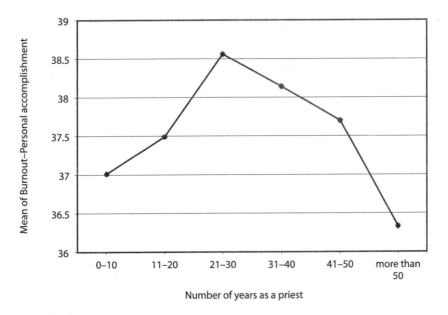

Figure 5.3. Years ordained and Burnout-Personal accomplishment

accomplishment, when looking to predict who will burnout in priesthood, one should definitely look more to childhood and emotional factors.

So, the first reason why younger priests are measuring higher on burnout is likely the psychological vulnerabilities they bring with them. They are more prone to anxiety and depression and come from more dysfunctional backgrounds, hence it is likely that the stress of active ministry is more difficult for them.

Second, with the reduced numbers of clergy and increasing demands of ministry, the experience of priesthood is changing. When I was ordained over twenty-five years ago, a priest did not become a pastor in our diocese until after his silver anniversary. He lived in a rectory with several priests and slowly learned the ropes.

Today, this has all changed. Young priests often become pastors after only a few years of ordination, not uncommonly three to five years. Thus, at a very early age they are thrust into running their own parishes, which is not unlike running a small business as the CEO with

Table 5.3. Correlations of Dysfunctional Childhood, Childhood Mental Health Problems, Time Off, and the three Maslach burnout scales

	Burnout-Personal accomplishment	Burnout-Emotional exhaustion	Burnout-Depersonalization
Dysfunctional Childhood			
Pearson correlation	-.116**	.316**	.234**
Sig. (2-tailed)	.000	.000	.000
n	2470	2472	2470
Childhood Mental Health Problems			
Pearson correlation	-.181**	.339**	.235**
Sig. (2-tailed)	.000	.000	.000
n	2465	2467	2465
Time Off			
Pearson correlation	.112**	-.046*	-.042*
Sig. (2-tailed)	.000	.024	.035
n	2462	2463	2462

* $p<.05$
** $p<.001$

the additional pastoral and spiritual challenges of being the shepherd of hundreds, maybe thousands, of people. This is not easy. The young priest is expected to be fiscally responsible, a good employer, a plant manager, as well as a good homilist and presider at liturgy, a gentle confessor, and a wise pastoral counselor.

These are tasks that take more than a few years with which to feel comfortable. Not only do the newly ordained have to adjust to priesthood, they have to adjust to pastoral leadership as well. I believe it is more difficult for the newly ordained simply to adjust to being a priest in our secular culture today. As one priest wrote on his survey, "Most Catholics are supportive, but the look and stares at Wal-Mart and restaurants by non-Catholics can be unnerving." Moreover, there is little support for the young priest's celibate vocation and his position as a leader in a large institutional religion. Our secular, sex-obsessed culture is often skeptical of anyone in authority, particularly a religious leader. On top of that, the new pastor must quickly learn how to be a successful leader of a "small business." With all that, it is no wonder they are stressed.

Overwhelmed with Work

The suggestion that younger priests are more likely to be overwhelmed with their ministry workload, especially new pastors, was supported by the findings of my first study, accomplished in 2004. This was a sample of 1,242 priests from sixteen dioceses, as noted in the introduction. The respondents were given the statement: "I feel overwhelmed with the amount of work I have to do." There was a statistically different response among ordination cohorts (ANOVA F=14.838, p<.001). Those who reported the highest levels of feeling overwhelmed were priests ordained 10–19 years. Figure 5.4 depicts the results.[5]

As some of the younger priests commented in writing on their surveys: "My biggest problem today is overwork" (Respondent ordained 1–9 years); "My biggest problem as a priest today is: 'Overworked and stretched to the limit'" (Respondent ordained 10–19 years).

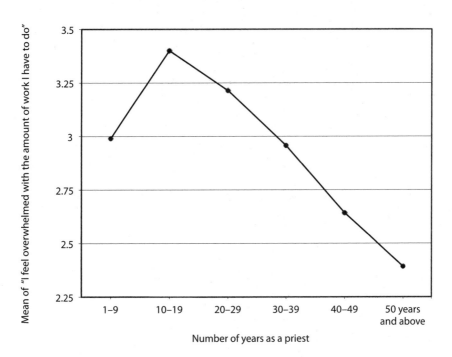

Figure 5.4. 2004 survey: Years ordained and "I feel overwhelmed with the amount of work I have to do"

Excessive workload was a very common theme in the comments section of the 2004 survey for all priests, including the newly ordained. For example, 42.3% of the entire sample of priests agreed or strongly agreed that they feel overwhelmed with their workload. However, for those ordained 10–19 years, this number jumps up to 54.9%.

Given the stress of adjusting to priesthood and often becoming pastors so soon in priesthood, plus carrying greater burdens from dysfunctional childhoods, it is now not difficult to see why the younger priests scored higher on burnout measures. It is very likely that they are experiencing higher levels of emotional exhaustion, given the intense adjustment and learning curve. They are less comfortable in their human relationships than the older priests as they learn how to develop good pastoral relationships without crossing dangerous boundaries (which must constantly be a threat in the back of their minds as they read media accounts trumpeting the sexual scandals of a few priests). Similarly, they are still adjusting to pastoral ministry and leadership and thus are likely less comfortable in their roles and may have less of a feeling of personal accomplishment than the older, more established priests.

These are important findings. Dioceses are instinctively becoming more concerned about the adjustment and mentoring of their newly ordained priests and new pastors. This study gives statistical support to their concern and perhaps increased incentive to reach out more strongly to priests ordained less than twenty years.

This increased level of burnout of the more newly ordained should be seen in context. First, the burnout scores of priests ordained in their first 1–9 years and also 10–19 years are still markedly better than their lay peers. Compared to medical personnel and people in the social services, as well as the general population, the youngest priests still score much less burned out than their lay counterparts. Nevertheless, of the entire priest sample, they are more at risk and thus deserve our increased attention.

Overall Workload and Burnout

As I travel around dioceses, priests in general are concerned about their workload and related stress. There are fewer priests and increasing numbers of Catholics. Instead of several priests living together in a single parish, they are now scattered around the dioceses and often cover more than one parish by themselves. These are significant changes to the lives of priests which are no doubt having an impact on their lives. It is clear to me that priests are concerned about the rising workload and their ability to keep up with it.

If we look at the responses in table 5.4 for the entire sample of the 2004 survey regarding the statement "I feel overwhelmed with the amount of work I have to do," the results are important.

It is striking that fully 42.3% of priests, as previously noted, would describe themselves as being overwhelmed with their workload (either agreeing or strongly agreeing). This is a very large percentage. These findings were echoed in the Center for Applied Research in the Apostolate (CARA) Priest Poll 2001. This poll said, "72 percent of non-retired diocesan priests and 62 percent of non-retired religious priests (68 percent overall) report that they experience the problem of 'too much work' either 'a great deal' or 'some.'"[6] It is also interesting that, in this CARA study, the recently ordained reported working slightly more hours per week than the entire sample of priests, a mean of sixty-five hours/week versus sixty-three hours/week for the general sample of priests. They concluded, "Still, the findings suggest that most priests are working an exceptionally large number of hours."[7]

A number of priests commented on their workload on the 2004 survey.

Table 5.4. 2004 survey results: "I feel overwhelmed with the amount of work I have to do"

	Frequency	Percent	Valid percent
Valid			
Strongly disagree	67	5.4	5.5
Disagree	508	40.9	41.7
Unsure	129	10.4	10.6
Agree	374	30.1	30.7
Strongly agree	141	11.4	11.6
Total	1219	98.1	100.0
Missing	23	1.9	
Total	1242	100.0	

"My biggest problem as a priest today is: feeling over-whelmed (timewise) in pastoring a large parish of 4,000-plus families."

"Priests are overworked, and expectations are too high."

"My biggest problem as a priest today is: more demands than I can satisfy."

There is no question that large numbers of priests are putting in long hours in their demanding pastoral ministries. Regardless of priests' scores on the Burnout Inventory, workload ought to be an issue of concern for both the priests themselves and the Church.

Conclusion

There are some important conclusions from the data in this chapter. First, the data clearly refute any notion that priests as a group are burned out. Regardless of which norm group we use—the general population, those in medical professions or social services, or males—priests score much lower on a widely accepted burnout test, the Maslach Burnout Inventory. On each of the three scales, Emotional Exhaustion, Deper-sonalization, and Personal Accomplishment, priests' scores are markedly better.

Given the intense workload of priests that has only been increasing in the past years, plus the declining numbers of priests, not to mention the intense, continuing, negative media coverage, one would expect the burnout rate to be higher. In fact, priests say that they have too much work to do and almost half feel "overwhelmed." But, as a group, their burnout scores are not high. In reality, they are lower than many other helping professions. Why?

The remainder of this book will shed some important light on the reasons for their low burnout scores. At this point, suffice it to say that burnout is not simply a matter of how much one works. If people are happy with their work, feel a sense of satisfaction with their lives, have a good set of friends and personal support, and also have a strong prayer and spiritual life, they are able to endure the toughest of circumstances.

Meaning. Victor Frankl

In the remainder of this book, we shall see how our priests measure up against these criteria.

Nevertheless, there are a few priests who are seriously burned out. Depending upon which norm group we use, 2.3% or fewer of priests would be considered in the upper third of the norm group of all three scales and thus considered to be seriously burned out. This is a small percentage. But if there are 150 priests in a given diocese, this means that approximately 3 or 4 priests in that diocese are in significant need of assistance.

How do we identify the few priests who are burned out or on the road to burnout? In what ways can we assist them? Each priest deserves the support of the Church, especially in his time of need. Moreover, having three or four pastors in such difficult mental shape can cause serious difficulty for hundreds or even thousands of parishioners. A problem with a single priest, as the spiritual leader of many hundreds or thousands of the faithful, can quickly become a serious problem for the entire diocese.

Our priests as a whole are holding up well under the increasing demands. They are dedicated, hearty souls who are generous in their giving of self for others. But if over 40% are feeling overwhelmed, it is time for us to address the issue of workload. As I go from diocese to diocese, one of the most common concerns I hear from priests is their heavy workload. Helping all priests to manage their challenging workload ought to be a priority. How can they integrate a demanding ministry with necessary time for prayer, study, and recreation? This challenge ought to be faced on the organizational level and faced directly.

In addition, priests themselves will need to cope personally with this challenge of rising workload. One priest wrote on his survey that his biggest problem as a priest today has been "realizing I can't do it all and letting go." This will be a challenge for most priests today.

Third, the results of this chapter found, surprisingly, that it is the younger priests who are experiencing relatively higher levels of burnout. There are echoes of this finding in the 1984 study by the United States Bishops' Committee on Priestly Life and Ministry that concluded, "If tension, worry, and stress are indicative of a lack of serenity at any stage of the priest's life, we are forced by the evidence to locate this problem in the early years of the priesthood."[8]

This again reminds us that burnout is not simply a function of how long one has been engaged in an intensive, caring ministry. Burnout is strongly affected by the health and background of the individual who is engaged in the ministry. Because of the increasing societal family dysfunction, an increasing number of younger priests report coming from dysfunctional backgrounds. A greater percentage is thus experiencing increased mental health problems in childhood. And, as the statistics in this study show, coming into priesthood with such a history makes one more likely to have difficulty with ministry, including the increased possibility of burning out, even after only a few years of priesthood.

Every so often, we hear of a promising young priest who leaves priesthood after only a very short time. While reasons are always given, the results of this study make one wonder if their experience of priesthood was just too personally emotionally overwhelming. Such a priest may have sunk into depression and/or been filled with anxiety. In fact, as we shall see later on in this study, two of the most powerful predictors of whether a priest will think of leaving the priesthood are the Maslach Emotional Exhaustion scale and the composite variable Dysfunctional Childhood. Thus, a priest who comes from a dysfunctional childhood and becomes emotionally exhausted as a priest is at higher risk of leaving the priesthood. These are some of our youngest priests.

The Church ought to look more closely at the challenges faced by our younger priests. Not only do some of them bring greater psychic vulnerabilities with them into priesthood, they are entering a lifestyle that has a decreasing amount of societal support. They are celibate in a sex-crazed society; they are leaders in an institutional religion when increasing skepticism is leveled at organizations and structured religion; they are CEOs of small corporations—that is, parishes—with very few years of experience; and they are Catholic priests at a time when the media continue to pound away in the public forum at the sins of a few. One can only admire the courage and faith of the ones who do face the pressures and the challenges of being a young priest and pastor today.

With all of our priests, their strength and faith is inspiring. Despite the sometimes intense and grinding challenges of a lifelong commitment to serving others, our priests as a group are strong and healthy. The results of this study ought to inspire mental health professionals and researchers to look more closely at what makes a healthy life. Under some of the most adverse of circumstances, people can endure and even prosper. For the keys to a healthy and holy life, we will look more deeply in later chapters of this book at the inner happiness and spiritual lives of our priests.

6

Happiness and the Priesthood

Overall Happiness and Morale

Are our priests happy? A staff writer for the *Hartford Courant* wrote in 2003, "In the wake of one scandal after another, the image of the genial, saintly cleric has given way to that of a lonely, dispirited figure living an unhealthy life that breeds sexual deviation."[1] There have been more than a few of these media accounts that have suggested that priests are an unhappy, dysfunctional lot. God knows we can all point to an unhappy priest. They stick out and sometimes are rather vocal. But it is important to investigate whether they represent part of a much larger group of unhappy priests or are an anomaly. One of the best ways to determine the overall satisfaction of priests around the country is to poll a substantial number of them, of all age groups and many racial and ethnic backgrounds. My two surveys did just that.

In the 2004 survey, 1,242 priests from sixteen dioceses around the country were surveyed; in the 2009 survey, 2,482 priests were surveyed from twenty-three dioceses around the United States. This is a lot of priests. Only two dioceses were sampled in both studies, thus there were thirty-seven different dioceses sampled. While this was not strictly a random sample, as noted previously, it contains a good cross-section of larger, middle-sized, and smaller dioceses from all the different areas around the country. With a bit more than 40,000 priests in the United States, this represents a large sampled portion of the entire population of priests and more than adequate for our studies.

Both surveys gave the respondents the statement, "Overall, I am happy as a priest." The results are found in table 6.1. The results are relatively stable over these five years with a modest increase of 3.3% in Strongly Agree and a slight decrease in Disagree.

The two surveys also asked a similar question about morale. The results are in table 6.2. Again, the results are largely stable but with a notable uptick of 12% in Strongly Agree and a concomitant decline in the other categories.

The message is clear: when asked directly, a large majority of priests say their morale is good and they are happy as priests. About 90 to 92.4% agree or strongly agree that they are happy as priests and 80 to 88.9% say their morale is good. In the wake of the 2002 abuse crisis, the decline in vocations, and the regular drubbing in the media, this is remarkable.

It is even more remarkable when one compares it to the job satisfaction rates of Americans, as reported in The Conference Board's 2009 report. In this comprehensive study of 5,000 households, only 45% of Americans surveyed said they were satisfied with their jobs. This percentage has been decreasing from 61.1% in 1987 when the study was first completed.[2]

Perhaps one of the reasons for the slight increase in happiness and larger increase in morale from 2004 to 2009 is the increased distance from the 2002 child abuse crisis. While the child abuse crisis obviously did not completely dismantle priestly happiness and morale, as some thought it might, *the crisis likely put a bit of a damper on their enthusiasm. We are currently seeing a rise in the number reporting to be the happiest of priests* (i.e., those who strongly agree that they are happy and their morale is good).

Table 6.1. "Overall, I am happy as a priest"

	Strongly agree (%)	Agree (%)	Unsure/ Neutral (%)	Disagree (%)	Strongly disagree (%)
2004 survey	39.2	50.8	5.2	4.5	0.3
2009 survey	42.5	49.9	5.0	2.1	0.5

Table 6.2. "My morale is good" (2004 survey); "My morale as a priest is good" (2009 survey)

	Strongly agree (%)	Agree (%)	Unsure/ Neutral (%)	Disagree (%)	Strongly disagree (%)
2004 survey	19.3	60.7	8.2	9.8	1.9
2009 survey	31.3	57.6	6.4	3.8	0.9

Some priests seemed able to distinguish between their overall happiness as a priest and their morale. Their happiness levels did not change substantially as the distance from the 2002 scandal increased, but their morale did. One possible interpretation is that these priests distinguished between their overall happiness with priesthood and the pain and sadness they felt in the wake of the crisis; the latter was apparently affected by the crisis, but the former showed little change. They still valued priesthood although they were suffering and, at times, their spirits sank. As one priest soberly wrote on the 2004 survey when asked about his evaluation of priesthood, "Nothing is perfect, not even the priesthood, but it is good."

Because these overall numbers are so positive, some have questioned their veracity. However, consistent research findings support them. First, this study was performed twice using two almost completely different samples. Second, other studies, both informal and formal, have found similar results. When similar findings occur in different surveys, accomplished by different organizations, and using differing samples, this argues strongly in favor of the accuracy of the findings.

For example, the *Hartford Courant*'s informal survey of 107 priests from the local archdiocese found that 94% of the priests agreed with the statement, "Most of the time, I am happy with my life as a priest."[3] In a survey of 1,854 priests by the *Los Angeles Times* published October 20 and 21, 2002, 91% of the priests were satisfied with the "way your life as a priest is going these days" and 90% said they would do it again.[4]

Similarly, in the National Federation of Priests' Council (NFPC) 2001 survey of 1,279 priests, 45% described themselves as "very happy" and 49% described themselves as "pretty happy" with only 6% saying they were "not too happy."[5]

Again, the CARA priest poll of 1,234 priests in March 2001 found 88% of priests "strongly agree" and 11% "somewhat agree" with the statement, "Overall, I am satisfied with my life as a priest." Similarly, 87% "strongly agree" and 12% "somewhat agree" with the statement "I am happy in my ministry."[6] CARA concluded, "Nearly all priests say they are happy in their ministry and they are satisfied with their lives as priests."[7]

The National Opinion Research Center (NORC) collected data on 32,029 adult Americans from the age of eighteen to eighty-nine years from 1972 to 1994.[8] They, too, were asked if they were "very happy," "pretty happy," or "not too happy." All age groups were consistently less happy than the priests, as noted in table 6.3.

In the 2001 NFPC study, Dean Hoge found that the levels of overall happiness of priests, that is, the percentage describing themselves as "very happy," has been steadily increasing from 28% in 1970 to 39% in 1985 to 39% again in 1993 and, finally, to 45% in 2001.[9]

In my 2004 study, the respondents were given the statement, "If I had a chance to do it over, I would become a priest again"; 81.5% agreed or strongly agreed, 5.4% disagreed or strongly disagreed. In the Hoge NFPC study, the same question was posed to the priests, and 88% said yes with only 4% saying definitely or probably not. The 2001 CARA study also found that 90% strongly agree and 8% somewhat agree with the statement, "If I had a chance to do it over again, I would still become a priest."[10]

Table 6.3. Percentage reporting happiness: comparing priests to laity of all adult age cohorts

	2001 NFPC Survey of Priests	Laity						
		18–27	28–37	38–47	48–57	58–67	68–77	78–89
Very happy (%)	45	28.3	30.9	31.7	33.3	36.0	37.9	34.1
Pretty happy (%)	49	58.9	58.6	56.6	53.4	51.2	49.9	52.4
Not too happy (%)	6	12.8	10.5	11.7	13.3	12.8	12.2	13.5

First, the statistics from all these studies are roughly similar. The great majority of priests, over 80%, would choose priesthood again. But it appears there was a slightly higher number of those who said unsure after the 2002 crisis with an increase from 8% in 2001 to 13.2% in 2003, and 6.5% decline in those who agreed. No doubt, the crisis precipitated a few priests, at least temporarily, wondering if they made the right choice. *Nevertheless, the large majority of priests remains committed to priesthood and would do it again if given the choice.*

What emerges from my studies and others is a consistent pattern. When asked, priests say their morale is good. They say that they are happy as priests, and the percentage is rising. Those who say their morale is definitely not good and report that they are unhappy is currently about 4.7%.

Having only 4.7% of priests currently reporting that their morale is not good is statistically a very positive finding. However, it still means that, taking a hypothetical diocese of 150 priests, seven priests would likely consider themselves to be dissatisfied. In this sample diocese, seven unhappy pastors would be a cause for concern. So, it is important to recognize the difference between statistical rates of satisfaction and the pastoral implications of those are who unhappy—for themselves, for their parishes, and for the diocese.

Nevertheless, these are very positive findings for the priesthood and, given its replicability, they are solid figures.

Perception of Priestly Morale

These findings do not mean that priests do not see any problems in priesthood nor does it even mean that if you ask priests about other priests' morale, they would agree that others' morale is good. For example, in the 2004 survey, priests were given the statement, "Morale in the priesthood today is good." The results are in table 6.4.

It is noteworthy that 80% of priests in the 2004 survey said their morale was good but only 38.3% of priests said other priests' morale was good. Essentially, a number of priests are saying, "My morale is good, but everyone else's is bad." How can we account for this?

It is obviously true that, in the wake of the crisis, priests have and continue to suffer. Many priests and bishops have told me that they have

Table 6.4. 2004 survey results: "Morale in the priesthood today is good"

	Strongly agree (%)	Agree (%)	Unsure (%)	Disagree (%)	Strongly disagree (%)
"Morale in the priesthood today is good"	3.9	34.4	28.4	28.8	4.5

been spit on in public, yelled at, called perverts and child molesters, and have watched mothers grab their children in fear as a priest walks by. This author himself has personally experienced such behaviors. Behind closed doors, priests share these shocking stories.

Priesthood is a sacramental brotherhood. It is a reality that priests love and to which they have committed their lives. They rejoice in their communion most especially when they gather around the altar. As St. Paul said so concisely, when one member suffers, all suffer together (1 Cor 12:26). Watching the public excoriation of the Church and the priesthood has been very painful for all priests.

Thus, it is not surprising that many people, including priests, would believe that the general morale of priesthood is low. Yet, it is a bit surprising that priests consider themselves to be such happy and satisfied people. As we shall see in a moment, when given the Satisfaction with Life Scale (SWLS), the results are likewise very positive. Priests are obviously able to make a distinction between public scandal with its subsequent suffering and their own happiness as a priest.

There are likely many reasons for this. One reason is undoubtedly that priests have an entire theology of dealing with suffering. One of the core images of Christianity is Christ upon the cross. Priests read time and again the beatitudes that promise, "Blessed are they who are persecuted for the sake of righteousness, for theirs is the kingdom of heaven" (Mt 5:10). Not only can priests incorporate this suffering into their Christian theology and priesthood, but the verse actually suggests that they are blessed because of such suffering. Many priests have told me that they believe it to be true in this case.

For example, in Michael Kane's qualitative survey of priests after the 2002 crisis, twenty-two priests were interviewed. Regarding the crisis, one of the respondents said:

It's had me question whether this is where I really belong. But overall, it's demonstrated that the priesthood exists and even thrives in the most arduous circumstances. Just when being a dishwasher looks good, God surprises me with a circumstance, and I'm reaffirmed and know that I am where I should be. I am where I belong; no matter what. Historically clergy have survived many difficult situations.[11]

Moreover, while priests may occasionally be spat upon and derided in public, their parishioners have largely stuck by them and supported them. Priests continue to feel much love and support from those whom they serve, and the people continue to stand behind their own priests. The people are able to distinguish between those who have molested minors and those who continue to serve them amid troubled times. Many have even greater understanding, compassion, and support for their parish priests because of it. And some laity actually go out of their way now to affirm their own priests in this difficult time.

We might want to bear in mind that the concept of "morale" is a multi-dimensional reality. Surveys cannot do complete justice to this complicated concept. When someone says their morale is good or bad, to what are they actually referring? It is my belief that when priests are speaking about other priests' morale, they are speaking about what they hear other priests saying in private and what they see. In private, they hear the priests talking about the challenges of the times, the pain and the suffering of these days, and the difficulties. For example, in my own priest support group, much of our time is spent listening to the challenges that each priest faces. So, it would be natural for priests today to wonder if morale of other priests is low.

But when you ask a priest about his own morale and happiness as a priest, I believe that he digs down deeper. While being very conscious of the current difficulties and pains, a priest thinks about deeper things when he assesses his own morale. He thinks about his relationship to God and to his brother priests and to the people. He thinks about his daily sacramental and ministerial life. He thinks about being with the people and being a part of their lives. When he looks at the core of priesthood and assesses its essence, he realizes that he likes being a priest and doing what a priest does. He feels blessed to be a part of such a life. And when asked about his own morale and happiness, he says it is good.

This was brought home to me concretely when I was helping out in a parish on a Sunday. The pastor was aware of the results of this survey that reported a high priestly morale. He was upset by this and told me in no uncertain terms that he disagreed and believed that morale in the priesthood was not good. I responded, "I understand what you are saying. But let me ask you this, Father. How about you? How is your morale?" "Well," he responded, "my morale is good. I like being a priest." "Exactly," I answered.

Satisfaction with Life Scale

Priests were also given a standardized psychological test called the Satisfaction with Life Scale (SWLS). This test is designed to measure a person's overall satisfaction with their lives. Psychometrics show that the test measures a construct different than psychopathology or emotional well-being. Rather, it measures an individual's overall judgment of his or her life based upon the person's own criteria.[12] One could say that it measures the cognitive dimension of subjective well-being.

It is a simple scale with five items: "In most ways my life is close to my ideal"; "The conditions of my life are excellent"; "I am satisfied with my life"; "So far I have gotten the important things I want in life"; "If I could live my life over, I would change almost nothing." Respondents were given the test's seven-point Likert scale to respond (strongly disagree, disagree, slightly disagree, neither agree nor disagree, slightly agree, agree, strongly agree).

It is interesting that the SWLS is known to be sensitive to events in the individual's life. If good or bad events occur, the respondents' scores on the scale will rise or fall accordingly.[13] Thus, giving this scale to priests in the wake of one of the most painful and difficult periods in Church history is particularly interesting, and one would expect the results to be markedly lowered.

The mean score on the SWLS for our 2,482 priests was 27.20 with a standard deviation of 5.218. The median score was 29. This means that most priests answered slightly agree or agree to each of the five questions. This score places them in the "satisfied" range.

How does this compare to others? Pavot and Diener have provided us with some standardized norms by which to compare the priests (see table 6.5).[14]

Pavot and Diener note that most individuals in Western countries fall in the range of 23–28, thus placing people from Western countries above the neutral score of 20 (choosing neither agree nor disagree in response to all the questions). We can see that priests scored in the upper part of this typical Western scoring range. Diener describes scores in the 25–29 range, which is where priests fell:

> Individuals who score in this range like their lives and feel that things are going well. Of course their lives are not perfect, but they feel that things are mostly good. Furthermore, just because the person is satisfied does not mean she or he is complacent. In fact, growth and challenge might be part of the reason the respondent is satisfied. For most people in this high-scoring range, life is enjoyable, and the major domains of life are going well—work or school, family, friends, leisure, and personal development. The person may draw motivation from the areas of dissatisfaction.[15]

Nestor also gave his sample of 101 Chicago priests the SWLS and the results were similar. For younger priests, those trained in 1970 and

Table 6.5. Satisfaction with life scale

	Mean scores	(Standard deviations)
2009 survey of priests	27.2	(5.2)
Religious women in active ministry	25.1	(7.2)
Military wives and nurses	25.0	(6.8)
Older American adults	24.2	(6.9)
American college students	23.7	(6.4)
Nurses and health care workers	23.6	(6.1)
Contemplative religious women	23.3	(7.3)
Elderly care givers	21.2	(7.7)

later, their mean score was 25.05 (*SD*=6.85) and for older priests, those trained before 1970, their mean score was 26.78 (*SD*=5.61). He, too, found that the mean scores for laity were lower. In his control sample of laity in the Chicago area, the younger laymen's mean score was 23.54 (*SD*=6.74) and the older laymen's mean score was 25.19 (*SD*=5.43).[16] Nestor adjusted the SWLS questions to assess "intimacy" and "relationships" rather than life in general. Thus, he made some substitutions of words on the scale. His scale adjustment to measure intimacy rather than life as a whole may have accounted for the slightly lower scores than my priest sample. But, in general, his results were similar: *priests' scores measuring overall satisfaction with life were significantly higher than the general population.*

Ordination Cohorts and Happiness

Given the significant differences among ordination cohorts of priests in previous sections of this study, it is important to investigate any ordination cohort differences in happiness and satisfaction with life. Figure 6.1 summarizes the findings for the 2009 survey (the graph for the 2004 survey was essentially the same).

The ANOVA shows that the differences are statistically significant (*F*=11.816, *p*<.001). Scheffe post-hoc results show significant differences between the oldest priests (those ordained over 40 years) and the middle groups of priests. Visual inspection shows the youngest priests, ordained 0–10 years, showing an apparent uptick in happiness, which is approaching a significant difference with the priests ordained 21–30 years (*p*=.071). Giving the numbers in percentages might help to make the difference more apparent: 46.9% of priests ordained 0–10 years strongly agree that they are happy as priests versus a lower 35.8% of priests ordained 21–30 years.

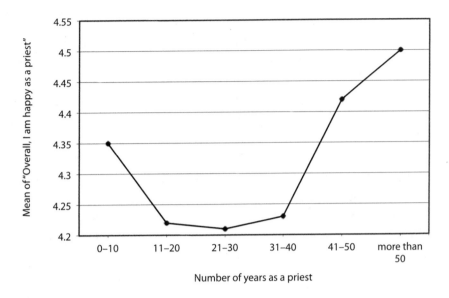

Figure 6.1. Years ordained and "Overall, I am happy as a priest"

These statistics support the findings of Dean Hoge in the 2001 NFPC study, previously cited. Hoge found that the rise in overall happiness of priests in his studies from 1970 to 2001 "was largely due to the large rise in happiness among younger priests—the 25–35-year-olds and the 36–45-year-olds."[17] He said, "Newly ordained priests feel needed today, and they are happier and more energized than they were three decades ago."[18] Hoge quoted a young priest in his 20s from 1966, over forty years ago, who said:

> It is difficult to sit in the rectory waiting for sick calls that never come. About all you can do is to think of some way of pushing yourself into special work. It's almost the only way to use your talents while you're still young. I don't think our bishops have any idea of the frustration felt by their younger priests.[19]

Things have changed greatly for the newly ordained. As previously discussed, the challenges facing newly ordained today are not a lack of work or not feeling needed. Rather, it is too much work, too much responsibility too fast, and being at risk for burning out. There are likely additional reasons as well for the rising morale of the younger priests, based on their theological and spiritual values, which we shall see in later chapters in this study.

It is also interesting to see which ordination cohort of priests is the happiest. While giving lectures on this material, one of my comments that the groups of priests always enjoy is, "And the happiest group of priests is the retired guys!" And then they laugh loudly.

Of course, they are thinking, "Wouldn't it be great to retire and stop working!" But actually, wouldn't it be a terrible indictment of priesthood if a man, after serving fifty years as a priest, became increasingly less happy? When entire dioceses or religious orders of priests gather and the younger priests see the joyful smiles on the faces of their eldest members, they see a wonderful sign of hope and encouragement.

Fifty years of priesthood and service are wearing well in the hearts of the older men. There is no better witness to the joy of priesthood than the happy faces of the most senior priests. We need their presence and their wisdom in our presbyterates. They have much to offer. The encouragement of their lives of faithful service and their joy-filled peace radiating in our midst is their greatest gift.

Summary

Despite impressions given in the media, the exceptionally high rate of priestly happiness and overall satisfaction with life should not be a complete surprise. If we take an objective look at other research findings for the past few decades, such high satisfaction rates of priests are consistent. In addition to the other research studies already cited, the 2006 General Social Survey of 27,000 Americans accomplished by the National Opinion Research Center found that *clergy in general (not simply Catholic clergy) had the highest level of job satisfaction (87% very satisfied) of any job holders and the highest level of overall happiness in life of any group in the United States.*[20] This is particularly remarkable at a time when more than 50% of Americans report being unhappy with their jobs.[21]

The CARA Priest Poll 2001 reasoned that the "relatively high levels of satisfaction among Catholic priests" is because "priests who are unhappy tend to resign."[22] However, unhappy people in all professions are more likely to resign. Do unhappy priests resign at a higher rate than, say, unhappy plumbers or teachers? I doubt it. In fact, one could argue that the permanent vows/promises of priesthood are a deterrent to resignations, a deterrent that other professions typically do not have. And priestly resignation rates, even in Dean Hoge's 2001 study of resigned priests, were not exceptionally high. CARA's stated reason for the high levels of priestly satisfaction does not square with the findings of the 2006 NORC study.

The plain facts consistently show that being a clergy member, in our case a Catholic priest, is a very satisfying vocation and a very satisfying life. As one priest summarized it in a written comment on his 2004 survey, "It (morale) is nowhere as bad as people or media think." Indeed, the statistics suggest that it is the most satisfying of any life, and a large majority of our priests agree. And there were no significant differences in happiness rates among the racial and ethnic groups surveyed. This is one thing they all agreed on: they are happy as priests!

The 2002 scandals were painful and traumatic for all priests, and the trauma continues to linger. But one might wonder if this crucifixion served, paradoxically, only to strengthen the priests. As one respondent wrote on his 2004 survey when asked about priestly morale, "It is no longer based on superficialities; it has had to go to a deeper level due to the crises." And another on the 2004 survey, commenting about priests: "They're at their best under fire." Indeed, they are.

7

Factors Contributing to
Priestly Happiness

M uch of what people commonly say about priesthood and happiness is based upon their individual experiences and anecdotal information. The extensive nature of the survey information provided in these two studies and modern statistical software together give us a chance to move beyond these individual experiences and investigate statistically the important contributors to priestly happiness for the 2,482 priests surveyed. What variables are predictive of priestly happiness? What makes a happy priest?

It might be interesting to begin by noting the relationship between workload and priestly happiness. As the previously cited CARA study noted, "Thus, the perception of having too much work is a predictor of priests' satisfaction, though not nearly the most important."[1] My findings are similar. In my 2004 study, the two survey items "Overall, I am happy as a priest" and "I feel overwhelmed with the amount of work I have to do" were only modestly correlated (r=.122, p<.001). As the CARA and my study both noted, there are factors other than workload that much more strongly predict priestly happiness.

In table 7.1, the variables in the 2009 survey that correlate mostly highly with priestly Happiness and Morale are listed (with r>.10). Recall that Happiness and Morale is a composite variable made up of

Table 7.1. Pearson's *r* correlations with Happiness and Morale

	Happiness and Morale
Inner Peace	.590
Relationship to God	.528
View of Celibacy	.468
Lonely and Unappreciated	-.458
Relationship to the Bishop	.375
Anger Problems	-.375
Dysfunctional Childhood	-.366
Obedience to Religious Authority	.364
Close Friends	.346
Childhood Mental Health Problems	-.345
Sexual Conflicts	-.305
Priests Support Each Other	.293
Difficulty Feeling Forgiven	-.281
Prayer and the Sacrament of Penance	.273
Devotion to Mary	.265
Attends Priest Gatherings	.265
Obesity and Unhealthy Coping	-.232
Family Support of Vocation	.199
Theological and Spiritual Reading	.183
Annual Retreat	.162
Work Out Problems Alone	-.113
Narcissistic Traits	-.104

Note: All correlations are highly statistically significant at p<.001. Only those correlations greater than .10 are listed. All of these variables are composite variables of several items and are listed in Appendix 3 except eight items: "Difficulty Feeling Forgiven" was a single question on the survey "I have difficulty feeling like I can be forgiven"; "Theological and Spiritual Reading," which was the survey item "I read theological or spiritual books/magazines regularly"; "Obedience to Religious Authority," which was the survey item "Obedience to religious authority is an important value for me"; "Priests Support Each Other," which was the survey item "Priests in my diocese/religious order are supportive of each other"; "Attends Priest Gatherings," which was the survey item "I attend priest gatherings in my diocese/order as often as I can"; "Annual Retreat," which was the survey item "I make an annual retreat"; "Family Support of Vocation," which was the survey item "From the beginning, my family has supported my vocation to the priesthood"; and "Work Out Problems Alone," which was the survey item: "When I have difficulties, I work out my problems by myself."

two survey items: "Overall, I am happy as a priest" and "My morale is good." The variable with the highest correlation is listed first and so on. The Pearson's *r* correlations are all highly statistically significant with *p*<.001 in each case.

These twenty-two variables were then entered into a multiple regression equation (*MR*) to put together a model to predict priestly happiness (see table 7.2). They were entered in stepwise fashion, which means that the software will first enter the variable that is the strongest predictor and subsequently move through the rest of the variables, entering them based upon which is the strongest predictor remaining.

We might be reminded again that correlation does not prove causation. We will need to use our psychological and theological background to help understand the underlying dynamics of the relationship of these variables. Once the statistical equations point out the significant relationships, I will present my best understanding of how these variables interrelate. The reader is welcome to posit a different set of underlying dynamics.

Table 7.2. Summary of multiple regression for variables predicting Happiness and Morale

Variable	B	SE B	ß	Sig.	Adj. R^2
(Constant)	1.818	.374		.000	
Neuroticism (control variable)	-.013	.005	-.037	.010	
Extraversion (control variable)	-.007	.005	-.021	.151	.025
Inner Peace	.302	.021	.276	.000	.351
View of Celibacy	.156	.014	.202	.000	.436
Relationship to God	.112	.012	.187	.000	.468
Relationship to the Bishop	.090	.014	.107	.000	.491
Lonely and Unappreciated	-.054	.010	-.102	.000	.502
Dysfunctional Childhood	-.028	.006	-.073	.000	.506
Obedience to Religious Authority	.122	.029	.073	.000	.509
Priests Support Each Other	.075	.024	.050	.002	.512
Close Friends	.016	.007	.036	.028	.513
Devotion to Mary	-.032	.013	-.043	.011	.514
Narcissistic Traits	.041	.016	.040	.008	.515
Annual Retreat	.039	.019	.030	.038	.516
Anger Problems	-.023	.010	-.040	.024	.517
Difficulty Feeling Forgiven	.051	.025	.033	.043	.517

Note: These numbers represent those from the final regression model.

Two variables were entered first as control variables: neuroticism and extraversion. These were two scales of the IPIP-NEO, a publicly available personality inventory. There is some research to suggest that happiness is affected by one's personality, such as neuroticism and extraversion. Thus, putting in these two variables first into the *MR* equation will parcel out the variance of these two variables thus enabling us to determine what the subsequent variables add to the prediction of priestly happiness. Simply put, this gives us more confidence that the subsequent results are valid.[2]

Taking out the two control variables of Extraversion and Neuroticism, *we see that the fourteen variables above account for 49.2% of the variance of Happiness and Morale* (.517-.025=.492). This is a very strong finding in social science research. We are able to predict almost half of what makes a happy priest using these fourteen variables. Of course, this means that there are other unaccounted-for variables that affect another half of what makes a happy priest. Nonetheless, *this 2009 research study has accounted for almost 50% of priestly happiness and thus is an important finding for anyone involved in priestly recruiting, formation, ongoing formation, and wellness.*

It is interesting to note that, in the *MR* equation, the twenty-two variables did not all contribute to the dependent variable Happiness and Morale and sometimes were entered in a different order than their correlations would initially suggest. This is primarily because of multicollinearity, that is, the independent variables were often highly correlated with each other. To view the correlations among all these variables, see Appendix 4. As to be expected, for example, Dysfunctional Childhood is highly correlated with Childhood Mental Health Problems (r=.59); Prayer and Sacrament of Penance is correlated with Relationship to God (r=.23); and Lonely and Unappreciated is strongly correlated with Dysfunctional Childhood (r=.40). Thus, when one of these intercorrelated variables enters the equation, it will significantly decrease the contribution by the next variable because it will have already parceled out part of its effect on the dependent variable Happiness and Morale.

There are other variables that were significantly correlated with priestly Happiness and Morale, as noted in Appendix 4. However, they did not enter the multiple regression equation. Again, this was because of multicollinearity. When an *MR* equation enters variables in a stepwise fashion, it first chooses the variable that is most predictive of the dependent variable, in this case, Happiness and Morale. It then looks for the second strongest variable, and enters it and so on. The equation builds upon itself, putting together the best predictive model. If two variables are highly correlated, as with multicollinearity, the first one entered into the *MR* equation will take out much of the predictive ability of the second variable. That is, much of the variance will have already been parceled out by the first variable.

Therefore, some variables will not be entered in the equation since their predictive quality has already been taken up by previous variables. For example, Childhood Mental Problems was not entered into the *MR* equation by the stepwise statistical routine, but its correlation with Happiness and Morale was high, $r = -.35$ ($p < .001$). This does not mean it is not important. Rather, it correlates highly with such variables as Dysfunctional Childhood ($r = .59$), which were already entered into the equation and accounted for much of the predictive ability of Childhood Mental Problems. The same is true for the variable Sexual Conflicts, which also correlates highly with variables already entered into the equation. Therefore, the *MR* equation did not enter them.

Thus, to understand what makes a happy priest, we should take into account both the *MR* equation with fourteen variables entered as well as table 7.1, which showed twenty-two variables having a significant correlation of $r > .1$.

Inner Peace

Looking closely at table 7.2, the results of the *MR* equation, we can begin to delve more deeply into those variables that predict priestly happiness. This will help us to understand better the nature of priestly life and its constitutive elements. It should help us to evaluate and modify as necessary our screening, formation, and ongoing formation of priests. And it can help priests themselves review their own lives and make any needed changes.

Reviewing the *MR* equation results, I was initially surprised by some findings. The first variable entered by the statistical routine was one of them. The composite variable Inner Peace was decidedly the strongest single predictor of priestly happiness of any variable in the entire study. The variable is composed of two items that loaded on a single factor: "I feel a sense of inner peace" and "I have a good self-image" (see Appendix 3).

This suggests that priestly happiness, more than anything else, is affected by what an individual himself brings to priesthood. This Inner Peace largely transcends the climate of the day, child abuse crises, and other external diocesan, religious order, or priestly factors. *First and foremost, we are happy in our priesthood if we are happy people inside.*

Upon further reflection, this is not completely surprising. Abraham Lincoln is often quoted as saying, "Most people are as happy as they make up their minds to be."[3] While we often think of the external world as being the source of our happiness or unhappiness, wise minds such as President Lincoln suggested otherwise.

A short time ago, I recall chatting with an elderly priest who was reflecting on his over fifty years of service. He candidly told me that he was happy with all of his assignments. He said, "Whenever I went into a place, I made up my mind to make the best of the assignment and enjoy it. And I did." He was a happy old priest.

This is a consoling finding. The most powerful predictor of our own happiness is something that we, eventually, have some control over. Rather than ceding our happiness to an external factor, we have some personal control over how happy we will be. It would be a shame to think that our life's happiness is primarily based upon the whims of external forces and the decisions of others. At the same time, it should make us reflect: "If I am not happy in my life, instead of blaming others, what am I going to do to change myself?"

Of course, it is true that some of what affects our inner peace and self-image are initially formed by forces outside of ourselves. So we do not have complete control over this. Nevertheless, they are inner realities that we as adults can and should work on as needed. And real change is possible.

Just about every priest has experienced this inner reality. We all know parishioners who appear to have few of the benefits of the world, and yet they are very happy. And, sadly, we all know others who are rich in the things of this world but are desperately unhappy. As one priest wrote on his 2004 survey, "Happiness is an inside job."

Happiness in priesthood is first and foremost affected by what we bring to the priesthood, not what is imposed upon us from the outside. Fortunately, priests report having a strong self-image and an equally strong sense of inner peace. Fully 86.0% agreed or strongly agreed with the statement, "I have a good self-image," and 87.4% agreed or strongly agreed with "I feel a sense of inner peace." *It is no accident that the overall happiness level of priests is very high since a large percentage of priests reports a sense of inner peace and self contentment, priestly happiness's strongest predictor.*

View of Celibacy

The interwoven nature of spiritual and psychological realities became very apparent to me as I reviewed the data over many months. The spiritual and the psychological are not two separate realities, but they are different lenses or aspects through which we view one whole person. While this is, in one sense, obvious since we are not two separate people—one psychological and the other spiritual—*the data in this study cannot be understood without recognizing the inseparability of these two interpenetrating aspects.*

The second most important variable entered into the *MR* equation predicting priestly happiness was the composite variable View of Celibacy. The data demonstrate that how a priest comes to grips with his commitment to celibacy, which he promises on the day of his ordination to the diaconate, is critical to how happy he will be as a priest. The variable View of Celibacy is comprised of two items: "Despite its challenges, celibacy has been a grace for me personally" and "I believe that God has called me to live a celibate life" (see Appendix 3).

These two items ask more than simply if the respondent accepts the requirement of celibacy. The items demand more from the respondent than believing celibacy is a discipline mandated by the institutional Church. Rather, they ask if respondent actually believes that God himself has called the priest to this life. Secondly, they ask if he has found, in this celibate life, more than only a functional reality that helps others.

Rather, it asks if he has come to recognize celibacy as a personal gift and grace. This requires a high level of integration and spiritual insight.

So often, celibacy is argued in the public forum on a rather mundane level, debating its historical roots and its efficacy or lack thereof. This variable View of Celibacy probes more deeply into the priest's personal connection with this commitment. Pope Paul VI, in his encyclical *Sacerdotalis Caelibatus*, speaks of celibacy as a gift to the priest and to the Church that can only be understood in the light of an intense spiritual life.[4] The variable View of Celibacy directly probes whether this deep integration has taken place.

Is celibacy too much to ask of our priests in this sex-crazed society? While not discounting the challenges and difficulties that celibacy brings, the responses of our priests were edifying (see figures 7.1 and 7.2).

Note that 75.1% agreed or strongly agreed that "Celibacy has been a personal grace" and 78.2% agreed or strongly agreed that "God has called me to live a celibate life." This level of deep commitment and spiritual reflection is impressive.

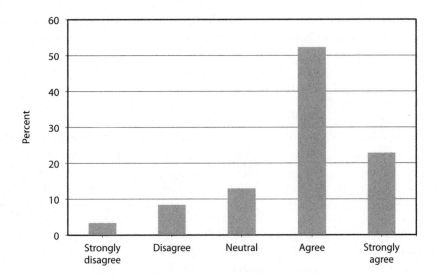

"Despite its challenges, celibacy has been a grace for me personally"

Figure 7.1. "Despite its challenges, celibacy has been a grace for me personally"

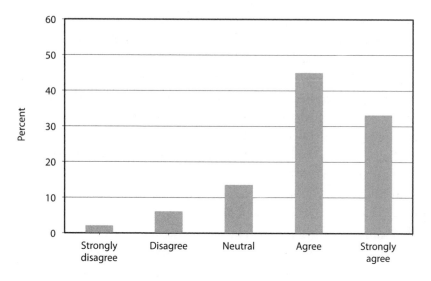

"I believe God has called me to live a celibate life"

Figure 7.2. "I believe God has called me to live a celibate life"

However, the data should also make us cognizant of the almost one quarter of priests who do not see celibacy in such a positive, personal, spiritual light. Surrounded by a society that, at best, does not understand the commitment and, at worst, actually works against it, the commitment to celibate living can be a particular challenge or even a burden to some. *Given this variable's importance for predicting the overall happiness of a priest, the Church might want to increase its efforts in forming, supporting, and assisting priests in living chaste celibacy with a positive integrity and peace.*

If a priest can come to view celibacy as a personal gift from God, he is much more likely to be a happy priest. Thankfully, a large majority have done so.

Relationship to God

The composite variable Relationship to God entered as the third predictor of Happiness and Morale. As we see in Appendix 3, Relationship to God is composed of five survey items that loaded onto a single factor in the factor analysis. The items are: "I feel that God loves me personally and directly"; "I feel a sense of closeness to God"; "I feel thankful for my blessings"; "From time to time, I feel a joy that is a grace from God"; and "I have a relationship to God (or Jesus) that is nourishing for me." One can easily see how these items are strongly related to each other and would subsequently make up a single factor.

Relationship to God was the second highest correlated variable with Happiness and Morale but was entered third in the regression equation by the SPSS routine because of multicollinearity. *It turns out that the strongest predictor of the first variable entered, Inner Peace, is, not surprisingly, Relationship to God.* The two are highly correlated, Pearson's $r=.55$ ($p<.001$). This, of itself, is important information. If Inner Peace is the most important predictor of priestly happiness, we would naturally ask ourselves, "Where do we find this inner peace?" The survey's first response, generated by the SPSS statistical routines, is, "In a relationship to God."

Thus, one cannot overstate the importance of a priest's personal relationship to God. It is the strongest predictor of the first variable, Inner Peace; it is strongly correlated with the second variable as well, View of Celibacy ($r=.36$, $p<.001$); and it stands alone as the third variable entered in the *MR* equation. In fact, a priest simply will not be a happy priest unless he has some kind of personal and direct relationship to God that is nourishing for him. As a priest wrote on his survey, "Your morale is high the closer you are to God." With this relationship, he will find much inner peace and he is liable to have a more positive understanding of celibacy as well.

To some, this might be a surprising finding. In modern social science, one would not normally look at one's relationship to God when investigating job satisfaction. I suspect we could look long and hard at social science studies before we would find a study that compared job satisfaction and relationship to God. But priesthood is no ordinary "job." In fact, we do not use such a term. We call it a "vocation," and a vocation comes from God; it is a "calling." And this calling begins and ends with a personal relationship with the God who calls.

When one views the essence of priesthood, it is then rather obvious that a relationship to God must be an essential part of any happy priestly life. How can one be and function as a priest without such a relationship? A few do . . . but not as a house built on rock.

What is exciting in this study is that these statistical routines could clearly demonstrate the strong connection between a priest's relationship to God and his happiness as a priest. And it suggests to us that if we want to raise priestly morale, one of the places to begin is with the priest's personal spiritual life. I have often thought that we spend a great deal of time in formation and ongoing formation of our priests with so many good and important things, but we leave his spiritual life to a kind of personal "catch as catch can" approach. The priest is often expected to squeeze it in, in his spare time.

Perhaps it is time to place formation and ongoing formation of a priest's relationship to God front and center. Have we ever discussed a seminarian's relationship to God as part of his fitness for ordination? While such things tend to be difficult to measure, the centrality of this relationship suggests we rethink its necessarily central place in formation. Later we will investigate, in greater depth, priests' perception of their Relationship to God in these survey results.

Relationship to Bishop

The fourth variable entered into the *MR* equation predicting Happiness and Morale was Relationship to Bishop. This variable was composed of two items: "I support my bishop's leadership" and "I have a good relationship with my bishop." These two items loaded on one new variable in the factor analysis. They obviously measure a priest's perception of his bishop and their relationship.

What is important is how central this relationship is for the happiness of an individual priest. I suspect many a bishop would be surprised to know just how important his relationship with each priest is for the man's personal happiness. However, when we look more deeply at what our Catholic theology says about the relationship of a priest to his bishop, the importance of this relationship becomes apparent.

Priests have no ministry apart from their bishops, as the *Presbyterorum Ordinis* from Vatican II noted. Priests minister "in the name of their bishop" (#6), and they are "coworkers with their bishops" (#4).[5] Priests and bishops are united in a "hierarchical communion" (#7). The ordination rite powerfully symbolizes this intense relationship with the conferral of the Holy Spirit upon the priest with the bishop's laying on of hands. Similarly, the priest folds his hands in his bishop's and promises obedience to him and his successors. For his part, the bishop is admonished to "regard priests as his brothers and friends" and "he should exercise the greatest care on behalf of the continual formation of his priests" (#7).

Priestly spirituality recognizes the deep bond between bishop and priest. Much more than a secular boss, a bishop is spiritual father, brother, coworker, and friend; his priests are an extension of his own apostolic ministry.[6] Therefore, it is no wonder that priests are strongly affected by their relationship with their bishop. I see this most obviously when I visit a diocese that is *sede vacante*, waiting for the appointment of a new bishop. The priests are anxious to know who they will be getting; much of their contentment as a priest will rest on who this person will be and what their subsequent relationship with him will be.

There has been much discussion of the relationship of bishops and priests, especially since the child sexual abuse crisis and the 2002 "Dallas Charter" (Charter for the Protection of Children and Young People), which the bishops adopted in its wake. In cases of child sexual abuse, the bishops put the needs of the victims first, and rightly so. Bishops have rightly obligated themselves to caring for victims first and to reporting all allegations of child abuse against priests to public authorities.

However, the result of these and other actions in the wake of the crisis is that more than a few priests feel that their rights would not be respected. In my 2004 survey, the sample of 1,242 priests was directly asked several questions about this. Only 27.1% of priests agreed or strongly agreed with the statement, "Priests with allegations of abuse are being treated fairly by the Church." Further, when given the statement, "I trust the Church to deal fairly with me if I am accused of misconduct," only 42.1% agreed or strongly agreed. And when asked if "The Church crisis has negatively affected my view of Church leadership,"

53.8% agreed or strongly agreed. Simply put, most priests do not believe that bishops will protect priests' rights, and this has had a chilling effect on the relationship of priests and bishops.

Priests are now wondering if their bishops will stand up for them and support them in difficult circumstances. Has the bond between bishop and priest therefore been irrevocably damaged? The two survey results, in table 7.3, are illuminating.

First, 74.9% of priests in the 2004 survey agreed/strongly agreed that their relationship with their bishop was good and 76.6% did likewise in the 2009 survey. So, the numbers are consistent, with a slight increase in 2009, that the large majority of priests view their relationship to their bishop as good.

For a supervisor, these are very high approval ratings. For example, a recent Conference Board survey of 5,000 American households found that 51% of Americans liked their supervisor. This was a marked decrease from the ratings of 60% they gave their secular bosses in 1987.[7] The statistics show that American bishops, as a whole, have a relatively very high approval rating by their priests.

These survey results were echoed in the *Los Angeles Times* poll of priests published in October 20, 2002, right during the middle of the crisis, which found that 76% of the priests said they approve "of the way the bishop who presides in your diocese is handling his duties."[8] Again, this is an independent survey reporting similar results, which gives additional credence to my findings.

There are similar findings in the 2001 CARA poll of 1,234 priests, which found that 70% of the priests strongly agree with the statement, "I have a good relationship with my bishop," and 24% somewhat agree, 3% somewhat disagree, and 3% strongly disagree.[9] While

Table 7.3. "I have a good relationship with my bishop"

	Strongly disagree (%)	Disagree (%)	Unsure/ Neutral (%)	Agree (%)	Strongly agree (%)
2004 survey	2.9	6.9	15.3	58.2	16.7
2009 survey	2.3	4.5	16.6	50.5	26.1

the Likert scaling is somewhat different than mine, these pre-2002 crisis CARA results confirm the high support bishops receive but also suggest that the crisis had a measurable impact on the relationship of priests and bishops. Although the scaling is different, the CARA results of 70% strongly agree and 24% somewhat agree to having a good relationship with the bishop seem noticeably higher than the 2004 and 2009 survey results in table 7.3.

The 2002 crisis has apparently affected the relationship, but the damage from the crisis may be waning slightly. From 2004 to 2009, we can see that the percentage of priests who agreed or strongly agreed that their relationship to their bishop is good has increased from 74.9 to 76.6% with the largest increase being in the strongly agree, an increase of 9.4%. It remains to be seen how lasting the damage will be, but there is a clear improvement in the relationship over the past few years.

CARA research results confirm that there was a similar dip in satisfaction among laity with the leadership of the Catholic Church in the wake of the crisis. In January 2001, 79% of Catholics said they were either somewhat or very satisfied with the leadership of the Church. This dipped to 55% in May 2002. Since then, it has rebounded to 77%, almost completely returning to its pre-crisis high.[10]

Overall, the relationship between a priest and his own bishop remains strong. It has a very strong positive rating currently of 76.6%. Nonetheless, the relationship between bishop and priest is a deep theological reality that is important for every priest's well-being. It remains a subject for continued reflection and work. As one priest wrote in his 2004 survey, "Morale is alright, but there needs to be healing in the relationship between bishops and priests in light of the last two years of scandal."

It might be good also to remind priests that a relationship is a two-way street. If your current relationship with your bishop is not what you would like, instead of passively leaving it all in the hands of the bishop, what can you yourselves do to make it better? Perhaps you might begin by praying for him, given his increasingly demanding and difficult ministry . . . much like your own.

Lonely and Unappreciated

The next and fifth variable to predict Happiness and Morale was the composite variable Lonely and Unappreciated. After the previous four variables, this was the next strongest predictor of whether a priest is happy or not. This variable is composed of four items: "I get angry when others criticize me"; "I suffer from loneliness"; "I am too hard on myself"; and "My special gifts are not being recognized" (see Appendix 3). Thus, if a priest is lonely and feels neglected and unappreciated, he is much more likely to be an unhappy priest.

If one looks at Appendix 4 for the correlations of the other composite variables with Lonely and Unappreciated, it is interesting that it is correlated more highly with other variables than View of Celibacy (r= -.31). Perhaps feeling lonely as a priest has less to do with celibacy and more to do with other variables.

Feeling lonely and unappreciated is more highly correlated with Anger Problems (r=.50), Childhood Mental Problems (r=.43), Dysfunctional Childhood (r=.40), and Sexual Conflicts (r=.37). *This suggests that the variable Lonely and Unappreciated springs as much, if not more, from one's personal problems than from trying to live a celibate life.*

To check these findings more closely, I correlated the individual survey item "I suffer from loneliness" by itself with the composite variables in the previous paragraph. The findings were confirmed that loneliness as a priest is as much if not more highly correlated with personal problems than it is with one's view of celibacy. The correlations with "I suffer from loneliness" are Anger Problems (r=.35), Sexual Conflicts (r=.35), Childhood Mental Problems (r=.34), Dysfunctional Childhood (r=.33), versus View of Celibacy (r= -.33).

We will look further at celibacy later in this book, but the initial findings suggest that loneliness appears to be closely connected to one's internal psychological deficits and relational problems. Rather than being the result of the imposition of celibacy, priests are particularly susceptible to feeling lonely and unappreciated when they have suffered from childhood dysfunction and grown up in dysfunctional families. Similarly, they are more likely to feel lonely and unappreciated if they have problems making relationships, have sexual problems, and have problems managing anger.

This certainly puts loneliness and feeling unappreciated in a new light. Will an exceptionally lonely priest stop being lonely if he left and got married? Perhaps . . . but I also know more than a few married people who have conflicts, anger, and relational problems. They, too, suffer from loneliness and feeling unloved. For these suffering married folks and our lonely priests, it may be that the trouble stems from human psychological deficits and that much inner healing is needed. *For those priests who suffer from loneliness, celibacy may be the venue, not the cause.*

Dysfunctional Childhood

The next and sixth variable to predict Happiness and Morale is the composite variable Dysfunctional Childhood. There are six survey items that comprise this composite variable: "I grew up in a dysfunctional family"; "I was emotionally abused as a child"; "Growing up, I had a good relationship with my mother"; "Growing up, I had a good relationship with my father"; "I was physically abused as a child"; "A member of my immediate family has suffered from psychological problems." As mentioned previously, coming from a dysfunctional background can be a significant liability to becoming a happy priest later in life. Of course, this does not mean that all those from dysfunctional backgrounds will be unhappy. But it does mean that it is a specific challenge for those who carry such childhood "baggage."

As demonstrated previously, due to the breakdown in the family and other societal dysfunctions, younger priests are saying that they are coming from dysfunctional families at a much higher rate than older priests. For example, we see in figures 7.3 and 7.4 how the different ordination cohorts of priests describe their relationship with their mothers and fathers. It is clear that there has been a marked decrease in positive parental relationships for priests since 1970 with younger priests reporting the least positive relationships with their parents.

In figures 7.3 and 7.4, the higher the mean number, the better the relationship. With an ANOVA, the differences were significant ("Relationship with Father" $F=19.096$, $p<.001$; "Relationship with Mother"

F=13.265, p<.001).[11] Therefore, we see a marked drop in good relationships with mothers and fathers in the younger cohorts of priests.

Could it be that younger priests are simply more willing than the oldest priests to recognize or admit to coming from a dysfunctional background? This is possible. However, earlier data showed the percentage of priests coming from divorced parents is rising rapidly. While this is only one factor, it is a significant one. Also, young priests are reporting higher levels of anxiety and depression on the BSI-18, as noted previously in figures 4.3 and 4.4, which is correlated with coming from a more dysfunctional background. Previously, in figure 4.6, we also saw younger priests reporting higher levels of having childhood mental health problems. And a common concern expressed among vocational and formation personnel today is the seeming greater psychological "baggage" of candidates for the priesthood. All of these factors suggest

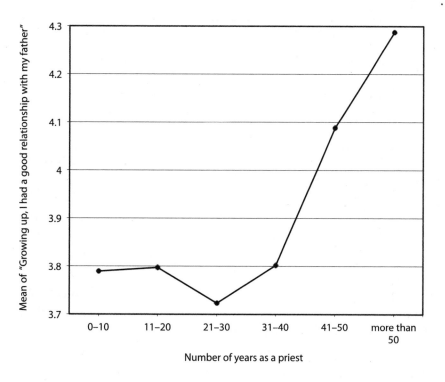

Figure 7.3. Years ordained and "Growing up, I had a good relationship with my father"

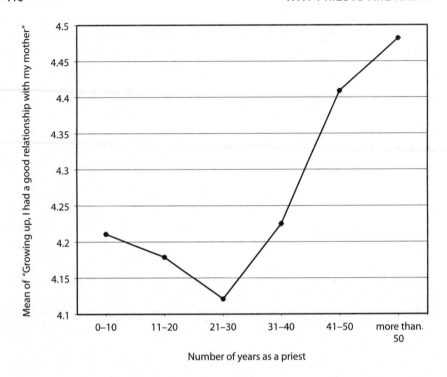

Figure 7.4. Years ordained and "Growing up, I had a good relationship with my mother"

that the reported increase in younger priests coming from dysfunctional backgrounds is, in fact, a real increase.

Nevertheless, we recall that it was actually the priests ordained 0–10 years that are experiencing an uptick in happiness as a priest. Shouldn't this dysfunctional background result in younger priests being less happy as priests, since Dysfunctional Childhood is negatively correlated with priestly happiness? However, Dysfunctional Childhood is only one variable among many that predict priestly happiness; if newly ordained are reporting higher rates of priestly happiness, then the factors affecting this must be found elsewhere.

These figures above should once again emphasize the sensitivity we ought to have in screening and forming candidates for the priesthood. Taking individuals with seriously dysfunctional backgrounds will likely have negative ramifications for their future well-being as priests.

Obedience to Religious Authority

It is interesting that one survey item, "Obedience to religious authority is an important value for me," had such a strong connection with Happiness and Morale (r=.36). It is the seventh variable entered in our *MR* equation predicting Happiness and Morale. As noted previously, the ordinand promises obedience to the bishop and his successors during the ordination rite. This is a solemn part of the rite and is considered a constitutive part of priestly life. For a religious priest, obedience is typically one of the three fundamental vows of religious life. A priest is not a "lone-ranger"; he is part of a religious order or part of a diocese. Obedience to religious authority is an essential element of his life.

It is significant that valuing this promise or vow correlates so highly with priestly happiness. One can only surmise what this connection might be. Why is it that priests who continue to believe in the importance of obedience to religious authority are happier priests? The answer is likely to be a complex series of factors.

One obvious reason is that priesthood is a life of humble service. Obedience and service are critical concepts in priestly life. When a priest wants to head off on his own and be served rather than to serve, he is in trouble. If his focus is more self-centered, a kind of clerical narcissism, then he is not able to give himself completely to the Church and to the people. However, when a priest humbly accepts his duty of service to the Church and to the people, in a full and complete self-gift symbolized and concretized in his promise/vow of obedience to his superiors, he is likely to be a happier man.

As we are beginning to see, many of the factors that make up priestly happiness are expressions of an authentic priestly spirituality. Simply put, *when a priest whole-heartedly embraces and lives his priestly vocation with integrity, he is a happier priest.* We will see this truth echoed again and again throughout this study.

The good news is that 72.8% of priests either agreed or strongly agreed with the statement, "Obedience to religious authority is an important value for me." Once again, we cannot overlook the ones who did not agree or were neutral. In this case, 7.6% disagreed or strongly disagreed with the statement. Not surprising, there was a rather strong correlation between Obedience to Religious Authority and composite variable Relationship to Bishop ($r=.38$). It may be that there is a small minority of priests who do not value obedience to the bishop or major superior and do not get along with him.

I decided to search the database for this subset of priests. How many of our 2,482 priests both do not value obedience and do not have a good relationship with the bishop? There were 47 diocesan priests (no religious) who disagreed or strongly disagreed with both statements; thus they do not value obedience and do not have a good relationship with the bishop. This represents a small 1.9% of the entire sample or 2.2% of the sample of diocesan priests. No doubt, these men must feel somewhat on the fringe of the diocese and perhaps even the priesthood.

Indeed, a relatively large percentage of this small group, 23.4% ($n=11$), is thinking of leaving the priesthood, and fully 31.9% ($n=15$) said they are unhappy as priests. This is opposed to only 3.1% of the entire sample of priests who said they are thinking of leaving the priesthood and only 2.6% who said they were unhappy. *If one does not have a good relationship with the bishop and does not value obedience, the individual is obviously much more likely to be unhappy as a priest and to consider leaving.*

But the large majority of priests continue to value their promise of obedience to their bishop or religious superior. At their ordination, they promised to be obedient and they continue to value their promise. And they are happier men for it.

Priests Support Each Other

The next and eighth variable to predict priestly happiness was, again, a single survey item, "Priests in my diocese/religious order are supportive of each other." The correlation was a solid $r=.29$ ($p<.001$). Those priests who perceived priestly mutual support as being good were happier priests. As one priest wrote on his 2004 survey, "The more healthy relationships priests have with each other, the greater their morale."

The CARA Priest Poll 2001 had similar findings: "Priests who perceive a lack of encouragement or support from fellow priests, who have relatively few close friends who are priests, and who view their bishop or superiors as unsupportive are more likely than others to express dissatisfaction."[12] Previously, we noted the close connection between one's relationship to the bishop or superior and one's priestly happiness, as also found in the CARA study. Now, this study also notes the strong connection between priestly mutual support and individual priestly happiness.

Priestly support is something that priests need and value. For example, priests who attended priest gatherings—such as the annual Chrism Mass, priest retreats, and convocations of priests—were more likely to be happy men (see Appendix 4, $r=.27$). Attending priest gatherings is one way that priests express their mutual support, and these important gatherings enhance priestly communion as well.

This, too, is indicative of the spirituality intrinsic to the priesthood. A priest is not ordained as a private professional, such as a doctor or lawyer. He cannot go wherever he wills and hang up his professional shingle. No. He is ordained into a presbyterate, a group of priests who minister side by side under the leadership of a bishop or superior. This is nowhere better symbolized than in the ordination rite. Typically, after the bishop lays his hands on the heads of the ordinands, most dioceses have all the priests come up and do the same. This emphasizes the priestly communion that he is entering.

This communion is more than simply a group of friends or coworkers. Rather, it is a deep spiritual bond uniting priests around the world. Wherever a priest goes, he is welcomed around the altar to concelebrate the Mass with his brothers. For example, when a priest goes to Rome and concelebrates the Mass with priests from many different countries, he is visibly reminded of this sacramental bond. And whenever he concelebrates with his brother priests in his own diocese, he is again reminded of and reexperiences this bond.

Just as all Christians are united in the sacrament of baptism into the one Body of Christ, so, too, are all priests united in their one sacrament of holy orders. When the bond among priests is kept strong, it strengthens all the priests in it. When it is weak, every priest suffers.

The 2004 and 2009 survey results suggest that the priestly bond is one area that needs work. The results from both surveys are found in table 7.4.

The results are relatively stable over time. Since 2004, there has been a modest increase in the percentage of priests who believe priests are mutually supportive. However, there are still 31.4% of priests in the 2009 survey who are neutral or disagree that priests are mutually supportive in their dioceses or religious orders. Given the centrality of this for the spirituality and happiness of priesthood, it is too low.

The fissures among priests in the United States are commonly discussed. Factors such as ethnic and racial diversity affect it. For example, Mass is said in some of our largest dioceses each Sunday in scores of different languages. One of the larger priestly divisions of our day is based on theology and age. Young priests are sometimes pitted against middle-aged priests—John Paul II priests versus Vatican II priests, and so on. As one who travels the globe meeting with priests, I can attest to the real fissures in the US presbyterate. They remind me of the intense fissures in American politics. While these fissures in the Church are everywhere around the globe, they seem to be particularly acute in the United States. As some American priests wrote on their 2004 surveys: "My biggest problem as a priest today is: divisions in the presbyterate" and "The most important thing I could say about the morale of priests is: *priests are really not supportive of one another.*"

With 68.6% of priests saying there is mutual support among priests, one should not consider the lack of harmony to be a concern expressed by all. Nevertheless, it is something that is important to priests and something with which they are often not completely content. As I meet with priests and ask them about their concerns, they will often mention two issues. They will first mention chronic excessive workload. But then they will often follow it up with lack of unity in the presbyterate. These

Table 7.4. "Priests are supportive of one another in my diocese" (2004 survey); "Priests in my diocese/religious order are supportive of each other" (2009 survey)

	Strongly agree (%)	Agree (%)	Unsure/ Neutral (%)	Disagree (%)	Strongly disagree (%)
2004 survey	7.9	52.8	20.0	15.1	4.3
2009 survey	10.0	58.6	17.7	10.4	3.3

are issues that priests are concerned with and I believe affect them more on a daily basis than the child sexual abuse scandal or any other erupting scandals in the media.

I share their concern and more than a few times have been stunned by the way some within the Church speak about their brothers and sisters in the faith. This lack of unity and civility spills over into the presbyterate and causes damage to harmony and unity among our priests. Many priests know it; they feel it, and they are unhappy with it.

Close Friends

The next and the ninth variable that predicts priestly happiness is the composite variable Close Friends. This variable is composed of six individual items that loaded on a single factor, which I have labeled as Close Friends (see Appendix 3). The items are: "Growing up I had close friends"; "I currently have close priest friends"; "I get emotional support from others"; "During the seminary, I made some close friends"; "I share my problems and feelings with close friends"; "I have good lay friends who are an emotional support for me personally."

As can be seen from visual inspection, these items all probe whether the respondent has had close friendships throughout his life. The correlation between the composite variables Close Friends and Happiness and Morale is positive and strong: $r=.35$ ($p<.001$). Thus, *priests who have good friends are much more likely to be happier priests.*

In the last few decades, the importance of celibate priests developing healthy, chaste friendships has been increasingly emphasized. It is increasingly understood that good, human relationships are important for all people including celibate priests. During their priestly formation programs, seminarians and priests are given workshops on forming and maintaining solid human relationships with other priests and with laity as well, yet maintaining appropriate celibate boundaries. This study gives concrete statistical support to the need for such relationships for priestly happiness and well-being.

In his Apostolic Exhortation *Pastores Dabo Vobis*, Pope John Paul II called the priest a "man of communion." This is true on many different levels. The priest is a man of the Eucharist, commonly called

Communion. Also, he is someone who is charged with building up the community or communion of the faithful in his local Church. Similarly, he is a man who gives himself to others, building solid human relationships not only as a pastor of souls but also as a member of the community himself who needs the life-giving warmth of human friendship.

I spent the last seventeen years working in a residential program for priests with personal difficulties. They came with many presenting issues such as alcohol addiction, depression, sexual boundary violations, personality disorders, and the like. Nevertheless, a common underlying theme among many of them was a difficulty forming healthy friendships. A significant part of our work was to help them heal from past wounds and begin to develop healthy, chaste friendships. When they were able to do so, they were happier men, better priests, and ultimately reported a stronger relationship with God (the latter will be directly addressed in a later chapter). As one priest wrote on his 2004 survey, "Priests need to keep connecting with people, bishops, and one another . . . to keep them strong, joyful, and peace filled."

It might be helpful to look at the percentages of priests from the 2009 survey currently reporting close friendships with priests and laity (see table 7.5).

First, we see that the overwhelming majority of priests report having good friendships, 93% with laity and 87.6% with other priests. This is a very strong percentage and no doubt contributes to the high rates of happiness and morale reported by the priests. Our priests are indeed "men of communion." They build good friendships both with other priests and with laity. As noted previously in this study, they are men who enjoy celibate intimacy with others, and it enriches their lives.

Table 7.5. Close priest friends and good lay friends

	Strongly agree (%)	Agree (%)	Neutral (%)	Disagree (%)	Strongly disagree (%)
"I currently have close priest friends"	45.9	41.7	7.7	3.9	.9
"I have good lay friends who are an emotional support for me personally"	40.7	52.3	4.4	2.0	.6

For example, the survey item "I share my problems and feelings with close friends" is designed to probe if priests actually do share on a deeper level with friends. It specifically asks if they share "feelings" with others. The results are reported in table 7.6.

The strong agreement with this modern kind of intimacy question among a group of male priests is interesting. Sharing feelings is not something that males in our society have traditionally emphasized as being important or even something that males should do. However, priests are comfortable with not only accepting it in general, but also indicating that it is a part of their own lives: 83.2% of priests agreed or strongly agreed that they do share their problems and feelings with close friends.

It might be interesting to see if there is a difference among ordination cohorts. If this is something that has been emphasized in recent years in seminary formation as well as in the general society, then one would expect to see differences among ordination cohorts of priests. The ANOVA was significant with $F=11.838$ and $p<.001$. Graphing the results visually demonstrates the difference (see figure 7.5).[13]

Priests ordained since 1980 are more likely to acknowledge that they "share their problems and feelings with close friends" than priests ordained before 1980. This is likely a cultural shift in the general male population and likely also an effect of the changes in priestly formation, emphasizing "human formation."

However, there was no significant difference in ordination cohorts of priests indicating that they had close priest friends or good lay friends, or in the composite variable Good Friends. Thus, the change in newer priests may be their willingness to engage in a deeper emotional intimacy with friends or it may simply be their willingness to admit to such

Table 7.6. "I share my problems and feelings with close friends"

	Strongly agree (%)	Agree (%)	Neutral (%)	Disagree (%)	Strongly disagree (%)
"I share my problems and feelings with close friends"	27.9	55.3	9.9	5.9	1.0

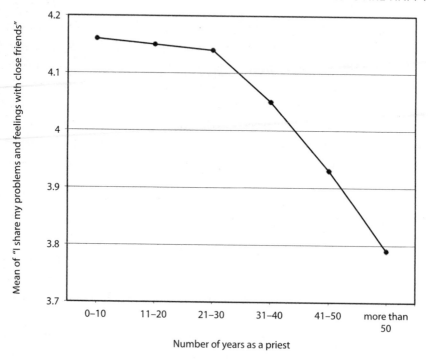

Figure 7.5. Years ordained and "I share my problems and feelings with close friends"

sharing, which seems to be more acceptable to males these days. But on having close friends, priests and laity, there were no significant differences between younger and older priests.

Devotion to Mary

The next variable to predict priestly Happiness and Morale was the composite variable Devotion to Mary. Despite being the tenth variable, the correlation between the two variables was still rather strong at $r=.27$ ($p<.001$). The composite variable is composed of two questions that loaded strongly together on the factor analysis: "Mary is an important part of my priestly life" and "I have a devotion to the Virgin Mary."

Once again, we are reminded that correlation does not mean causation. Nevertheless, the strength of the correlation and the fact that this variable, Devotion to Mary, provides some unique predictive capability to priestly happiness not supplied by the previous nine variables, suggests that there is something important at work here. But what?

A devotion to the Blessed Virgin Mary has traditionally been not only an important part of Catholic spirituality, but even more intensely an integral part of the spiritual lives of Catholic priests. While Catholics consider Mary to be a spiritual mother to all the faithful, she is thought to be particularly close to her priests, who are uniquely configured in their ordination to the image of her divine Son. When Mary looks upon a priest, she sees the face of her own beloved Son.

And priests have looked to Mary as a Mother and a special source of affection. For celibate males, Mary is sometimes considered to be the "woman" in the priests' lives. Pope John Paul II echoed the timeless truth that Jesus gave his Mother to all the faithful on the cross when he said, "Behold your Mother." But he added that it was no accident that the person to whom Mary was given was an apostle, John. Thus, she was given to all the faithful, but especially to priests.

While all priests do not have a devotion to the Blessed Virgin, it has long been an integral part of priestly spirituality. Since the Second Vatican Council, we have typically heard less about Marian devotion from the pulpits in the United States. In my 2009 survey, how did our priests measure up? We see the results in table 7.7.

The large majority of priests, about 72%, agree that Mary is an important part of their priestly and spiritual lives. Again, this high percentage of concurrence in a variable that is predictive of priestly happiness can only strengthen priestly morale and happiness.

Table 7.7. Devotion to Mary

	Strongly agree (%)	Agree (%)	Neutral (%)	Disagree (%)	Strongly disagree (%)
"I have a devotion to the Virgin Mary"	24.5	48.1	16.1	9.1	2.2
"Mary is an important part of my priestly life"	26.7	45.0	16.3	10.0	1.9

It is interesting how important spiritual values are for priestly happiness and morale. It is clear that being a happy priest means much more than simply taking care of one's psychological needs. Already we have seen variables with spiritual overtones—such as View of Celibacy, Relationship to God, Relationship to Bishop, Obedience to Religious Authority, and now Devotion to Mary—being of critical importance to a priest's well-being. A priest who does not focus a major part of his life on the spiritual is obviously not going to be a happy priest. It would be no secret to speak of priesthood as a spiritual vocation. However, this study offers concrete statistical support to the centrality of the spiritual dimension of a priestly life.

And now we see that Devotion to Mary contributes significantly to priestly happiness. Taking a strictly social science perspective, one might speculate about the internal motivations of a priest with a Marian devotion and how this might predispose him to priestly happiness. But we might also ask ourselves, "Might not Mary be a real person in the lives of these priests and could it not be that she actually is a conduit of grace and consolation for them?" While such spiritual realities cannot be proven in a statistical study, these findings point in that direction. Priests and dioceses/religious orders who have given a diminished place to Mary in the wake of Vatican II may want to reflect upon these findings.

In a book I edited in which priests reflected upon their own devotion to Mary, one of the priests shared an experience he had as a young priest. Praying with a young woman who had lost a child, like Mary did, he invoked Our Lady's intercession. Then, the priest wrote, "As I was encouraging her to confide in this special, loving woman, I felt a presence enter my office, a presence of ineffable sweetness. . . . The experience was real and perceptible, palpable for both of us. . . . Mary was real."[14]

Narcissistic Traits

The next and eleventh variable to predict priestly happiness and morale is Narcissistic Traits. As we move toward the end of the multiple regression equation, the strength of the correlations is necessarily declining. In this case, the correlation between Happiness and Morale and Narcissistic Traits is $r = -.11$ ($p<.001$). Of course, the relationship is negative (-). There is an inverse relationship: as the priest increasingly has narcissistic personality traits, he is less likely to be a happy priest.

The items that comprise this composite variable are two: "I use people to satisfy my own needs" and "Others are often envious of me." They loaded together in a subsequent factor analysis, and those familiar with personality disorders will recognize that these two items are aspects of a narcissistic personality structure: using other people to satisfy their needs and believing that others are envious of them. It should be noted that this is not a fully developed narcissistic scale nor should it be viewed as such. However, it does pull for narcissistic aspects, hence its name Narcissistic Traits.

This composite variable correlates significantly with several other composite variables, most highly with Lonely and Unappreciated ($r=.29$), Anger Problems ($r=.28$), Sexual Conflicts ($r=.20$), Dysfunctional Childhood ($r=.18$), and Childhood Mental Problems ($r=.18$). It is not surprising that these men would be more likely to feel lonely and unappreciated, have anger problems and sexual conflicts, and come from dysfunctional childhoods, experiencing mental problems growing up. Incidentally, these psychological dynamics are not inconsistent with narcissism, which again supports the use of the word narcissism with this variable.

As noted previously, priesthood is a life of humble, obedient service. This runs counter to any narcissistic trends of self-aggrandizement and believing oneself to be superior to others. We are all aware of individuals with such traits and perhaps see streaks of it in ourselves. But these temptations are contrary to the spirit of priesthood. This study suggests they negatively impact one's happiness as a priest.

Fortunately, the percentage who endorsed these traits in this study was low: only 8.9% agreed or strongly agreed "I use people to satisfy my own needs," and 13.3% agreed or strongly agreed "Others are often envious of me." For those who suffer from narcissistic wounds in childhood that later translate into a narcissistic personality structure, priesthood is likely to be less satisfying than for others without such wounds.

Annual Retreat

Once again, we see a variable entering the *MR* equation that is strongly related to the priest's spiritual life: Annual Retreat. This was the twelfth variable to enter the equation. It was based on a single survey item which said, "I make an annual retreat."

The previously cited CARA study did not find a significant relationship between spiritual activities—such as prayer and priestly retreats—and priestly happiness.[15] My 2009 survey found a significant albeit modest relationship: $r=.16$, $p<.001$. Similarly, there was a modest relationship ($r=.18$, $p<.001$) with the single survey item: "I read theological or spiritual books/magazines regularly." Given the larger sample size, my 2009 survey has more statistical power and thus is more likely to find a smaller but significant relationship.

Similarly, this 2009 study found a significant relationship between the composite variables Prayer and the Sacrament of Penance and priestly Happiness and Morale ($r=.27$, $p<.001$). The composite variable is composed of the three items: "I receive the Sacrament of Penance about: at least weekly, monthly, every three months, every six months, yearly, less than yearly"; "I pray privately each day about: not daily, 1–15 min., 16–30 min., 31–59 min., 60 min. or more"; and "I pray most or all the Liturgy of Hours daily." (As will be noted below, however, this composite variable was not entered into the *MR* equation by the statistical routine since its variance was previously parceled out by antecedent variables entered into the equation.)

The priests self-reported that 80% almost all the time or usually make an annual retreat. While this is good news for the strong majority of priests, 20% are not consistent in this important spiritual practice. Does it need more emphasis from presbyterates and Church leaders?

Clearly, taking the time to make an annual retreat, to pray, to do spiritual reading, and to receive the Sacrament of Penance are all positively correlated with priestly happiness and important priestly spiritual practices.

Anger Problems

The thirteenth variable to be entered into the *MR* equation by the SPSS program is Anger Problems. This is a composite variable comprised of the following four items: "I have consistent problems getting along with people"; "I have trouble managing my anger"; "My relationships seem to have more conflict than others have"; and "I have angry outbursts which upset others." After having spent many years working with priests in difficulty, I saw a commonality that surfaced in treatment was priests with interpersonal problems, particularly those with anger issues and often in conflict with others. Since the priest is a "man of communion," as noted previously, if he cannot develop good relationships and is plagued by anger and conflict, then his priesthood and his own happiness will suffer.

This raises an important issue for screening and formation. In our screening we ought specifically to check if priestly candidates have anger issues and relational problems. These problems are particularly devastating in priestly life. Our residential treatment programs work hard to heal priests with such buried anger and to facilitate them making healthy relationships.

Having anger issues and relationship conflicts is strongly correlated to Childhood Mental Problems ($r=.46$) and Dysfunctional Childhood ($r=.42$). While we have known about the devastating effects of growing up in dysfunctional backgrounds, it may be that we have underestimated its impact in later life and the difficulty of moving beyond it. Although spiritual and psychological healing can go a long way in bringing inner healing and peace, *these survey findings are increasingly showing that priestly screening and formation personnel should be more cautious in accepting candidates who come from seriously dysfunctional backgrounds.*

In my initial interviews of incoming priest-clients at a residential program, I was struck with how much anger plays a central role in many of their problems. At the end of treatment, I would interview them all again. If the priest was still stuck in his anger, I knew that he did not "get it" and would likely continue to have problems. But if the client sat before me with a twinkle in his eyes and peace in his heart, I knew that he had found peace and that the pervasive anger was gone. Then I knew he would do well upon his return to priestly ministry.

Difficulty Feeling Forgiven

The last and fourteenth variable entered into the *MR* equation was the individual item Difficulty Feeling Forgiven. The item specifically was "I have difficulty feeling like I can be forgiven." It significantly and negatively correlates with priestly Happiness and Morale ($r= -.28$, $p<.001$). Those who are mired in a feeling of not being able to be forgiven are likely to be less happy as priests.

This item also correlates strongly with a number of other composite variables such as Relationship to God (-.39), Anger Problems (.37), Inner Peace (-.36), and Lonely and Unappreciated (.34). Thus, those who have difficulty feeling forgiven are more likely to have anger problems and a lack of inner peace, and to feel lonely and unappreciated, plus to have a perceived decreased relationship to God.

However, since all those variables were already entered into the equation, and Difficulty Feeling Forgiven was subsequently entered as statistically significant, then it must be accounting for an aspect of priestly happiness in a unique way from these other variables. What is its unique contribution?

One might hypothesize that people who have difficulty feeling forgiven may be suffering from some inner guilt or shame that continues to haunt them. Or they may be currently engaged in some behavior that they see as sinful, and they are not currently able to break free of such behavior. There are likely to be other possibilities as well. But its core contribution, like Inner Peace, probably relates to an inner personal state which is largely independent of external structural factors in the priesthood. It is not something the priesthood needs to deal with per se; rather it is something with which the individual priest personally needs to come to grips.

What the specific issue is cannot be determined by this study. However, it is positively correlated with the composite variable Sexual Conflicts ($r=.31$) so we can assume that some of the priests are suffering from conflicts with their sexual orientation, sexuality in general, and/or behaviors now or in the past. But the correlation is not 1.0, so there are other conditions that are leading some priests to have Difficulty Feeling Forgiven.

Nevertheless, the percentage of priests who suffer in this way is low. Only 7.6% of the priest sample either agreed or strongly agreed with the statement: "I have difficulty feeling like I can be forgiven." Still, it remains an important issue for a number of priests.

Forgiveness is a very human issue but especially challenging for priests who hold themselves to a very high standard. My experience is that priests tend to be hardest on themselves. While they readily speak to their parishioners of the love and mercy of God, they often omit themselves from being eligible for such divine forgiveness. As one priest coming into residential treatment told me, "I am very good at preaching and teaching about God's mercy, but I cannot apply it to myself." One of the most exciting changes that can take place in a priest's spiritual life, when he suffers from feeling outside of God's mercy, is for him to experience directly and personally the mercy of God, that God loves him just as he is. More than one priest has spoken to me of such an experience during residential treatment and how it changed their lives.

Summary

The model that was generated by the 2009 survey was strong in its ability to predict the variable Happiness and Morale. It was able to identify fourteen variables that predict 49.2% of what makes a happy priest, even after controlling for two personality variables (neuroticism and extraversion). Of course, there is another 50.8% of priestly happiness that we cannot account for in this study, but the findings are strong and should be an important part of future priestly screening, formation, and ongoing formation.

The fourteen variables that surfaced help us to understand why research studies continually find that priests, as a group, are very happy in their lives and vocations. As the 2006 National Opinion Research Center study found, more so than any other job or vocation in the entire United States, clergy rank number one in job satisfaction and life satisfaction. The priests responded very positively to almost all of the fourteen variables in the 2009 study. For example, in their Relationship to the Bishop (the number four factor), 76.6% felt they had a good relationship with him. We will see in later chapters that almost unanimously priests report a nourishing relationship to God, which was the number three factor. As we saw in earlier chapters, the mean psychological health of our priests is slightly better than the health of the general population. Each of these positive factors contributes to making a happy presbyterate, and, as a group, our priests score well on all of them.

At the same time, we would do well to note that priests were not unanimous in their happiness nor did they all report being content on each of the variables. There was a small but significant minority that struggles with priesthood, is unhappy, feels isolated from brother priests and the bishop, and has internal and relational problems. We often speak of the "multiplier effect" of priests: one happy priest can positively affect the lives of thousands of others to whom he ministers and one unhappy priest can do the same, but negatively. One unhappy employee in a large corporation might have little impact on the company's performance, but one unhappy, maladjusted priest can be devastating to a diocese, of which we have recently been reminded. For the welfare of every priest and for the people, we ought to strive for unanimity.

As I review the variables that correlated highly with Happiness and Morale, there are several summary findings that are noteworthy:

1. *Being happy first and foremost comes from within.* If a priest finds himself to be unhappy as a priest, he should first look within. If he is carrying within himself a lack of self-esteem, a poor self-image, and a lack of inner peace, he is likely to be unhappy, wherever he goes. As one priest wrote on his survey, "Happiness is an inside job."

2. *A priest will not be happy unless he has a strong spiritual life.* There were a number of factors that strongly demonstrated the importance of a priest's spiritual life for his personal happiness. His relationship to God, devotion to the Blessed Virgin Mary, annual retreat, prayer, going to confession, spiritual reading, and the like all contribute strongly to his priestly satisfaction. The study suggests that the priest with a vibrant spiritual life will likely be a happy man.

3. *Understanding celibacy as a gift from God is essential to priestly happiness.* The happiest priests were the ones who came to see their

celibate commitment as something asked by God and ultimately a source of grace and gift for the priest personally. Rather than seeing it as a burden imposed by the Church, the happy priest moved to a positive spiritual integration of this important reality in his life.

4. *The bishop is a very important figure in the life of a priest.* The findings highlighted the importance of a priest's relationship to his bishop, especially for his personal happiness. If he has a good relationship with his bishop and continues to value his promise of obedience, he is much more likely to be a happy priest.

5. *The challenges of personal pathology should not be underestimated.* A common theme in some of the unhappy priests was individuals with considerable psychological baggage. Priests from dysfunctional childhoods, anger problems, mental health problems in childhood, sexual conflicts, and narcissistic traits were much more likely to be unhappy as priests. Screening and formation of candidates ought not to underestimate the impact of these personal problems.

6. *A happy priest is a man who builds healthy relationships.* A number of the variables highlighted the identity of a priest as a "man of communion." A happy priest is one who has close priest and lay friends and shares his life, emotions, and challenges with others. A happy priest is someone who values priestly fraternity and mutual support. A priest whose relationships are often conflictual and/or who is isolated and alone will be less fulfilled. An important question for future candidate screening for the priesthood is: Can this person build and foster healthy relationships? Building communion and community is a constitutive part of priestly life.

8

Those Thinking of Leaving the Priesthood

Previous studies have looked at the percentages of priests who are thinking of leaving the priesthood. For example, in the 2001 NFPC study, Hoge and Wenger reported that "Only 1% said they 'will probably leave,' and another 4% said they are 'uncertain.'" They added, "This question was asked in 1970, 1985, 1993, and 2001, and the number saying 'I will definitely not leave' rose from 59% to 79% during this time. The level of unrest among priests has subsided."[1] The October 2002 *Los Angeles Times* poll of priests, conducted right in the middle of the sexual abuse crisis, concluded, "Virtually all priests say they would not leave the priesthood if they had a chance to choose again (71% definitely, 19% probably), while 7% say if they had to do it over again, priesthood would not be their choice."[2]

Both my 2004 and 2009 surveys asked a similar question. The results were comparable to these other studies. In table 8.1, we see the results.

In 2004, 5.9% of priests agreed/strongly agreed that they were thinking of leaving the priesthood. In 2009, this number dropped almost in half to 3.1%. The largest change was in those who strongly disagreed with this statement, increasing from 64.1% in 2004 to 77% in 2009. This suggests an even stronger commitment to priesthood and supports

Table 8.1. 2004 and 2009 survey results: "I am thinking of leaving the priesthood"

	Strongly agree (%)	Agree (%)	Unsure/ Neutral (%)	Disagree (%)	Strongly disagree (%)
2004 survey	1.9	4.0	5.0	25.0	64.1
2009 survey	1.4	1.7	4.1	15.7	77.0

the Hoge and Wenger conclusion, "The level of unrest among priests has subsided."

At this point, it should be noted that this study has found a consistent although modest improvement from 2004 to 2009 in a number of variables related to priestly happiness. The percentage of priests reporting (1) a strong positive relationship to the bishop, (2) priests being mutually supportive, (3) feeling happy as a priest, (4) reporting one's morale as good, and now (5) thinking of leaving priesthood, all modestly improved. Given the nature of these variables, the obvious hypothesis for this improvement is the increasing distance from the horrendous 2002 sexual abuse crisis and its concomitant media barrage. The fact that so many priests reported being happy and content as priests immediately in the wake of the crisis was remarkable. As the crisis slowly wanes, one would expect an even stronger reporting of priestly happiness and morale, priestly unity, and a positive relationship to the bishop. There are clear signs of this trend.

If we investigate the incidence of priests thinking of leaving priesthood by ordination group using the 2009 data, we see a similar graph (figure 8.1) to the three charts depicting the three burnout scales by ordination cohort (see figures 5.1–5.3). The shape of the graph using the 2004 data was identical. The highest scores are those most likely to consider leaving. It should be noted that the differences in the means were not large and should not be overemphasized, but they were statistically significant. The ANOVA was $F=14.628$, $p<.001$.[3]

An example of the differences using percentages might be helpful, and they suggest that the differences, while small, should not be overlooked (see table 8.2).

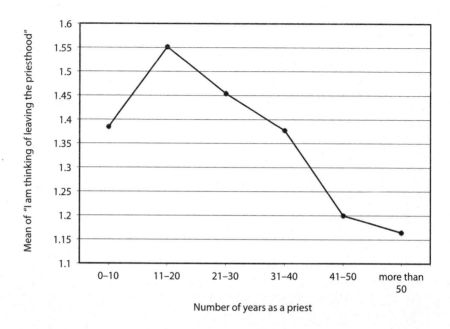

Figure 8.1. Years ordained and "I am thinking of leaving the priesthood"

In table 8.2, for those priests ordained 11–20 years, the percentage thinking of leaving is 5.7%; this is almost twice as high as those ordained 31–40 years (3.0%), and it is considerably above the overall average for all priests at 3.1%. Thus, the most at-risk group for leaving priesthood is those ordained 11–20 years.

Overall, most priests are not thinking of leaving. In any work or ministry, there will always be some. But the idea that large numbers of priests are unhappy and thinking of getting out is not founded. The percentage was 5.9% in 2004, and it dropped to 3.1% in 2009. This low number of those thinking of leaving is a reflection of the high percentage of those who are happy in priestly life and ministry.

Nevertheless, it would be devastating to lose 3% of our priests because of resignations due to unhappiness. Losing even one of our brothers is always a source of sorrow and pain for the presbyterate. We should continually ask ourselves, can some resignations be

Table 8.2. Numerical count for years ordained and "I am thinking of leaving the priesthood"

| | "I am thinking of leaving the priesthood" | | | | | |
	Strongly disagree	Disagree	Neutral	Agree	Strongly agree	Total
Number of years as a priest						
0–10						
Count	267	57	20	8	4	356
%	75.0	16.0	5.6	2.2	1.1	100.0
11–20						
Count	213	78	20	12	7	330
%	64.5	23.6	6.1	3.6	2.1	100.0
·21–30						
Count	253	81	28	8	2	372
%	68.0	21.8	7.5	2.2	0.5	100.0
31–40						
Count	418	106	24	9	8	565
%	74.0	18.8	4.2	1.6	1.4	100.0
41–50						
Count	451	39	8	5	8	511
%	88.3	7.6	1.6	1.0	1.6	100.0
More than 50						
Count	299	26	3	1	5	334
%	89.5	7.8	0.9	0.3	1.5	100.0
Total						
Count	1901	387	103	43	34	2468
%	77.0	15.7	4.2	1.7	1.4	100.0

prevented? Therefore, it is important to investigate factors contributing to a desire to resign from priesthood.

Variables' Correlations

The individual survey item "I am thinking of leaving the priesthood" correlates very strongly and, of course, negatively to the composite variable Happiness and Morale ($r= -.49$, $p<.001$). Not surprisingly, those who are most unhappy as priests are most likely to think of leaving the priesthood. Thus, the same variables that strongly predict Happiness and Morale also strongly predict whether one is thinking of leaving the priesthood. The strongest correlations are listed in table 8.3.

There are some strong spiritual factors that are obviously connected to priestly happiness and, inversely, to one thinking of leaving. In table 8.3, we see such spiritual values as View of Celibacy, Relationship to God, Relationship to Bishop, and Devotion to Mary as being strongly predictive of one's desire to leave priesthood. Those without such solid priestly values are likely less connected to priesthood and more apt to leave.

However, it continues to be interesting how strongly psychological factors influence one's priestly happiness and whether one is thinking of leaving. Three of the four BSI-18 psychopathology scales are strongly correlated ($r > .20$) with thinking of leaving, the depression scale, the anxiety scale, and the global severity index scale. The only BSI-18 scale

Table 8.3. Pearson's r correlations with "I am thinking of leaving the priesthood"

	"I am thinking of leaving the priesthood"
View of Celibacy	-.384
BSI-18 DEP	.316
Burnout-Emotional exhaustion	.302
Inner Peace	-.296
Lonely and Unappreciated	.294
Dysfunctional Childhood	.275
Childhood Mental Health Problems	.265
BSI-18 GSI	.251
Relationship to God	-.251
Prayer and Sacrament of Penance	-.236
Anger Problems	.235
Burnout-Depression	.231
Relationship to Bishop	-.228
Devotion to Mary	-.218
BSI-18 ANX	.213

Note: Only those variables that correlated at $r=.20$ and higher with $p<.001$ were included. These correlations were tested for significance using two-tailed tests.

that did not correlate as strongly was the somatization scale, but it was still a significant correlation ($r=.15$, $p<.001$).

As we look at these numbers, such findings might impress upon us once again the significance of psychological health for a well-adjusted and happy priesthood. While the spiritual factors were strongly predictive and must not be overlooked, so too were these psychological factors. I am wondering if, at times, the importance of psychological background has been underestimated in screening candidates for the priesthood.

At times, there is a temptation to see the dysfunction in some applicants' backgrounds and yet to overlook it because the candidate in front of the vocation director seems, at least on the surface, to be functioning well enough. But these research findings indicate that candidates who suffer from seriously dysfunctional childhoods and bring with them a propensity to struggle with depression and anxiety are much more likely to become unhappy priests. Despite their own good will and sincere faith, they may not have the human capacity to live priesthood effectively. These findings continue to serve as a warning to us when we are considering candidates with significant psychological deficits.

Burnout and Leaving the Priesthood

It is important to note that each of the three burnout scales was significantly correlated with a priest thinking of leaving the priesthood. See table 8.4.

Priests who score higher on the Maslach Burnout Inventory are more likely to think about leaving the priesthood. The strongest predictor is

Table 8.4. Pearson's r correlations of burnout scales with "I am thinking of leaving the priesthood"*

	Emotional exhaustion	Depersonalization	Personal accomplishment
"I am thinking of leaving the priesthood"	.302	.231	-.145

*All correlations are strongly significant at $p<.001$.

the Emotional Exhaustion scale. Priests who feel emotionally exhausted, more emotionally hardened, and less empathetic, with a reduced sense of being effective are more likely to consider leaving ministry. Burnout is a serious risk for leaving the priesthood.

As noted in the previous chapter on burnout, the percentage of priests who would be considered at high risk for burnout is low. But these individuals are at greater risk for leaving priesthood. Recall, too, that those who scored highest on burnout scales were the priests ordained less than 20 years. We can see that this, too, reinforces the findings in this chapter. The priests who scored highest on thinking of leaving priesthood were those ordained 11–20 years. Once again, we see the finding reinforced that those priests perhaps most in need of support and assistance are our younger priests. Many are young men holding great responsibility as new pastors and struggling to adjust to priesthood, leadership, and living as a celibate priest in an often unfriendly world.

Summary

A picture is becoming clearer of the priest who is likely to seriously consider leaving priesthood. His spiritual life may be struggling: he feels less connected to his bishop, to God, and to Mary. He is likely to pray less and go to confession less often. Psychologically, he is more likely to come from a distressed childhood and carry within him significant problems. He may be prone to feelings of anxiety and depression. As he begins to experience the stresses and challenges of priesthood, he may begin to feel anxious and depressed. He may become burned out and emotionally exhausted. He is likely to feel lonely and unappreciated. In such a state, he is more vulnerable to seek comfort and to become romantically involved with another person. To such a person, celibacy can feel like a great burden. In short, he is psychologically and spiritually "sinking." It is little wonder that he is seriously considering leaving priesthood. He is in significant internal distress and needs to find a way out of it.

As Dean Hoge noted in his study of priests who resigned, "An important lesson here is that all . . . have one condition in common—that the man felt lonely or unappreciated."[4]

What is the priest's way out of this morass? Naturally, he will wonder if leaving priesthood would be a fix. But before he does, the survey findings suggest another path (see the steps below). Will he be happy out of priesthood and as a married person? As any married person can affirm, marriage does not take away one's childhood traumas nor one's propensity for depression and anxiety, nor does it automatically connect one to others in a healthier way. These are all personal challenges that must be faced both in priesthood and in marriage. To be a successful and happy priest or a successful and happy married person, an individual needs to learn to connect to God, to others, and to self in a healthy and holy way.

For the priest who is considering leaving priesthood, this study suggests the following steps:

1. An assessment of levels of depression and anxiety should be performed. If clinical levels are reached, then appropriate clinical interventions should be implemented.

2. Levels of burnout ought to be assessed. Is the person emotionally exhausted and feeling useless, ineffective, and hardened? A period of sabbatical/leave might be offered with close mentoring and assistance by a senior pastor.

3. The health of his spiritual life should be investigated. This might include his personal prayer life and personal use of the sacraments, relationship to God, Mary, other priests, and his bishop/major superior. If he is not in spiritual direction, this should begin as soon as possible.

For a priest who leaves, celibacy is sometimes pointed to as the cause, particularly if he leaves for a relationship. However, as Dean Hoge rightly pointed out, the cause of a priest leaving priesthood is much more complex. He wrote, "Happy and fulfilled priests rarely resign, even if they find themselves in love. We concluded that more than one motivation is present in almost all cases of priestly resignation."[5] It would be important for an individual's formation and ongoing formation to address these underlying issues before they precipitate a crisis in the priest's vocation. And priests who are considering leaving because they believe that celibacy is the cause of their problems may want to investigate their lives more deeply before making such a radical change.

9

The Spiritual Lives of Priests

Priests' Relationship to God

The previous chapters have demonstrated the importance of the spiritual lives of priests for their happiness and well-being. It is time to look more deeply into their spiritual lives. First, there were five items in the survey that loaded highly onto one factor that were made into a composite variable called Relationship to God. These five items are listed in table 9.1 along with one similar item from the 2004 survey.

The overwhelming positive response of the priests to these five questions about their relationship to God is important. The priests almost unanimously say they feel a sense of closeness to God, that God loves them personally, that they feel a joy from God, and that their relationship to God is nourishing for them, the latter being steady over both the 2004 and 2009 surveys.

Since Relationship to God is one of the most powerful predictors of a priest's happiness, this high level of their reported relationship to God gives one strong reason for their exceptionally high levels of happiness and satisfaction with life. This is consistent with other studies as well. For example, a Duke University study of more than 4,000 Americans over the age of sixty-five found that those who attended church weekly were much less likely to be depressed. They tended to have better physical health

Table 9.1. Relationship to God

	Strongly agree (%)	Agree (%)	Neutral/ Unsure (%)	Disagree (%)	Strongly disagree (%)
"I feel that God loves me personally and directly"	56.3	40.2	2.7	0.5	0.2
"I feel a sense of closeness to God"	36.1	57.1	5.4	1.3	0.1
"I feel thankful for my blessings"	53.2	45.2	1.3	0.2	0.1
"From time to time, I feel a joy that is a grace from God"	34.3	60.6	3.9	1.1	0.2
"I have a relationship to God (or Jesus) that is nourishing for me" (2009 survey)	40.8	55.3	3.2	0.5	0.2
"I have a personal relationship with God (or Jesus) that is nourishing for me" (2004 survey)	34.1	60.1	4.2	1.3	0.3

and to live longer. As journalist John Allen summarized it: "Put simply, religious people tend to be healthier, live longer, and be happier than everyone else."[1]

Do the findings in this survey confirm that one's relationship to God does, in fact, help one's personal sense of mental health and well-being? The correlations in table 9.2 say yes.

This table shows us that as a priest's relationship to God strengthens, his level of somatization (BSI-18 SOM), depression (BSI-18 DEP), and anxiety (BSI-18 ANX), thus his mental health in general (BSI-18 GSI), tend to be better. Similarly, as his relationship to God improves, he is less likely to be burned out; that is, he has a greater sense of Personal Accomplishment (Burnout PA), and lower levels of Emotional Exhaustion (Burnout EE) and Depersonalization (Burnout DEP). Also, his overall Satisfaction with Life (SWL) is much higher as well.

Table 9.2. Pearson's *r* correlations of Relationship to God to mental health and well-being*

	Relationship to God
BSI-18 SOM	-.108
BSI-18 DEP	-.299
BSI-18 ANX	-.216
BSI-18 GSI	-.255
Burnout PA	.341
Burnout EE	-.205
Burnout DEP	-.216
SWLS	.382

*All correlations are significant at $p<.001$.

This study confirms previous studies that one's spirituality or, in this case, relationship to God is good for one's mental health and for one's happiness and satisfaction with life. Since priests reported exceptionally strong levels of a relationship to God, this likely contributes very positively to their generally good mental health scores. *Also, given priests' reported exceptionally strong relationship to God, it is little wonder that clergy report the highest levels of job satisfaction and personal happiness over any other vocation/job in the United States, as noted in the 2006 NORC study.*

Factors Contributing to Relationship to God

The following thirteen variables correlated significantly to Relationship to God (with $p<.001$ and $r>.10$). These variables were chosen based upon a combination of their hypothesized connection to one's relationship to God and based upon the statistical correlations in this 2009 study. See table 9.3.

These thirteen variables were then entered into a multiple regression equation (*MR*) to assemble a model to predict a priest's Relationship to God. As previously done in this study, the variables were entered in stepwise fashion. This means that the software first entered the variable that was the strongest predictor and subsequently moved through the rest of the variables entering them based upon which was the strongest predictor remaining, in the sense that it added more to the prediction of Relationship to God than any of the predictors not already in the regression model.

Table 9.3. Pearson's *r* correlations with Relationship to God

	Relationship to God
Close Friends	.46
Anger Problems	-.35
Relationship with Mother	.35
Devotion to Mary	.32
Sexual Conflicts	-.31
Obedience to Religious Authority	.30
Relationship with Father	.26
Attends Priest Gatherings	.25
Theological and Spiritual Reading	.24
Private Prayer	.22
Liturgy of the Hours	.17
Sacrament of Penance	.15
Annual Retreat	.12

Note: All correlations are significant at p<.001 and only correlations above .10 were selected. "Relationship with Mother" was the individual survey item "Growing up, I had a good relationship with my mother"; "Relationship with Father" was the item: "Growing up, I had a good relationship with my father"; "Attends Priest Gatherings" was the survey item "I attend priest gatherings in my diocese/order as often as I can"; "Theological and Spiritual Reading" was the survey item "I read theological or spiritual books/magazines regularly"; "Private Prayer" was the item: "I pray privately each day about: not daily, 1–15 minutes, 16–30 minutes, 31–59 minutes, 60 minutes or more"; "Liturgy of the Hours" was the survey item "I pray most or all the Liturgy of Hours daily"; "Sacrament of Penance" was the individual survey item "I receive the Sacrament of Penance about: at least weekly, monthly, every three months, every six months, yearly, less than yearly" (this item was coded in reverse for ease of interpretation); "Annual Retreat" was the individual item "I make an annual retreat: almost all the time, usually, sometimes, rarely, almost never" (this, too, was coded in reverse for ease of interpretation).

Again, two variables were entered first as control variables: neuroticism and extraversion. Putting these first into the *MR* equation parceled out the variance due to these two personality variables thus giving us greater confidence in the subsequent variables' ability to predict truly a priest's Relationship to God, independent of some personality issues. See table 9.4.

Taking out the two control variables of Extraversion and Neuroticism, we see that the *MR* equation used eleven of the variables and accounted for 36.9% of the variance of Relationship to God (.387-.018=.369). This is a strong finding in social science research. We are able to predict almost 37% of a priest's relationship to God using the eleven variables above. Of course, this means that there are other unaccounted-for variables which affect another 63.1% of a priest's relationship to God.

Table 9.4. Summary of multiple regression for variables predicting Relationship to God

Variable	B	SE B	ß	Sig.	Adj. R²
(Constant)	13.282	.615		.000	
Neuroticism (control variable)	-.004	.009	-.007	.659	
Extraversion (control variable)	.016	.010	.026	.109	.018
Close Friends	.215	.013	.288	.000	.219
Devotion to Mary	.216	.024	.175	.000	.286
Anger Problems	-.108	.017	-.112	.000	.323
Relationship with Mother	-.403	.053	-.133	.000	.342
Attends Priest Gatherings	.270	.040	.111	.000	.358
Theological and Spiritual Reading	.263	.044	.100	.000	.368
Sexual conflicts	-.087	.017	-.091	.000	.376
Obedience to Religious Authority	.284	.052	.103	.000	.382
Sacrament of Penance	-.088	.032	-.052	.006	.384
Private Prayer	.155	.041	.073	.000	.386
Liturgy of the Hours	-.082	.035	-.048	.020	.387

Nonetheless, this is important information when trying to understand and assist priests in their relationship to God. It also should be very useful in the selection and formation of candidates to the priesthood.

Similar to the previous *MR* equation in chapter seven, all the thirteen variables inputted did not contribute to the dependent variable, Relationship to God, despite having a significant correlation with the dependent variable. Moreover, they sometimes were entered in the regression equation in a different order than their correlations would initially suggest. Again, this is primarily because of multicollinearity, that is, the independent variables were often highly correlated with each other.

Close Friends

The variable entered first by the statistical program and thus the strongest predictor of Relationship to God was the variable Close Friends. I must admit I was surprised. I did not expect the composite variable Close Friends to be the strongest predictor of a priest's Relationship to God. It is markedly so. Its $ß=.288$, which is much higher than the other variables in the equation, and it accounts for the "lion's share" of the overall variance explained, that is, the *Adj. R^2*=.201 for Close Friends, which is over half of the entire variance predicted by the above model. Thus, we can say that it single-handedly accounts for slightly over 20% of a priest's Relationship to God, a strong finding indeed.

But why? Perhaps my experience working with struggling priests can help to illuminate some of this. When priests finished the residential treatment program, I individually asked them how their time in treatment went and what, if anything, changed for them during this time. The priests almost always mentioned their relationships with other people in the program as being critical. Many had never had true friendships before or any real chaste intimacy. When they experienced real human connection in their lives it was an important and healing experience. Toward the end of the conversation, I would ask them about their relationship to God: has it changed at all during their stay? They would invariably say, "Yes, it has deepened." When I asked how it deepened, they would use very similar words to the ones they used to describe their relationships with others. It was clear to me that as they grew in their interpersonal relationships and mutual intimacy with others, their intimacy with God grew in similar and parallel ways.

In the Gospel of Matthew, we read about Jesus being asked what is the greatest commandment. He responded that there are two: "You shall love the Lord, your God. The second is like it: You shall love your neighbor as yourself" (Mt 22:37–39). There are many times that Jesus equated the love of others with the love of God. "Whatever you did for one of these least brothers of mine, you did for me" (Mt 25:40). Again, when Paul was persecuting the Christians, Jesus spoke to him and said, "Saul, Saul, why do you persecute me?" (Acts 9:4). Or more directly, "For whoever does not love a brother whom he has seen cannot love God whom he has not seen" (1 Jn 4:20). The New Testament consistently speaks of love of God and love of neighbor as being part of one reality. They go together. The findings of my survey suggest the words of Jesus are an ongoing dynamic reality in people's lives.

This research supports the New Testament notion that one cannot really love God without loving one's neighbor. And if one wishes to improve one's relationship to God, s/he might start with improving relationships with other people. It makes sense when we consider the notion that the human person is made in God's image. We are made in the likeness of God. So, if people cannot love the "God images" in front of them, how can they love the fullness of God? Coming to love the "God images" in front of us leads us directly to loving God more. The New Testament says this. My experience with priests in treatment has supported this. The current study underscores this truth.

Devotion to Mary

The second variable entered into the *MR* equation predicting Relationship to God was Devotion to Mary. Once again, we see that the very Catholic practice of Marian devotion is strongly and directly connected to a priests' relationship to God. *As a priest's Marian devotion increases, so too does his relationship to God.*

This has long been a tenet of Catholic spirituality. Catholics say that Mary's "job" is to lead us to her son Jesus. As theologian Hans Urs von Balthasar put it, "The veneration of Mary is the surest and shortest way to get close to Christ in a concrete way."[2] The findings of this study support von Balthasar's claim.

The correlation of the two variables Devotion to Mary and Relationship to God is a strong, positive $r=.32$. If we want to improve our relationship to God, we should first improve our relationships with others. Second, we might also want to improve our relationship with the Mother of Jesus, whom Catholics dare to call the Mother of God since her Son is both human and divine. Knowing and loving God's Mother helps us to know and to love God better.

It should be no surprise that loving Mary brings us closer to God. If all human beings are made in the image of God, and thus loving them helps us to love God better, then how much more is it true with Mary. After Jesus, considered in his humanity, Mary is the most pure member of the human race; indeed, she is totally pure, sustained in the beautiful image of God due to having been conceived without sin (the doctrine of the Immaculate Conception).

The study suggests that if we do our "job" and love Jesus' mother—as Jesus commanded us, "Behold your mother" (Jn 19:27)—she will do her job and bring us closer to her divine Son.

Anger Problems

The third variable entered into the *MR* equation predicting Relationship to God was Anger Problems. The Letter to the Ephesians admonishes us: "Be angry but do not sin; do not let the sun set on your anger, and do not leave room for the devil" (Eph 4:26). Of itself, anger is not necessarily a sin. It is a human passion that can be used for good or for ill. We should be angry when we witness injustice and oppression. Child sexual abuse should make us angry. From time to time, Jesus became angry; witness the scene of him shouting and throwing money changers out of the temple with a whip of cords. But there is also a kind of anger that can be deadly.

I had an old pastor who once said to me, "I am beginning to see how destructive anger is for people." I, too, while working with struggling priests, have seen the same. Perhaps the most common underlying current in these men's unhealed lives was anger. It was not the passing emotion we feel at injustice, but rather it is a deep-seated anger that sticks in their souls and eats away at them. They are stuck in their anger, and it drives their lives in dysfunctional ways. Only after this anger has been largely healed can they move on in a healthier way.

The four items that made up the composite variable Anger Problems were: "I have consistent problems getting along with people"; "I have trouble managing my anger"; "My relationships seem to have more conflict than others have"; and "I have angry outbursts which upset others." These all suggest a deep-seated anger that the individual is not managing well and is damaging his relationships with others. And, as we noted in this chapter, damaging one's relationships with others results in damage to one's relationship with God.

Heaven—where God "lives," or rather we should say, where God *is*— is a place of communion and peace. Hell, on the other hand, is a place of isolation and rage where there are no deep human connections and no inner peace. It is a place consumed with rage. We see the dynamics of heaven and hell being played out in this statistical study of the lives of priests. Those who find inner peace and communion, move closer to God. Actually, the fact that they find this inner peace and communion means *ipso facto* that they are connecting with God. But when they fall into isolation and anger, they are drifting into hell.

Some do not believe in the existence of hell. Others do not even believe in heaven. But I have witnessed the seeds of both on this earth. Some people through faith and struggle come to know communion and peace. Thus, they begin to know God and begin to taste heaven. But others do not and their path leads them into increasing isolation and anger. As the isolation and anger increase, so, too, the experience of hell.

Sometimes people wonder why there is so much anger and violence in this world, even in the very wealthy nations. There is much of this "hell" everywhere: road rage, shootings in schools, family violence, abuse of children, not to mention the constant wars and violence among nations. Maybe some people are angry because there is no peace in their hearts. Where does this peace come from? Jesus said, "My peace I leave with you; my peace I give you." In this study we have seen a strong positive correlation between a relationship to God and inner peace ($r=.55$), plus a strong negative correlation between a relationship to God and anger problems ($r= -.35$). As long as God does not dwell in our hearts, there will never be peace and there will always be anger and violence.

But the end is not foreordained for us. We can choose. I have seen many priests come through a healing program remarkably changed and at peace. And, after much struggle, loving God and others with a newfound joy. While the variable Anger Problems correlates highly with Dysfunctional Childhood ($r=.42$), and thus anger problems increase markedly when one comes from a distressed background, healing is more than possible. This journey requires and begins with a choice; we must choose to live. As one man told me, "All my life I have unconsciously, and sometimes consciously, wanted to die. I ran away from people and relationships. Now, after all these years of healing and growth, I finally want to live."

Relationship with Mother

The fourth variable entered into the *MR* equation was the variable Relationship with Mother. It is noteworthy that this single survey item, "Growing up, I had a good relationship with my mother," correlated so strongly with one's Relationship to God, $r=.35$. So, having a good relationship with one's mother is a strong predictor of a priest's Relationship to God. In fact, it is an even stronger predictor than a relationship with the father, $r=.26$, although both are solid predictors.

A relationship with one's parents is an important influence on one's relationship to God. While those who do not have a good relationship with parents are not destined to have little or no relationship with God, it is a detriment. Catholic theology speaks of the family as the domestic church and tells parents that they are the first teachers of their children in the ways of faith. These statistical findings suggest that one of the most important ways they can teach their children about the faith is by loving them and having a good relationship with them. In this way, they will certainly have shown them something about God who loves them and desires to be in a similar kind of loving relationship.

This study found that priests typically have better relationships with their mothers than their fathers. A large 91.3% of priests agreed or strongly agreed that they grew up with a good relationship with their mothers as opposed to 76.1% of priests saying they grew up with a good relationship with their fathers. Given that Relationship with Mother is a stronger predictor of Relationship with God, then this is a good thing for the priests, at least in this regard. Perhaps these priests as children were taught more about the faith by their mothers. This is likely since it is adult women who, more than men, highly populate Catholic churches and assist with Church ministries. Could we speculate that a priest's vocation more often is transmitted through the mother? I can think of more than a few examples where this has been so.

Attends Priest Gatherings

The fifth variable to predict Relationship to God was Attends Priest Gatherings. This variable is made of the single survey item "I attend priest gatherings in my diocese/order as often as I can." The correlation between the two variables is a solid $r=.25$ ($p<.001$). In the previous chapter on priestly happiness, we saw its similar correlation with priestly Happiness and Morale as well ($r=.27$).

Since previous variables entered in this *MR* equation already parceled out the variance due to close friendships including priest friendships, then this variable Attends Priest Gatherings must be accounting for a slightly different aspect of a priest's relationship with God than the effect of developing friendships. While these priestly gatherings are about friendship and priestly fraternity, they touch other realities as well.

Each year, I typically speak at several annual diocesan convocations of priests. In these priest gatherings, the priests congregate around their bishop in priestly communion. The liberals and the conservatives are both present, as are the young and the old. The laity are usually not invited. The door is closed and priests relate in a way that is unique to them. It includes not only the typical priestly humor and camaraderie, but also touches their priestly communion in the faith, sometimes explicitly, certainly implicitly.

These gatherings not only bolster priestly communion, they also bolster priestly spirituality and are a support to their faith. Convocations may address such mundane subjects as parish finances and personnel practices. But they often address more deeply theological topics such as priestly spirituality and teaching and preaching the faith. Daily Mass is a part of these gatherings as is a communal recitation of the Liturgy of the Hours and other prayers. These gatherings are much more than simply meetings of priests. When successful, they are an expression and an affirmation of their spirituality and identity as priests and men of faith.

For these reasons, I have been stressing the importance of attending such gatherings to the priests. Typically, about 80% attend, which is a good turnout. In fact, the 2009 survey results confirmed that 80.9% of priests agreed or strongly agreed that they attend priest gatherings. The survey results did not show any significant differences among ordination cohorts. The young priests and the old priests reported showing up in similar percentages.

Sadly, there are some, young and old, who rarely, if ever, show up. However, the statistical findings in this study and my own experience indicate how important they are. *Priests do well not to absent themselves from priestly gatherings except for serious reason.* I recommend that it be emphasized to seminarians and newly ordained how important it is to attend these gatherings even if the speakers or subjects are of little interest to them. They ought to attend not only for the health of the entire presbyterate, but also for their own spiritual well-being.

And for those that typically do not show up, I would hope that diocesan leadership as well as brother priests could reach out to these men before the next gathering. We all know who these individuals are. They might be contacted by the local vicar or priest friend and encouraged to attend with such words as, "We missed you last time the priests gathered. You are important to us. We are hoping you can make it to the next one. Can I pick you up so we can go together?"

Dioceses should continue to sponsor these gatherings, despite the declining numbers of priests. In fact, priestly gatherings are needed now more than ever. Ultimately, they strengthen a priest's relationship, not only to the priestly communion and his bishop, but also to God.

Theological and Spiritual Reading

The sixth variable is made up of the single survey item "I read theological or spiritual books/magazines regularly." I recall one priest who had boasted that he had not picked up a theological text since leaving the seminary. This, obviously, is a very poor idea. Those who continued to read theological and spiritual material also reported a stronger relationship to God. The correlation was $r=.24$, which is not a minor finding.

Why is theological and spiritual reading so important to one's relationship with God? Priestly formation does not end at ordination any more than the relationship of a husband and wife stops growing at the wedding ceremony. It is obvious what would happen to a married couple if it did. The formation of a priest is a lifelong process just as the marriage relationship grows throughout life. There are many things that feed a priest's ongoing formation, and continued theological reading and reflection is one of them. Such reading not only keeps the priest current in theological thought, but also promotes his spiritual reflection and personal spiritual growth.

The word *theology* actually means "study of God." All theological disciplines ultimately point to God. Whether it is liturgy, scripture, patristics, moral theology, ecclesiology, dogmatics, pastoral or any branch of theology, all sacred disciplines have their ultimate focus and compass pointing toward God. Each comes at God from a different direction, but in the end the compass needle directs one to the Source. As we continue to read and study, we refine our theological sensibilities and take in nourishment for our own journey toward God. Theological reading is good for a priest's ministry. It is also good for his own spiritual journey. Ultimately, it is good for his relationship to God.

These days many diocesan bishops are giving a well-chosen theological book to all of their priests as a Christmas gift. The findings of this study suggest that this gesture of thoughtfulness to their priests is a good one for many reasons.

As a husband and wife continually get to know each other better down through the years, so too a priest must learn to know God better as his priesthood grows. The mind and the spirit hopefully expand as the years pass. We move into deeper understandings of God as the horizon of our consciousness expands. At times, we are invited into a wordless communion, transcending the limitations of the written word. But as long as we are on this side of eternity, our minds need to be fed with penetrating insights and the study of God.

Sexual Conflicts

The seventh variable is Sexual Conflicts. This composite variable was made up of three items: "I know my sexual orientation, and I am at peace with it"; "Growing up, I had difficulty coming to grips with my sexuality"; and "I feel some conflict around my sexuality." This variable looks for overall challenges with one's sexuality. Its correlation with

Relationship to God was an inverse $r= -.31$; that is, those who had sexual conflicts were less likely to have a good relationship with God.

As we look at its interrelationship with a number of the composite variables, we can see that Sexual Conflicts has strong interconnections with some of the other variables, such as with Childhood Mental Problems ($r=.39$), Inner Peace ($r= -.38$), Lonely and Unappreciated ($r=.37$), Dysfunctional Childhood ($r=.36$), Anger Problems ($r=.34$), and Happiness and Morale ($r= -.31$). Typically, priests with sexual conflicts were more likely to come from dysfunctional childhoods, have anger and emotional problems, feel isolated, and lack inner peace. They are less likely to be happy as priests.

Theologically speaking, there are more serious sins than "sins of the flesh." Nonetheless, we particularly feel ashamed when we have sexual problems. In the book of Genesis when Adam and Eve sinned, they covered themselves and hid from God. God had to go searching for them, "Where are you?" (3:9). All sin fills us with shame and we hide from God. When our sins are sexual, these kinds of sins have a unique ability to make us feel ashamed.

This is especially true of priests. Priests with sexual conflicts are particularly in conflict and often filled with shame. They have said to me many times, "If people really knew me, they would despise me." What they mean to say is that if the laity knew about their sexual struggles and sins, they would be rejected and loathed—declared a hypocrite. It also means that they are already filled with self-loathing.

Priests with sexual conflicts tend to "hide" from others as well. The correlation between Sexual Conflicts and Close Friends was $r= -.23$. As sexual conflicts increase, one's close friendships decrease.

It is little wonder, then, that struggling with sexual conflicts and sins can be devastating to one's relationship with God and others, especially for priests. In today's climate of publicly trumpeting the sexual sins of priests, the entire dynamic is loaded with an even stronger negative intensity. When the sexual sins involve minors, the effect is extreme; over fifteen priests in the United States committed suicide in the wake of allegations of child molestation.

There are many, many reasons for a priest to strive with all his might to live his priestly promise of celibate chastity with integrity. This study highlights several of them, which must also include an awareness of damage done to others. In this chapter, we have demonstrated the damage caused to a priest's relationship to God, even when he only struggles with his sexuality. Should it become acted out in unchaste ways, devastation can follow. Just as Adam and Eve hid from God after they had sinned, the priest struggling with his sexuality, consciously or unconsciously, is more likely to try to hide from God and from others.

It is important for priests' lives and spirituality to integrate their sexuality in a healthy, chaste way. When they are at peace with their sexuality, then they are likely to have a stronger relationship to God and closer friends. *Sexual integration* are important words for priests today. Another very important word is *integrity.*

Obedience to Religious Authority

The eighth variable to predict Relationship to God was the single survey item "Obedience to religious authority is an important value for me." The correlation was a significant $r=.30$. This item also strongly loaded on priestly Happiness and Morale as discussed previously.

There are four composite variables with which this item most strongly correlates: View of Celibacy ($r=.49$), Devotion to Mary ($r=.43$), Prayer and the Sacrament of Penance ($r=.42$), and, as noted before, Relationship to Bishop ($r=.38$). Thus, we might say that a priest who values religious obedience is likely someone who also values his commitment to celibacy, has a devotion to Mary the humble servant of God, engages in prayer and the sacrament of penance, and has a good relationship to his bishop.

What kind of man is this? The portrait emerges of a priest who is a humble man of God and gives himself completely in service to the Catholic Church, particularly to its representative, the bishop or major superior, and to its people. He is willing to be obedient and engages in a self-sacrificing love. He nourishes himself with daily prayer and regularly confessing his own sins.

Ultimately, all sins really can be subsumed under the broad umbrella of the sin of pride. All violations of the divine law separate us from God and are rebellions against God. Satan would rather arrogantly reign than humbly serve, and so he created his own hell. Heaven, on the other hand, is a blissful communion with God where we are overjoyed to serve the One who, in turn, gives of the divine self completely. And so, in a manner of speaking, we serve God who, surprisingly, turns around and humbly gives to and serves us. If we are asked to be humble and to serve, we who are made in God's image, it is because we are only reflecting the divine nature. The divine nature is to humbly serve, as Jesus taught and showed us.

Humility and obedient service bring us closer to God and, ironically, make us happier people. To verify this statement, I checked this variable of Obedience to Religious Authority with the Satisfaction with Life Scale (SWLS), the latter previously discussed in chapter 6. Indeed, the two correlate positively and significantly, $r=.26$, $p<.001$. Thus, those who value their promise of religious obedience are much more likely to say they are satisfied and happy with their lives. The survey findings confirm: we are happier people when we humbly serve our God in the Church.

Sacrament of Penance

The ninth variable to predict Relationship to God is the Sacrament of Penance. This is the individual item "I receive the Sacrament of Penance about: at least weekly, monthly, every three months, every six months, yearly, less than yearly." Those who went to confession more often reported a stronger relationship to God ($r=.15$, $p<.001$). See table 9.5.

Has this changed since the 2004 survey that asked a similar but slightly different question? See table 9.6.

Table 9.5. 2009 survey results: Reception of the Sacrament of Penance

	Weekly (%)	Monthly (%)	3 months (%)	6 months (%)	Yearly (%)	Less than yearly (%)
"I receive the Sacrament of Penance..." (2009 survey)	4.2	24.8	28.4	19.1	12.3	11.2

Table 9.6. 2004 survey results: Reception of the Sacrament of Reconciliation

	Within 1 month (%)	1–3 months (%)	4–8 months (%)	9–12 months (%)	1–3 years (%)	More than 3 years (%)
"How long ago did you last receive the Sacrament of Reconciliation?" (2004 survey)	33.7	27.2	16.8	10.2	7.8	4.2

The results are fairly stable over time. About 29% of priests in the 2009 survey go to confession at least monthly compared to 33.7% in the 2004 survey. The number of priests who do not go yearly (considered a minimum for all Catholics) is a fairly consistent 11.2% in the 2009 survey and 12% in the 2004 survey.

I found the latter to be a surprisingly high figure. Catholic priests are the instruments of this special sacrament; only they can dispense it. The sacramental life is an integral part of the priest's spirituality. One could argue that the findings are strong in that about 88% of the Catholic priests themselves receive this sacrament at least yearly. However, the response is that one would expect the priest himself to be a promoter of this sacrament and one who encourages others to use it frequently. This, of course, presumes that he himself strongly believes in the sacrament and frequents it himself. This is the case for most priests, but not for about 11–12%.

Perhaps it is no coincidence that Pope Benedict XVI began the 2009–2010 Year for Priests by emphasizing the need for frequent reception of the Sacrament of Penance. Given the above statistics, this exhortation is well-directed not only at the laity, but also at the priests themselves. One could hardly expect a priest to be a promoter and effective celebrant of confession if he himself does not frequently avail himself of its use.

I had mentioned earlier that the findings of this study seem to be pointing out that a priest's happiness and morale rises as he lives his life with integrity, that is, in harmony with an authentic priestly spirituality and theology. As a dispenser of sacraments, especially this sacrament, this is an integral part of a priest's life. Does it therefore predict his over-all happiness? Yes. As noted above, there is a positive correlation ($r=.15$) between Sacrament of Penance and Relationship to God and a positive correlation with Happiness and Morale ($r=.18$).

Private Prayer and the Liturgy of the Hours

The final two variables to predict Relationship to God were two more spiritual practices, Private Prayer and the Liturgy of the Hours. Relationship to God correlates positively and significantly with Private Prayer ($r=.22$) and Liturgy of the Hours ($r=.17$). Thus, the more one prays privately and also prays the Liturgy of the Hours, the more the priest is likely to report a strong relationship to God.

A relationship to God or to any person is precisely that: a relation-ship. It needs to be fostered from both sides. We know that God is completely active on his part. It is up to us to reciprocate. Prayer is our way of connecting with God. Teresa of Avila called prayer a "conversa-tion between friends." In order to strengthen our relationship with our divine Friend, we must pray.

In table 9.7, the first striking fact is that almost one-fifth (19.7%) of our priests are praying more than one hour each day. Are they con-sciously doing a daily holy hour? It is likely.

But what also must strike us is that another one-fifth (19%) of priests are praying privately 15 minutes a day or less. This is equally notewor-thy. For a man of God whose life centers around spiritual realities, this is not much and, I dare say, too little.

When a priest in difficulty came for long-term residential treatment, we usually began him on a minimum of 20 minutes of private prayer a

Table 9.7. "I pray privately each day . . ."

	Not daily (%)	1–15 minutes (%)	16–30 minutes (%)	31–59 minutes (%)	60 minutes or more (%)
"I pray privately each day . . ."	4.2	14.8	30.2	31.1	19.7

day and gradually increased it. It is easy to forget the centrality of God in our lives and to be absorbed in daily duties. Now, more than ever, prayer keeps us balanced and focused in the midst of the ever-increasing demands of ministry.

The results in table 9.8 were similar to the 2004 survey findings. In the 2004 survey, when asked if they pray the Liturgy of the Hours most or all of the time, 53% of the priests said yes. In the 2009 survey above, 58% agree or strongly agreed with daily saying most or all of the Liturgy of the Hours. So, the results are relatively stable with a modest increase of 5%.

Overall, this number is surprisingly low since the priest, at his diaconate ordination, explicitly promises to pray the Liturgy of the Hours for the Church and for the world. It is a solemn part of the ceremony, and it is considered to be an integral part of the cleric's ministry.

Among some priests in the past, this promise has been controversial. Unfortunately, some see it only as an onerous duty imposed upon them. However, like the requirement to live a celibate life, if the priest is able to see this liturgical prayer as a gift and nourishment for himself, as well as for the people, it might take on a whole new meaning and importance in his life. To set aside various moments of the day to recite passages of sacred scripture, especially the psalms, can be restful, recentering, grace-filled moments. It can be a time to refocus and to reconnect with God, who is the center of our priestly lives.

Moreover, the Liturgy of the Hours primarily is meant to be a part of the priest's ministry. The first reason he prays it, as the ordination rite notes, is not for himself but for the people whom he serves and for the whole world. If a significant portion of priests have left these books on the shelves, it may be that they have not made the connection between

Table 9.8. "I pray most or all of the Liturgy of Hours daily"

	Strongly agree (%)	Agree (%)	Neutral (%)	Disagree (%)	Strongly disagree (%)
"I pray most or all of the Liturgy of Hours daily"	30.1	27.9	9.6	23.9	8.5

their own prayer and its efficacy for others. But the people have not forgotten. What is the most common request every priest around the globe receives from the people? "Father, please pray for me." In the Liturgy of the Hours, he does so and he ought not to omit it.

Prayer and the Sacrament of Penance

The previous three variables, Sacrament of Penance, Private Prayer, and the Liturgy of the Hours, were combined into one composite variable called Prayer and the Sacrament of Penance. In the previous chapter on priestly happiness, it was noted indeed that this composite variable Prayer and the Sacrament of Penance significantly correlated at $r=.27$ with priestly Happiness and Morale. When combined, confession, private prayer, and the Liturgy of the Hours are a stronger predictor of one's relationship to God. Individually the correlations are slightly less: Sacrament of Penance $r=.15$, Private Prayer $r=.22$, and Liturgy of the Hours $r=.17$, but together the correlation with Relationship to God is a bit higher at $r=.27$. *This confirms that as a priest receives the Sacrament of Penance more often and prays more, including the Liturgy of the Hours, he is more likely to report having a good relationship with God.* And the most predictive of one's relationship with God is a combination of all three. Together, the three spiritual practices of private prayer, Liturgy of the Hours, and confession may have a synergistic effect in strengthening one's relationship to God.

It is also important to look at the effect that Prayer and the Sacrament of Penance is likely to be having on a number of other variables. See table 9.9.

Like the effect of the variable Relationship to God on mental health as noted previously, Prayer and the Sacrament of Penance is modestly but significantly correlated with better mental health as well. It includes slightly lower levels of burnout and lower levels of anxiety, depression, and somatization. Similarly Prayer and the Sacrament of Penance is associated with a greater sense of personal accomplishment, greater inner peace, and greater satisfaction with one's life. Again, the effects are modest but significant.

Table 9.9. Pearson's *r* correlations of Prayer and the Sacrament of Penance*

	Prayer and the Sacrament of Penance
BSI-18 SOM	-.086
BSI-18 DEP	-.190
BSI-18 ANX	-.117
BSI-18 GSI	-.160
Burnout PA	.052
Burnout EE	-.144
Burnout DEP	-.100
SWLS	.190
Inner Peace	.174

*All correlations are significant at $p<.001$ except Burnout PA where $p<.009$.

If people, especially priests, want to increase their mental health and life satisfaction, one area to investigate is one's spiritual life. *Developing a stronger relationship to God and including a stronger regimen of daily prayer and receiving the sacraments would likely be an effective part of any wellness plan.*

Summary

Priests report a very strong spiritual life. They are almost unanimous in their personal belief that God loves them and has a close personal relationship with them, and that this relationship is personally nourishing to them. At times, they feel a "joy that is a grace from God." There are very few who do not feel part of this relationship, less than 2%.

This is an important finding. Why are priests so happy? Secular studies have consistently shown that having a religious or spiritual life makes one less depressed, healthier, and happier. One could easily hypothesize that having a strong relationship to God would be even more essential to a Catholic priest whose life is dedicated to the service of God, the Church, and its people. The fact that these men do profess having such a strong relationship must be a source of strength, inner peace, and happiness for each one of them.

It might remind one of the parable of the buried treasure. Jesus compared the kingdom of heaven to a buried treasure "which a person finds

. . . and out of joy goes and sells all that he has and buys that field" (Mt 13:44). The priest appears to give up so many things—spouse, home, children, worldly success—but he does so for a greater good. In fact, it is "out of joy" that he "goes and sells all that he has and buys" it.

This study demonstrates clearly that priestly happiness is directly tied to their relationship to God. And the priests' report that this relationship is strong, direct, personal, and nourishing, and that it occasionally opens into a feeling of joy.

This Relationship to God is especially important for a priest. And since it is so important, dioceses and religious orders will want to promote and encourage priests in this relationship. The correlations and multiple regression equation give some suggestions as to how to foster this relationship to God:

- Working on relationships with other people and developing close friendships will be very important. Also, attending priest gatherings and making priest friends is necessary.
- Rekindling a devotion to Mary will be a strong help.
- Finding healing from psychic damages may be necessary for some people, including healing any residual anger, sexual conflicts, and relational conflicts.
- While most will not be able to change any dysfunctional aspects in their relationships with their mothers and fathers, they can pray for their parents, and ask God for the grace of a forgiving heart where needed.
- Developing a healthy sense of religious obedience and relationship to one's bishop or major superior is a solid help.
- Frequent reception of the Sacrament of Penance, more time in private prayer, faithfulness to the Liturgy of the Hours, regular theological and spiritual reading, and an annual retreat all contribute to growing one's relationship to God.[3]

A strong theme to emerge from these findings is the theme of relationship. Almost all of these variables surface the concept of relationship whether it is a relationship to God, parents, friends, brother priests, Mary, or bishop or major superior. The priest truly is a "man of communion" and thus a man of relationships. Those who know how to make and grow good relationships are likely to do well as priests. Those who cannot make or sustain healthy relationships are at a serious disadvantage in priesthood.

The ability to make and to sustain healthy relationships both spiritually and psychologically ought to be a focus area for screening, formation, and ongoing formation of priests. One cannot be a successful, healthy, and happy priest without solid spiritual and personal relationships.

As one steps back a little from the data and sees a bigger picture, it appears that there are two different ways to God, which might be related to the way of Martha and the way of Mary in Luke 10:38–42. Martha is busy about the household tasks while Mary sits at the Lord's feet and listens. In one possible interpretation of this passage, they have often been used as symbols of the active life and the contemplative life. Both are praiseworthy but Mary "has chosen the better part."

Similarly, in this statistical study, there are two ways to get to God, either more directly through prayer, retreats, spiritual reading, sacraments, and Marian devotion, that is, a more contemplative way. Or one can go through others—lay friends, priest friends, and relationships in general, that is, the more active life. When done in grace, all lead us to God. Is one better than the other? The study suggests we should use them both; together they give us the strongest and most complete spiritual life and foster the strongest relationship to God.

Nevertheless, it is true that the single greatest predictor was Close Friends. For most of us, we encounter God in many ways but most consistently we encounter God in others whom we meet. It is the best predictor of priests' relationship to God because most of them are in active ministry. It is the rare but important vocation where God is almost solely encountered in solitary prayer. These are the great hermits and anchorites who live even in our own day.

God meets most of us in a variety of ways, through others, through Jesus' Mother, through brother priests, through our religious superiors, through our lay friends, and through our parishioners. But he also meets us directly in the sacraments, most of all the Eucharist and also in the confessional. He meets us in the sacred psalmody that we pray each day, and he meets us in the silence of our own prayer and on retreat. All of these together form a solid, multidimensional spiritual life and invariably lead us closer to God.

As priests are faithful to each of these pathways to God, they become spiritually stronger and closer to God. Each day, they come a step closer to a God who radiates love and joy. Is it any wonder that they too are increasingly happy and joy-filled men? We should not be surprised that the happiest priests in this study were the oldest, those moving closest to the Lord. As one ninety-plus-year-old saintly priest recently told his bishop after kindly being asked about some of his worldly needs, "Bishop," he said, "my thoughts are elsewhere." A few weeks later he died.

10

Priests and Prayer

I t is important for priests, from time to time, to reflect upon their own private prayer practices. Working with priests in difficulty for many years, I assessed their use of private prayer and sometimes found it wanting. Given the importance of prayer for one's psychological and spiritual health, as documented in the previous chapters, it is clearly important for priests to take the time to engage in private prayer.

What does the 2009 survey tell us? First, the mean self-report private prayer time for priests is approximately 30–45 minutes per day. The priests' aggregated responses are shown in figure 10.1.

It seems to this researcher that if a busy priest in ministry is able to pray privately more than 30 minutes per day, this is a good finding.

Figure 10.2 shows us time spent in private prayer by ordination cohorts. On the y axis, the scale is as follows: 1=not daily; 2=1–15 minutes; 3=16–30 minutes; 4=31–59 minutes; and 5=60 minutes or more. The mean for the entire sample was 3.47, which is almost half-way between 3 (16–30 minutes) and 4 (31–59 minutes). Thus, we can approximate the average time in prayer for priests, as noted above, as 30–45 minutes daily.

The ANOVA showed that differences among ordination cohorts were significant ($F=20.565$, $p<.001$) with the post-hoc Scheffe results showing significant differences between the oldest priests and all the other ordination cohorts. Plus, the results for the priests ordained 0–10 years

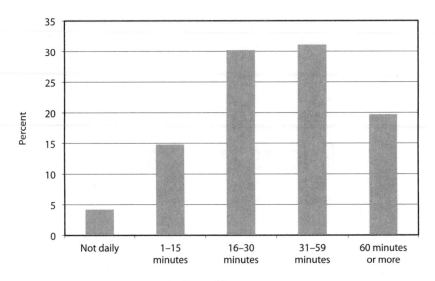

Figure 10.1. "I pray privately each day . . ."

were significantly different from those ordained 21–30 years and trending toward significance (p=.08) with those ordained 31–40 years.

Figure 10.2 shows that the oldest of priests, presumably retired or semi-retired, are praying the most. It is edifying that these retired priests who now have more time to pray are, in fact, doing so. It is commonly thought that one of the important ministries of our older priests is the ministry of prayer. They are taking this part of their priestly ministry to heart.

Priests Who Do Not Pray Privately

What about those on either ends: those who do not pray and those who pray the most? First, what about those priests who said they do not pray privately each day. Who are they?

Comparing diocesan and religious priests, diocesan priests are more likely to fall into this category with 4.6% reporting that they do not pray daily and 2.1% of religious priests reporting the same. There were

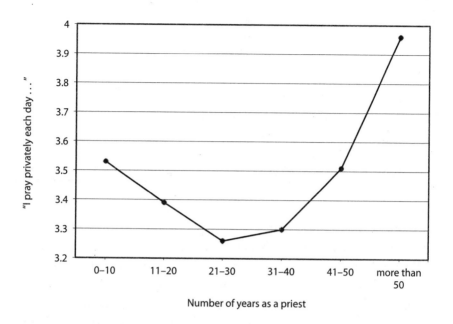

Figure 10.2. Years ordained and "I pray privately each day . . . "

also important differences among ordination cohorts as shown in table 10.1.

The ordination cohort that is mostly likely to stop praying daily is those ordained 11–20 years. From previous chapters we noted that this group scored higher on burnout measures and was more likely to think about leaving priesthood.

Given the importance of private prayer, as demonstrated in this chapter as well as earlier chapters, a bishop or major superior should be concerned for any priest who stops praying, but especially those ordained 11–20 years. They are at greater risk for burnout and leaving the priesthood. The correlation between time in private prayer and the survey item "I am thinking of leaving the priesthood" is modest but significant ($r = -.15$, $p < .001$). The study also suggests that any priest who is considering leaving the priesthood ought to ask himself, "Have I stopped praying? Am I feeling burned out?"

There were 105 of the 2,480 priests who responded to this question who said they did not pray privately each day. This was 4.2% of the

Table 10.1. Years ordained and those who do not pray privately

	Number of years as a priest					
	0-10 (%)	11-20 (%)	21-30 (%)	31-40 (%)	41-50 (%)	More than 50 (%)
"I pray privately each day…" Response: not daily	3.9	7.0	5.7	4.2	3.3	1.8

sample. Only 79.1% of this group agreed/strongly agreed with the survey item, "Overall, I am happy as a priest." This is much lower than the remainder of the sample, of which 93.1% said they were happy.

Figure 10.3 shows clearly that the more a priest prays, the more likely he is to be happy as a priest (when the individual survey items of private prayer and happiness as a priest are correlated, the results are $r=.20$, $p<.001$). The ANOVA was statistically significant (ANOVA $F=27.487$, $p<.001$).[1] As noted in chapter 7, prayer is a solid predictor of priestly happiness.

Again, correlation does not prove causation. Do priests stop praying because they are unhappy or does being unhappy leads them to pray less, or is there a third factor at work? I suspect that it is a vicious circle. It is likely that private prayer helps the priest in many ways including increasing his mental and spiritual health, which contributes to his being a happy priest. And, being a happy priest further aids his health and well-being, which is likely to express itself in many ways, including personal prayer.

Moreover, third factors are probably also involved. For example, if a priest is suffering from inner turmoil and inner psychological pains, it may be that he is likely to pray less. It is difficult to sit in silence and pray when what comes up to consciousness is pain and trauma, or sexual problems. More than a few struggling priests have told me they do not pray because they are afraid to face what will come up from within. For example, priests who suffer from inner sexual conflicts tend to pray less ($r=-.15$, $p<.001$) and those who come from a dysfunctional childhood likewise are less likely to pray ($r=-.12$, $p<.001$). A life of prayer is not

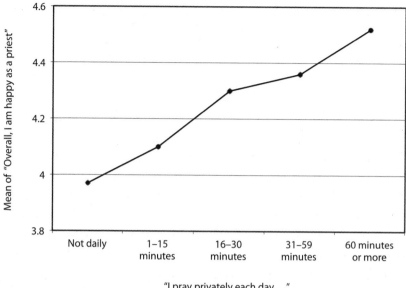

Figure 10.3. "I pray privately each day . . . " and "Overall, I am happy as a priest"

always easy. It means facing and working through one's inner "demons" in order to find the God of peace who dwells within.

Only 69.5% of these priests who do not pray privately each day agreed or strongly agreed with the item "I feel a sense of inner peace." This is compared to 87.4% of the entire sample who reported feeling a sense of inner peace. It is difficult for a priest, or anyone, to sit quietly in private prayer with a sense of inner turmoil. However, one could argue that such individuals need private prayer all the more in order to find a sense of inner peace. The individual survey item "I feel a sense of inner peace" and private prayer are positively significantly correlated with each other (r=.21, p<.001). Inner peace is enhanced by private prayer and inner peace can make it easier to pray privately.

In treatment, I often found that priests who do not pray privately need a regimen of assisted and structured private prayer to help them begin to make private prayer an important part of their lives. In addition, they often need spiritual direction, perhaps even counseling, to help them work through whatever is causing their inner turmoil. This direct interconnection between spiritual and mental health has been a consistent finding in this study.

A Daily Hour of Prayer

How about those who pray the most? There were 19.7% of the priests sampled who reported praying 60 minutes or more daily. There is a noticeable movement today among some priests to do a daily Holy Hour. Of the ordination cohorts, the groups that are most involved with praying at least an hour a day are the newest ordained: ordained 0–10 years=23% and ordained 11–20 years=20.6%, and the eldest of priests ordained over 50 years=35.3%. However, this is not to say that no priests in the middle years are praying an hour a day. Of those ordained 21–30 years, 13.2% are praying 60 minutes or more each day; of those ordained 31–40 years, 13.3%; of those ordained 41–50 years, 18.4%. But, as a group, the oldest and youngest priests are praying privately significantly more.

There have been famous individuals who have advocated a daily holy hour for priests including Archbishop Fulton Sheen. He preached a well-known retreat advocating this practice and one in which he himself engaged. He quoted Jesus' words in the Garden of Gethsemane, "So you could not keep watch with me for one hour?" (Mt 26:40).

Does this survey suggest that praying a holy hour each day makes a noticeable difference, at least as discoverable in this survey? After reviewing the statistics, the answer is decidedly yes. However, it appears that the benefits of prayer steadily increase the more a priest prays, not just with those doing Holy Hours. For example, figure 10.3 shows consistent improvement in priestly happiness the more a priest prays.

Moreover, it is not surprising that private prayer directly aids one's relationship to God as well. The results in figure 10.4 were statistically significant (ANOVA $F=32.882$, $p<.001$).

Figures 10.3 and 10.4 show a relatively straight arithmetic progression demonstrating consistent improvement as prayer time increases. In addition, as private prayer time increases, the priest's score on the

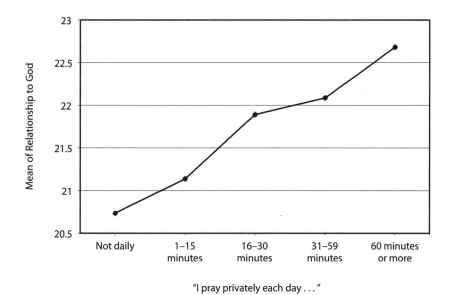

Figure 10.4. "I pray privately each day . . ." and Relationship to God

Maslach Burnout Inventory for Emotional Exhaustion decreases (the ANOVA F=9.533, p<.001), figure 10.5.

Those who engage in Holy Hours, for example, are much less likely to suffer from emotional exhaustion. This is likely true because prayer not only allows time away from the demands of ministry but is often refreshing for the person's spirit and psyche.

It is very interesting that those who pray more are significantly less likely to say they feel lonely as a priest (ANOVA F=21.89, p<.001). Figure 10.6 demonstrates the point.

It has long been said that private prayer connects us to ourselves and to God. The survey results show that time spent in private prayer correlates positively with the composite variables Relationship to God (r=.22, p<.001) and Inner Peace (r=.18, p<.001). The more we pray privately, the stronger our relationship to God and to ourselves, both of which foster an inner sense of peace.

Those who regularly know an intimacy with God and self in private prayer are thought to be able to connect with others better as well. True prayer moves us beyond loneliness to solitude. In this spiritual solitude

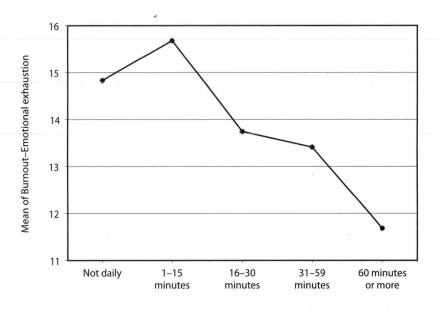

Figure 10.5. "I pray privately each day . . ." and Burnout-Emotional exhaustion

we find God and our true selves. Then we are able to connect more deeply with others.

Also, as one of this book's priest reviewers related to me, "The priest who prays is not alone. He spends time with someone he loves."

Summary

The priests who are praying the most are the elderly priests. Part of their priestly ministry at this age is a ministry of prayer and intercession. As a group, they are faithful to this ministry and are a fine example to their younger brothers in the priesthood.

At the same time, it appears that there is a trend toward an increase in private prayer time among the newly ordained. After the priests ordained over 50 years, the newly ordained are most likely to pray for an hour or more a day. Presumably, many are consciously doing a daily Holy Hour.

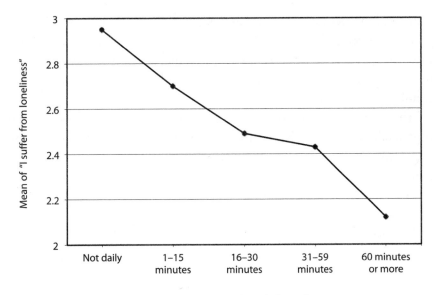

Figure 10.6. "I pray privately each day . . . " and "I suffer from loneliness"

The importance of private prayer in the life of a priest is statistically and strongly affirmed by this study. Private prayer is directly correlated with improvement in both one's psychic and spiritual health. The research suggests that as priests' time in private prayer increases:

- They are less emotionally exhausted.
- They are less depressed (see chapter 3).
- They deal with stress in less dysfunctional ways (see chapter 3).
- They are less likely to be obese (see figure 3.1).
- They are less likely to be lonely.
- They have a greater sense of inner peace.
- They are happier as priests.
- They experience a stronger relationship to God.

How much time should a priest devote to private prayer each day? This is obviously a personal question and the answer will vary based upon each priest's spiritual life and ministry. But it is striking that the statistics here demonstrate that as one's time in private prayer increases up to and over an hour per day, the priest's life improves as noted above. Presumably, there will be a point at which increasing one's time in prayer no longer has any benefit and may even be detrimental, but that point is not available in this study.

The findings of this study are that praying privately one hour a day is generally recommended (with the support of one's spiritual director) and is directly correlated with increased psychic and spiritual health of a priest.

11

Young Priests, Old Priests, and Those in the Middle

uch has been said about different generations of priests.[1] In *Evolving Visions of the Priesthood*, Hoge and Wenger drew distinctions between priests ordained in the 1960s and 1970s versus those ordained after, that is, the "new priests." They said, "The main difference is clearly ecclesiological."[2] They stated that the young priests hold to a "sacramental and cultic theology of the priest" and emphasize that the "priest is distinct from the laity, and that emphatically includes ontological as well as institutional distinctiveness." They are likely to stress a "strong prayer life to sustain him in his special role, and this requires nourishment from the breviary and from confession."[3]

On the other hand, Hoge and Wenger described "Vatican II priests" as ones who stress "the need to be flexible, collaborative, and open" and who are more likely to speak of the "spirit of Vatican II." A priest is seen by them as a "community leader and coordinator, a person who calls forth the gifts of the faithful to serve the parish." They are likely to emphasize "the ministry of all the baptized and the need that it be done collaboratively."[4]

Of course, it must be noted that these two ecclesiological approaches are not mutually exclusive. In fact, both are vital parts of the priesthood and of the Catholic Church. A priest ought to hold to a strong cultic and sacramental theology of the priesthood that is in part sustained by prayer and the sacraments. At the same time, he should also be a community leader and one who calls forth the gifts of the laity. However, being the limited human beings that we are, we tend to emphasize some aspects of the Church's theology to the detriment of others.

Hoge and Wenger ask the question, "Is the current attitude shift a return to older forms, or is it something altogether new?"[5] Without actually fully answering the question, they quote some who call it a return to the pre–Vatican II cultic model of priesthood, whereas "many of the newly ordained see it as an innovative blending of pre–Vatican II and post–Vatican II elements into a new vision of priesthood."[6] The findings in this study add statistical information to help respond to this question.

Ordination Cohorts and Priestly Happiness

First, as noted previously in figure 6.1, cohorts of priests reported significantly different levels of priestly happiness. It is worth looking at the 2009 survey figure again (see figure 11.1).

It is noteworthy that 46.9% of priests ordained 0–10 years strongly agreed with the statement "Overall, I am happy as a priest" while only 35.8% of priests ordained 21–30 years strongly agreed.

As Hoge and Wenger noted, there is an increase in happiness among the younger priests which is beginning to be reminiscent of the older, pre–Vatican II priests, that is, those ordained in the 1950s and 1960s. What is remarkable from this graph (figure 11.1) is the clear dip in happiness among the middle group of priests. Let us see how these cohort differences manifest in other variables.

In figures 11.2 and 11.3, the composite variables Prayer and the Sacrament of Penance and Devotion to Mary have similar U-shaped curves, with the highest levels of positive response by the very oldest and the very youngest priests.[7] Visual inspection shows the lowest point in these traditional spiritual practices to be those ordained 31–40 years, that is, approximately 1970–1979. The differences were strongly significant (figure 11.2 Prayer and the Sacrament of Penance ANOVA $F=41.214$ $p<.001$; figure 11.3 Devotion to Mary ANOVA $F=30.247$ $p<.001$).[8]

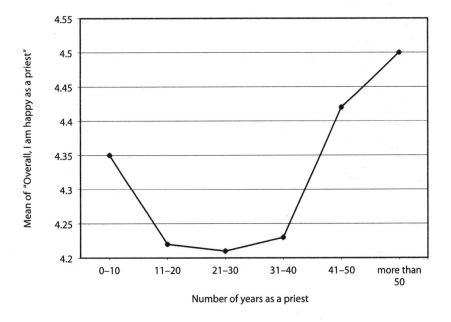

Figure 11.1. Years ordained and "Overall, I am happy as a priest"

For those priests ordained in the period immediately after Vatican II and the tumultuous 1960s in the United States, it is likely that they were affected by the social forces of the 1960s and the winds of change in the Catholic Church in the direct wake of the Second Vatican Council. Catholic literature often refers to these men as "Vatican II priests." Some of them, but certainly not all, are feeling "out of step" with today's Church and with the newly ordained. Written comments from priests ordained shortly after the Vatican Council reflected a bit of this dissatisfaction:

- "My biggest problem today is celibacy; I cannot see a contradiction between priesthood and marriage."
- "I feel as if I live in a bubble of time that is passing and that the future leadership of the Church is moving retrograde to my orientation and formation."
- "Morale is shattered."
- "I feel I need more intimacy in my life."

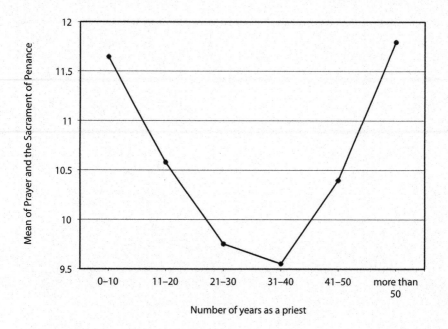

Figure 11.2. Years ordained and Prayer and the Sacrament of Penance

Given the U-shaped curves, it appears that the newer priests are actually returning to some of the spiritual practices of priesthood before Vatican II, such as a stronger devotion to Mary, faithfulness to the Liturgy of the Hours, private prayer, and more frequent reception of the Sacrament of Penance. And, as we have seen, these variables are directly and positively correlated with priestly happiness and morale as well as strengthening their relationship to God.

Putting a few of these in percentages might be helpful. For priests ordained 0–10 years, 52.5% pray privately more than 30 minutes per day, whereas for priests ordained 31–40 years, the figure is less (43.2%). For priests ordained 0–10 years, 66.2% pray all or most of the Liturgy of the Hours daily compared to only 48.5% of the priests ordained 31–40 years. Similarly, 57.3% of the 0–10 year priests receive the Sacrament of Penance at least monthly compared to 16.8% of 31–40 year priests, which is a large difference. Additionally, 4.5% of the 0–10 year priests receive the Sacrament of Penance less than yearly compared to a rather

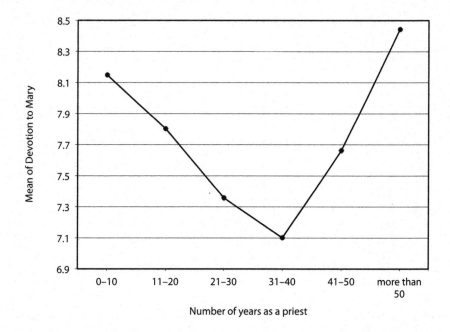

Figure 11.3. Years ordained and Devotion to Mary

large 17% of the 31–40 year priests. Finally, 86.5% of the 0–10 year priests agree or strongly agree that obedience to religious authority is an important value for them compared to 63.3% of 31–40 year priests; again, this is a large difference. These numbers highlight the consistent differences between the younger priests and those priests in the "middle."

Similarly, we see the same U-shaped curve with other values as well. The results concerning relationship to one's bishop and their support for the value of religious obedience are in figures 11.4 and 11.5.

Younger priests appear similar to the oldest of priests in the strength of their positive support for and relationship to the local bishop (the ANOVA was statistically significant with $F=4.113$, $p<.001$). If we look at their support for obedience to religious authority, we see a similar U-shaped curve, and the differences are again statistically significant ($F=25.804$, $p<.001$). Young priests appear to be returning to some of the spiritual values and practices of their "grandfathers" in the priesthood, not their "fathers." Scheffe post-hoc tests showed significant differences

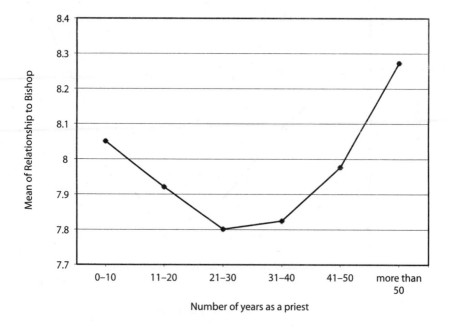

Figure 11.4. Years ordained and Relationship to Bishop

between the oldest and youngest priests and those priests in the middle for the item on support for religious obedience. The composite variable Relationship to Bishop showed significant differences between the oldest priests and those in the middle.

Of course, these are only a few of the aspects of priesthood, but they reflect a wider rift, which has been much discussed. One can say with some assurance that the newly ordained are returning to some of the values of the pre–Vatican II Church, particularly when it comes to the traditional priestly spiritual values and practices such as prayer, devotion to Mary, support of celibacy, and religious obedience. Given these variables' significant correlations to priestly happiness and priestly spiritual life, the increase among young priests in these areas is a positive trend.

Some authors, including John Allen Jr. in *The Future Church*, have referred to these newer priests and laity as "evangelical Catholics." He said the words *traditionalist* or *conservative* do not completely fit. Allen said they are not really trying to conserve cultural Catholicism or to return to a better day in the past, but rather it is a conscious attempt to

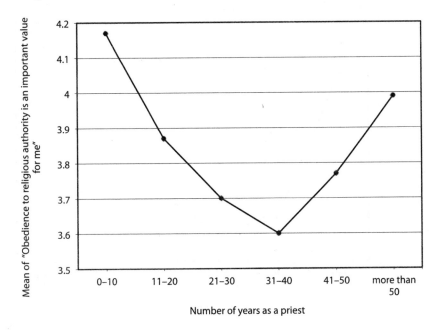

Figure 11.5. Years ordained and "Obedience to religious authority is an important value for me"

resist the secularism of today. He said it has three major elements: (1) "clear embrace of traditional Catholic thought, speech, and practice," (2) "eagerness to proclaim one's Catholic identity to the world," and (3) "faith as seen as a matter of personal choice rather than cultural inheritance."[9] In the face of societal secularism, evangelical priests boldly proclaim they are Catholic and hold fast to a strong and clear Catholic identity.

These survey results supported this notion. For example, in the 2004 survey priests were given the statement: "I feel proud to be a priest today." This was taken within one year of the public thrashing of the Church and the priesthood in the 2002 scandals. The results in figure 11.6 again showed the same U-shaped curve.

In figure 11.6, younger priests are trending to a stronger personal appropriation of being proud to be priests. (The ANOVA results were trending toward the .05 level of significance but not quite with $p < .061$.) For priests ordained 1–9 years, 41.5% strongly agreed that they were

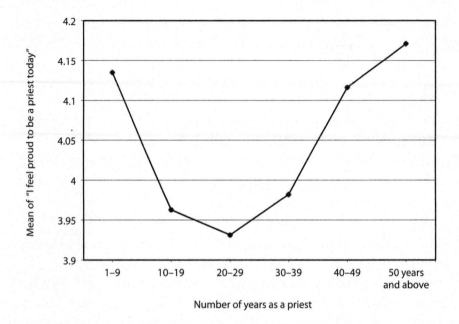

Figure 11.6. 2004 survey: Years ordained and "I feel proud to be a priest today"

proud to be priests today while only 24.8% of priests ordained 20–29 years similarly strongly agreed.

This unashamed and uncompromising embrace of priesthood and Catholicism are essential elements of modern evangelical Catholicism. As one younger priest, ordained 1–9 years, wrote on his 2004 survey: "Celibacy is not part of the problem, it is part of the solution. The problem is a lack of priests because the culture values fornication, adultery, divorce, abortion, hedonism, and does not value virginity, purity, marriage, self-control, children."

This strong and proud proclamation of one's Catholic identity is also seen in figure 11.7 from the 2004 survey.

These young priests not only profess to be proud to be priests today, they report being much more likely to encourage other men to become priests. The differences are statistically significant with the ANOVA's $F=7.587$ and $p<.001$.[10] While the curve is roughly the same U shape, the spike upward for the newly ordained is readily apparent. It is possible

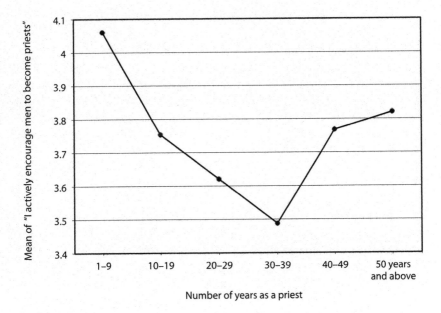

Figure 11.7. 2004 survey: Years ordained and "I actively encourage men to become priests"

that this is an indication of their stronger evangelical tendencies than any of their recent predecessors.

The respondents were given the statement, "I see a positive future for priesthood in the United States." Again, in figure 11.8, we see the same U-shaped curve. The ANOVA was significant at $p<.001$ with $F=4.604$. Scheffe post-hoc tests showed significant differences between the youngest priests and those ordained 20–29 years and a trending toward significance with the very oldest priests and those ordained 20–29 years ($p=.07$). For example, 83.4% of priests ordained 1–9 years said they see a positive future for priesthood while a lower 67.8% of those ordained 20–29 years would agree.[11]

The youngest priests are returning to a more positive evaluation of priesthood and are more likely to encourage others to become priests as well.

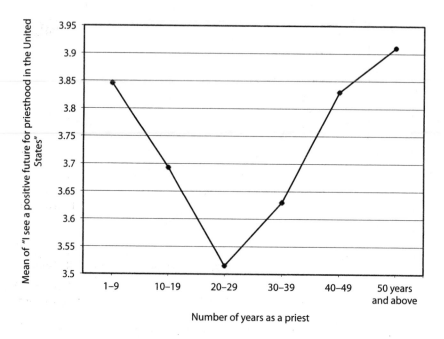

Figure 11.8. 2004 survey: Years ordained and "I see a positive future for priesthood in the United States"

Celibacy and the New Priests

Perhaps one of the least publicly understood and most discussed realities of priesthood in the Roman Catholic Church is mandatory celibacy. Whenever a priest is accused of some sort of sexual misconduct, invariably some will malign the practice of celibacy. When the issue of the reduced numbers of priests in some countries arises, again, celibacy is often fingered as the culprit. In a *New York Times* poll released May 4, 2010, only 35% of Americans believed that celibacy was "not a factor" contributing to child sex abuse by priests.[12]

However, there is no data to suggest that celibate priests are more likely to abuse children than other people are. As noted previously, the John Jay study found 4% of priests had been accused of molesting minors. While one case is one too many, this figure is not likely to be any higher than the rate for adult males in the United States in general.

A recent poll suggests that this is generally understood in society: in the same *New York Times* poll, 72% of Americans did not believe that "child sexual abuse is more common in the Catholic Church than in other walks of life."[13] This latter statistic seems somewhat contradictory to the earlier poll figure citing celibacy as a factor. Nevertheless, celibacy remains a contested public issue.

The first question to probe should not be how the public views mandatory celibacy but rather how the priests themselves view it. They are the ones who live it. The results of my two surveys were interesting. Only 52.8% of priests in the 2004 survey agreed/strongly agreed, "I support the requirement that priests live a celibate life." So, when asked about their support for mandatory celibacy in general, slightly more than half supported it.

However, when asked about celibacy for themselves personally, a different picture emerges. In tables 11.1 and 11.2, we see the results for both surveys. A large majority of priests, 66.6% in 2004 and 75.1% in 2009, actually experience celibacy as being a grace and a positive experience, despite its challenges. Also, it is interesting to note the increase from 2004 to 2009 of 8.5%.

Sometimes when I do public interviews, the media will speak to me about celibacy and its challenges. They suggest that it is too difficult. While agreeing that it is difficult, especially in our sex-crazed society, I respond that marriage is no easier. I have three married brothers, and I witness first-hand the challenges of being a good spouse and a good father while holding down a full-time, demanding job. As a priest, I sometimes think I have been called to the easier path. Nevertheless, each way of life has its own challenges and its own graces. Both of my surveys

Table 11.1. 2004 survey: "Overall, celibacy has been a positive experience for me"

	Strongly agree (%)	Agree (%)	Unsure (%)	Disagree (%)	Strongly disagree (%)
"Overall, celibacy has been a positive experience for me"	20.1	46.5	17.1	11.9	4.3

Table 11.2. 2009 survey: "Despite its challenges, celibacy has been a grace for me personally"

	Strongly agree (%)	Agree (%)	Neutral (%)	Disagree (%)	Strongly disagree (%)
"Despite its challenges, celibacy has been a grace for me personally"	22.8	52.3	13.0	8.4	3.4

indicate that the majority of priests have found a personal grace within their commitment to celibacy.

In the 2004 survey, space was given to the respondents to write in personal comments. Some of the comments about celibacy were particularly illuminating, both positive and negative:

- "I have grown into it."
- "It has helped me reach out to others, freed me for ministry, led me to a closer relationship to God."
- "Celibacy has meant little more for me than 'stifling it.'"
- "It has been difficult."

It is true that celibacy, like marriage, is something that the individual grows into as the days pass. At times, it is difficult. Natural intimacy and sexual needs must be managed and directed in a healthy, chaste way. As many of the priests' written comments noted, celibacy does indeed free the priest to develop chaste, deep relationships with others, and it should be a spur to developing a deeper relationship with God. Hopefully, a priest can move beyond the merely negative stance of "stifling it" but, as we have seen, not all do. In the 2009 survey, 11.8% of priests reported that they did not experience celibacy as a grace.

But to think that a large percentage of priests is waiting for celibacy to become optional so that they can get married is not accurate. In the 2004 survey, the priest respondents were given the statement: "If priests were allowed to marry, I would get married." The results are in table 11.3.

Only 17.9% of priests indicated that they would marry if celibacy were optional. This is similar to the Hoge and Wenger 2001 results in which 12% of priests answered certainly or probably yes to the same

Table 11.3. 2004 survey: "If priests were allowed to marry, I would get married"

	Strongly agree (%)	Agree (%)	Unsure (%)	Disagree (%)	Strongly disagree (%)
"If priests were allowed to marry, I would get married"	5.2	12.7	28.5	29.8	23.8

question.[14] So, while many priests favor optional celibacy, few would marry if given the opportunity by the Church.

It might be surprising for some in our society to learn that support for mandatory celibacy and satisfaction with celibate life among priests is not deteriorating among priests in the United States but actually getting stronger. It is the younger priests, as noted in the last section, who are returning to a stronger support of mandatory celibacy as did their "grandfathers" in the priesthood. As two of the younger priests, ordained 10–19 years, wrote:

- "Celibacy impresses on me what my vocation is."
- "Celibacy has been confirmed as a gift of the Spirit for me, an invitation to spousal union with the Lord."

Looking at the results of the 2004 survey broken down into ordination cohorts, we see that support for celibacy rising to previous high levels among pre–Vatican II priests. In figure 11.9, the higher the score, the greater the support for mandatory celibacy.[15] The ANOVA results are statistically significant with $F=24.843$ and $p<.001$ with the post-hoc Scheffe test showing statistically significant differences between the newly ordained priests and all the other cohorts. Once again, we see the U-shaped curve. Overall, the younger priests (ordained 1–19 years) strongly support mandatory celibacy at the same rates or greater than those ordained before the Vatican Council.

Table 11.4 breaks these numbers down into percentages. For example, 81.4% of priests ordained 1–9 years agree or strongly agree with mandatory celibacy whereas for priests ordained 30–39 years this number drops sharply to 37.9%. *This is a huge drop.*

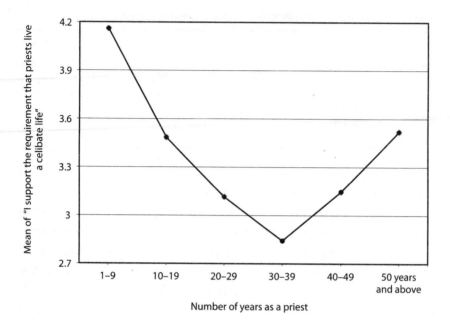

Figure 11.9. 2004 survey: Years ordained and "I support the requirement that priests live a celibate life"

In the time immediately after Vatican II, there was expectant talk in some seminaries and among some priests of an impending shift to optional celibacy. Some priests said that they were told as seminarians that celibacy would become optional during their priesthood. This did not happen. Some felt disappointed and even misled.

Again, highlighting the differences among ordination cohorts, in figure 11.10 we see the same U-shaped curve for support for celibacy, that is, belief that it is a personal grace and that God has called the priest to live a celibate life. In figure 11.10, the ANOVA again showed strong significant differences ($F=20.319$, $p<.001$). Younger priests are returning to a stronger positive evaluation of celibacy. Post-hoc Scheffe tests showed the youngest priests significantly different from the "middle" priests and not statistically different from the priests ordained more than fifty years.

But the newer priests are not simply a return to former days. Times have changed. While the newer priests reflect many of the good qualities of their "grandfathers," they are not the same. Many realities in today's

Table 11.4. 2004 survey: "I support the requirement that priests live a celibate life"

Number of years as a priest	Strongly agree (%)	Agree (%)	Unsure (%)	Disagree (%)	Strongly disagree (%)
1–9	48.2	33.2	8.5	6.5	3.5
10–19	32.6	25.6	11.2	19.1	11.6
20–29	19.5	25.7	18.0	20.3	16.5
30–39	17.9	20.0	12.1	28.6	21.4
40–49	24.7	22.2	12.6	23.7	16.7
50 and above	29.9	31.2	11.7	15.6	11.7

Church are taken for granted by these younger men, which were not present before the Council such as lay ministries, Mass in the vernacular, parish councils, finance boards, active participation of the laity at Mass, and many other reforms that are all firmly embedded in the mainstream of today's Catholic Church. These reforms are largely accepted by the mainstream of younger priests, albeit with exceptions.

The younger priests are much more strongly supportive of celibacy. They believe that celibacy is more than a discipline imposed by the Church. They believe that God has personally called them to a celibate life. Rather than seeing it as a burden, they are more likely to experience celibate living as a grace, although a difficult one. To support themselves in this celibate lifestyle, they rely heavily upon prayer, a relationship to God, devotion to Mary, frequent reception of the Sacrament of Penance, and chaste intimate sharing with friends.

These findings regarding celibacy noted in this chapter suggest that mandatory celibacy is fading in this country as a "hot button" issue among priests.

Summary

These new evangelical priests and the pre–Vatican II priests share many similar values. The U-shaped curves in this chapter gave statistical witness to the young priests returning to some traditional values, reminiscent of our oldest priests. However, the cultural reality they are coming from and the day-to-day reality of priestly life have changed.

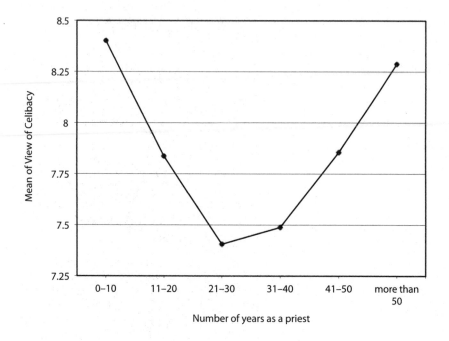

Figure 11.10. Years ordained and View of Celibacy

These changes have profoundly affected these younger priests so that they cannot be, nor should they be, exact mirror images of pre–Vatican II priests.

For example, as noted previously in chapter 4, a much higher percentage of these younger priests, compared to older priests, reports coming from dysfunctional backgrounds with more mental health problems in childhood. As newly ordained, they have higher rates of anxiety and depression as well as higher rates of burnout than the oldest of priests. While they mirror their "grandfathers" in their spiritual practices, the dysfunctional families that some are being brought up in are having a negative effect on their mental health.

A concrete expression of that reality was seen in our residential program. In the beginning of my tenure starting in 1993, priests typically came to us in distress later in life, often being well over forty years of age. Toward the end of my work there, at the turn of the millennium, we began to see more relatively newly ordained needing residential care, some after only a few months of priesthood. This was noticed and remarked upon by the clinical staff. It was a striking change.

But understanding the environment the newly ordained come from and then adding the current stresses and challenges of a young priest, it becomes more understandable. They are more likely to come from dysfunctional backgrounds; they are ordained celibate priests in a society that often does not support their celibate commitment nor their commitment to being part of an institutional religion; and they are quickly put in positions of responsibility, running parishes with all their concomitant administrative and leadership challenges. *The young priest of today is coping with adjusting to priesthood, adjusting to celibacy, adjusting to leadership, and doing all this surrounded by a sometimes hostile society.* It is little wonder their burnout scores are among the highest of any priests.

In some ways, the newly ordained priests look like their "grandfathers" in the priesthood. However, these similarities are limited to spiritual practices and some traditional values. Their reality is a new one and a much different one. They are a new breed of priests.

These younger seminarians and newly ordained strongly hold to the values of the Catholic Church while surrounded by a society that, at best, ignores such values and, at worst, is hostile. They profess to be priests in their public dress and are proud to be called such in a day when the image of priest-pedophile continues to be splashed incessantly on the media's front page. They are not afraid to say that they are happy in their vocations and in their celibate commitment, which they claim to have received from God. This is in contradistinction to a society that is registering its lowest job satisfaction rates in decades and for whom sex has become obsessively bartered and banal.

Of course, this does not mean that these new evangelical priests are perfect or without need of formation. *While this cohort is strong in traditional Catholic values, learning to translate these values into pastoral service and shepherding the local Church is important and sometimes difficult for them. As one now ministering in forming seminarians to become priests, I have sometimes witnessed that their uncompromising holding of values can be tainted with a bit of judgmentalism and their zeal for the faith, at times for some, can be laced with signs of pastoral harshness. A small number are tempted to bring back externals of the faith that have become inappropriate anachronisms. This cohort, like every one before it, needs a strong priestly formation program and solid mentoring during its initial years of priesthood.*

The "Vatican II priests" have spent a lifetime ministering in the Lord's vineyard. They have learned how to build an active community of the faithful and have themselves become exemplary shepherds. Now these Vatican II priests can help our younger priests learn to be compassionate shepherds and loving pastors of souls. Moreover, they can help them expand their ecclesiology to be more completely "Catholic" by not only holding to a strong sacramental and cultic vision of priesthood, but also incorporating a vision and skills to build a community of faith that calls forth the proper gifts and roles of the laity.

Moreover, the younger priests are suffering higher rates of burnout and carrying more psychological baggage from childhood. Some are particularly vulnerable to burning out and leaving the priesthood. On the other hand, the Vatican II priests have learned how to live a healthy life and balance the many and growing challenges of priesthood. The younger priests need to learn from these older men how to "survive and thrive" in decades of demanding service.

It can be argued that these new evangelical priests have the raw material that is needed today. The Holy Spirit inspires and forms men to become priests not in isolation from the world but as men who are raised in this world and yet are born anew in the Spirit. Thus, they are "in" the world but not "of" the world. And they can preach to this world as one of them but also as one who has been touched and transformed by the Holy Spirit. As one young priest wrote on his survey, "Our joy needs to be seen by all."

12

Recommendations

As a result of the findings of this study, I offer a few recommendations to vocation/formation personnel, to priests, and to bishops. These are not exhaustive. There is much rich material in this entire study for further reflection and study. Throughout, I have attempted to present as much of the data as I am able. I invite others to dig into this data and to offer their own insights, reflections, and recommendations.

To Vocation and Formation Personnel

- *Get the word out: priesthood is a very fulfilling and happy vocation.* The sometimes negative image of priesthood is largely a myth.
- *During the formative years, work intensely with seminarians on their spiritual formation, fostering a direct, personal relationship with God.* Seminarians study philosophy and theology; they often engage in a pastoral year and regularly are involved in pastoral work. These are important. But spiritual formation is sometimes left to the seminarian and his spiritual director as a hidden and perhaps even peripheral part of his preparation for the priesthood. While the relationship to a spiritual director must remain in the internal forum, the survey results suggest that spiritual formation is central and crucial to the well-being and happiness of a priest. The seminarian needs to be

directly and intensively formed in the spiritual life. This ought to be a priority.

- *Train the seminarians and young priests to see celibacy as a gift from God and as a personal grace.* To accept celibacy simply because it is necessary for priesthood in the Roman rite is not enough for a truly fulfilled and happy priesthood. Perceiving celibacy as a gift from God and a personal grace is important for the happiness and well-being of a celibate priest. These survey results suggest that direct training in celibacy will be one critical element of a seminarian's spiritual formation.

- *Assist seminarians in their development of good friendships, and screen out seriously isolated men.* The presence of good friendships is a key marker in the suitability of a man for the priesthood. An isolated priest is unlikely to do well personally, spiritually, and pastorally. Formation personnel should foster the development of healthy, chaste friendships and not call to orders any who cannot develop such life-giving relationships.

- *Do not underestimate the impact of a dysfunctional childhood and a background of childhood mental problems on the future success and happiness of a priest.* It would be unwise to "lower the bar" on taking candidates with a seriously dysfunctional history, even if the need for new priests is great. In fact, these research findings suggest that some vocation personnel will want to raise the bar they are currently using.

- *Screening prospective priestly candidates for a history of sexual problems remains critical.* There was likely a period in the recent history of the Church when unsuitable candidates with significant sexual conflicts were admitted to priesthood. The devastating results speak for themselves. Direct screening for a history of sexual problems and direct formation in a healthy, chaste psychosexual development are essential for the health and integrity of the priesthood.

- *Do not overlook the presence of obesity in a candidate.* What does a candidate's or priest's obesity mean? It is possible that, for some, their weight problems are a symptom of underlying unresolved issues that need to be addressed. It is unwise to ignore the presence of obesity.

To Priests

- *Give thanks for your vocation to the priesthood!* It is a wonderful life. Most priests are happy in their priesthood, very satisfied with their lives, and would do it all over again. While there are challenges, as in any life, the real happiness of our priests is remarkable, especially given the stresses of these past few years. It is a credit to the commitment and faith of our priests.
- *Let people know about the joy of your priesthood.* It is time to break this "secret" of priesthood and to tell people about the true satisfaction and happiness of priestly life. This is good for vocations; it is good for the People of God to know; and it is good for priests to tell their story. As one priest wrote on his survey, "When we're happy, we don't share it." Sharing their joy is an essential part of priestly ministry and the new evangelization.
- *Give primacy to your relationship to God.* A priest's relationship to God is critical for his happiness and priestly life. Without this rock, a priest will find himself in difficulty, the findings suggest. Many priests would likely benefit from even more time and energy directly focused on fostering a deeper personal relationship with God.
- *Foster good friendships.* The presence of good friendships for a priest is strongly predictive of having a good relationship to God. Having such friendships with other priests and laity is also important for your psychological well-being and happiness. Friendships, including priestly friendships, are integral to a priest's life and ought to be a priority.
- *The traditional elements of a priest's spiritual life are important:*
  - Receive the Sacrament of Penance frequently
  - Pray privately each day; consider a daily Holy Hour
  - Pray the Liturgy of the Hours daily
  - Regularly do theological and spiritual reading
  - Take an annual retreat
  - Foster a devotion to Mary

  All of these were directly and significantly related to the psychological and spiritual well-being of a priest. Moreover, a number of priests wrote on their surveys how important their sacramental ministry was to them, especially the Eucharist. Thus, I would add to that list: deepen one's love of and connection to the Eucharist.

- *Priestly unity needs to be improved.* Priestly unity is a big issue for priests. Many are unhappy with it and priestly divisions are harmful to the priesthood and to the Church. Priests say this area needs work, and it is only priests themselves who can improve it. It is time to listen to our brothers, especially those with whom we disagree, and to begin to mend the fissures in priestly unity.

- *Mutual priestly support is critical and should be fostered.* Attend priestly gatherings. Create priest support groups. Support brother priests. Priestly gatherings such as annual convocations and Chrism Masses are important moments for priests and should not be missed. Priest support groups remain a helpful way to promote mutual support. As one priest wrote on his survey, "We need to spend more time together in prayer and fraternity."

- *Love and support the bishop.* The bishop is an important person in a priest's life. Priests ought to nurture actively this important relationship. Priests can attend liturgies and functions led by the bishop. Understanding his hopes and goals for the diocese can be helpful. Praying for him and supporting his leadership are essential. Also, valuing the promise of obedience is an integral part of a solid priestly spirituality.

- *Different ordination cohorts need to help each other.* Today's senior pastors need the younger priests. These younger priests are full of evangelical fervor and profess a strong adherence to the faith. They are the new breed of evangelical Catholics, and these gifts are much needed today. Welcome them and guide them. And these younger evangelical Catholics need to respect and listen to the older priests. They need to be guided and mentored by them. These older men need to teach the younger priests how to manage their lives and prepare for a lifetime of demanding priestly service. As one priest wrote on his survey, the priesthood "needs more fraternity between younger and older priests."

- *Be aware of the signs of burnout.* If a priest becomes aware of the symptoms of burnout in himself or in another priest, assessment and pastoral care are needed.

- *When present, depression and anxiety need to be managed.* The findings strongly suggest that priests who become depressed and suffer from anxiety are less likely to be happy and are more at risk for having problems or leaving priesthood. Symptoms of anxiety and depression cannot be ignored but ought to be dealt with in a direct and effective fashion.
- *Learn to deal with stress in healthy ways.* A significant percentage of priests, nearly one quarter, indicated that they have unhealthy ways of coping with stress, such as excessive food and/or alcohol consumption. Learning to deal with stress is important for many priests.
- *Exercise and lose weight.* Too many priests are obese and do not exercise enough. If you are obese, ask yourself why. Perhaps there are underlying issues that need attention. But regardless, physical self-care is important for your physical and mental health.
- *Take your weekly day off as well as an annual vacation.* A priest will be healthier and happier if he takes regular time away for rest and rejuvenation.

To Bishops

- *Affirm your priests often.* Their happiness, commitment, and faith amidst an increasingly secular world is remarkable and a testament to the power of God's grace and their own greatness. Affirm them.
- *Be encouraged that the majority of your priests love you, support you, and obey you.* While there are some important issues that need to be addressed regarding the relationship between bishops and priests in the wake of these last few years, the essential relationship between a bishop and his priests remains solid.
- *Bishops are important to their priests.* Bishops are tied together with their priests in a sacramental bond that is critical for their nourishment and happiness. The bishop's first role for his priests is to love them. Do not underestimate how important you are to your priests. A kind word, a remembrance for one's ordination anniversary, a hospital visit, a call upon the death of a parent, a birthday wish, and other such small acts of kindness are not small to priests.

- *Make supporting priests' spiritual lives a priority.* This study consistently demonstrated the centrality of a priest's spiritual life for his personal happiness and well-being. A bishop and diocese would do well to emphasize, support, and dedicate resources to the spiritual lives of its priests including fostering an authentic diocesan priestly spirituality. Religious superiors and their orders will likewise want to investigate ways of similarly emphasizing the spiritual life. Oftentimes, we leave the subject of developing a spiritual life to the individual. However, would not some institutional or group presbyteral effort be advisable? Ongoing formation programs might not just be continuing education efforts but might also include continuing formation in the spiritual life. There are many possible ways for a diocese and/or a presbyterate to begin to emphasize the spiritual life such as highlighting the annual diocesan retreat, providing and training spiritual directors, focusing some annual convocations on the spiritual life, making the sacrament of penance a part of the annual priest convocation, praying the Liturgy of the Hours together, and a variety of other supports. These will likely be time, effort, and money well spent for the health of the priests and thus for the diocese or religious order as a whole.

- *Priests need help with their workload.* Most priests are not burned out, but a large percentage of them feels overwhelmed. This remains of great concern to priests today and needs to be acknowledged and faced directly.

- *Priests need to know they will be dealt with fairly.* In the wake of the crisis, a large percentage of priests is not confident that their human rights will be respected if they are accused of sexual misconduct. While we do not want to reduce our improving efforts to hear and respond to alleged victims, priests also need to know they will be heard and treated fairly.

- *Younger priests today need solid mentoring and support.* This includes priests up to twenty years ordained. They are at greater risk for burnout and thinking of leaving priesthood. It is difficult to adjust to a celibate, demanding priesthood today surrounded by a secular, sex-crazed culture. This is especially true for new young pastors with only a few years of priestly experience. They are placed in these complex and challenging pastoral positions with limited experience and fewer personal resources. They need the special attention of the bishop.

- *Continue to make healing resources readily available.* Some priests come from dysfunctional backgrounds and/or suffer from psychological difficulties. Ready access to healing regimens is needed for them. Helping priests in difficulty manage depression and anxiety and other problems is important. The study suggests that priests do avail themselves regularly of such assistance. This is encouraging and ought to be continued.

- *If a priest is considering leaving, first help him to assess his personal and spiritual life.* A priest who is considering leaving priesthood may be suffering from burnout, depression, and/or anxiety. The priest himself may be only slightly aware of these underlying feelings. Before a priest can discern his future, he must first deal with these realities, or else his discernment will be skewed and priesthood may be precipitously abandoned.

- *Have diocesan programs to ensure that priests maintain a proper weight, exercise, eat healthy foods, have regular medical checkups, and take the proper time off.* Physical self-care is sometimes overlooked by our priests who often live alone and are engaged in a busy ministry with increasing responsibility and fewer priests. Healthy living and sufficient time away, including sabbatical programs, will ultimately increase the availability of priests, not decrease it. If these healthy living programs come from the "top," it gives the priest permission to take better care of himself.

Conclusion

The Secret of Their Joy

The overall findings of this study are clear and, when combined with similar findings in other studies, incontrovertible: *Priests, as a group, are very happy with their lives and their vocations. They are among the happiest of any people in the country.*

Priests also scored well on standardized psychological tests. They scored modestly better than general samples of the lay population on tests measuring depression, anxiety, somatization, and overall functioning. Given that such symptoms comprise the large majority of psychological complaints in community and residential settings, these are good markers of the overall psychic health of priests.

In the wake of the sexual abuse crisis, the issue of mental health in the priesthood has resurfaced. Some would suggest that priests are psychologically stunted or less healthy than others. But the results indicated otherwise.

Moreover, the scores of priests as a group on standardized burnout measures were not elevated. In fact, they were markedly below secular norms, a positive finding. Despite the challenging if not overwhelming workload of our priests, they are bearing up well under the load and, by all measures, are actually prospering. Why are they not burned out, given their often excessive workload? Clearly, the great satisfaction with their lives and ministry that priests report is important in understanding their low burnout rates. In addition, their strong spiritual lives must also be taken into account; they find much nourishment in their relationship to God and in their spiritual lives in general.

This does not mean that there are no challenges or difficulties. Nor does it mean that there are no unhappy, burned out, or psychologically unwell priests. There are, and always will be, some of our number who are struggling. Priests are men not angels. And they are subject to all the frailties and temptations of any human life. Bishops and priests will want to continue to reach out to their wounded brothers and offer them love, support, and healing.

But the modern secular rumor that our celibate priesthood is an unhappy, lonely life is simply not borne out by the facts. The opposite is true. As a group, priests are much happier than their lay counterparts. I suspect the rumor that priests are dissatisfied is a projection of a secular mentality that has difficulty imaging happiness in such a celibate life of self-giving in faith to the Church and to the people. Moreover, the Church has a problem in getting this message out. As one priest wrote regarding morale, it is "good but this is not communicated." As this priest is implying, it is time to spread the word.

Where does their happiness come from? The findings in this study noted that a combination of psychological and spiritual factors contributes to priestly happiness. However, priestly scores on psychological tests were only modestly better than the general population and could not account for their extraordinarily high rates of happiness. To account for their happiness, one needs to look into the pastoral and spiritual lives of our priests.

Regarding their pastoral and spiritual lives, there were many sources of support and nourishment experienced by priests, such as good friendships with other priests and laity and a personal love of their vocations and pastoral ministry, especially their Eucharistic and sacramental ministry. The centrality and strength of their faith and pastoral commitment were critical to understanding our priests. Often unseen to the public, the spirituality of our priests is integral to their peace, happiness, and, at times, joy.

Their relationship with God is very much alive and a strong source of their inner peace and happiness. Priests reported having a strong nourishing relationship to God, feeling personally loved by God, feeling a sense of inner peace and even joy, and being grateful for these blessings.

The impact of their spirituality on the rest of their lives was remarkable. A powerful predictor of priestly happiness was their relationship with God. One could conclude that a priest simply cannot be a happy and effective priest without having a solid relationship to God. And this strong relationship to God is one of the major reasons they are so happy. *Priesthood is a human life, it is true, but it is more.*

The words of Paul VI, which began this work, seem a fitting summary of so much of what this research found. It is striking to this researcher that a written survey and modern quantitative statistical techniques could cross over into the realm of the spiritual and affirm the insights on the scriptures spoken by one of our pontiffs over thirty-five years ago. While Paul VI's words were speaking of the life of Jesus, they also directly apply to our priests as well. The life of a priest is simply that of imaging Christ, of being configured to the One who is in a loving relationship with the Father. Paul VI tells us what the secret of Jesus' joy is and thus the secret joy of the priesthood as well:

> But it is necessary here below to understand properly the secret of the unfathomable joy which dwells in Jesus and which is special to Him. It is especially the Gospel of Saint John that lifts the veil . . . if Jesus radiates such peace, such assurance, such happiness, such availability, it is by reason of the inexpressible love by which He knows that He is loved by His Father. (*Gaudete in Domino*)

Appendix 1

The 2004 Survey of Priests

This survey is completely ANONYMOUS and CONFIDENTIAL. There are no right answers; just be as honest as you can about how you really feel. For each statement, please indicate the extent to which you agree or disagree by checking the appropriate box. Please do not leave any blank unless they do not apply.

	Strongly Agree	Agree	Unsure	Disagree	Strongly Disagree
If I had a nephew, I would encourage him to be a priest.	☐	☐	☐	☐	☐
I see a positive future for priesthood in the United States.	☐	☐	☐	☐	☐
Compared to the Church of the past, today's Church is better.	☐	☐	☐	☐	☐
I support the requirement that priests live a celibate life.	☐	☐	☐	☐	☐
Overall, I am satisfied with the priests that we have in the Church today.	☐	☐	☐	☐	☐
Overall, I am satisfied with my current bishop.	☐	☐	☐	☐	☐
If I had a chance to do it over, I would become a priest again.	☐	☐	☐	☐	☐
If priests were allowed to marry, I would get married.	☐	☐	☐	☐	☐
I feel appreciated by the Church leadership.	☐	☐	☐	☐	☐
The Church crisis has negatively affected my view of priesthood.	☐	☐	☐	☐	☐
Priests are supportive of one another in my diocese.	☐	☐	☐	☐	☐

	Strongly Agree	Agree	Unsure	Disagree	Strongly Disagree
I feel alienated from the Church hierarchy.	☐	☐	☐	☐	☐
Priests are angry these days.	☐	☐	☐	☐	☐
I feel that people now look at me with suspicion.	☐	☐	☐	☐	☐
The Church crisis has negatively affected my view of Church leadership.	☐	☐	☐	☐	☐
Priests with allegations of abuse are being treated fairly by the Church.	☐	☐	☐	☐	☐
My morale is good.	☐	☐	☐	☐	☐
I actively encourage men to become priests.	☐	☐	☐	☐	☐
I trust the Church to deal fairly with me if I am accused of misconduct.	☐	☐	☐	☐	☐
I feel adequately informed by Church leadership.	☐	☐	☐	☐	☐
Overall, I am happy as a priest.	☐	☐	☐	☐	☐
I approve of the way my bishop is leading the diocese.	☐	☐	☐	☐	☐
Morale in the priesthood today is good.	☐	☐	☐	☐	☐
I feel supported by Church leadership.	☐	☐	☐	☐	☐
Overall, I feel fulfilled ministering as a priest.	☐	☐	☐	☐	☐
I am satisfied with my current living arrangement and conditions.	☐	☐	☐	☐	☐
Relationships among priests today are good.	☐	☐	☐	☐	☐
I feel proud to be a priest today.	☐	☐	☐	☐	☐
I am thinking of leaving the priesthood.	☐	☐	☐	☐	☐
My life and ministry as a priest make a difference in the world.	☐	☐	☐	☐	☐
I have good relationships with other priests.	☐	☐	☐	☐	☐
I have a good relationship with my bishop.	☐	☐	☐	☐	☐
I feel overwhelmed with the amount of work I have to do.	☐	☐	☐	☐	☐
I am satisfied with my current salary and benefits.	☐	☐	☐	☐	☐
There is a lack of unity in the priesthood today.	☐	☐	☐	☐	☐
I am worried about the future of the priesthood.	☐	☐	☐	☐	☐
My psychological health is good.	☐	☐	☐	☐	☐

	Strongly Agree	Agree	Unsure	Disagree	Strongly Disagree
I live under an unhealthy level of stress.	☐	☐	☐	☐	☐
I have close friendships with other priests.	☐	☐	☐	☐	☐
I am happy in my current ministry.	☐	☐	☐	☐	☐
I am committed to the ministry of the Catholic Church.	☐	☐	☐	☐	☐
I am satisfied with my spiritual life.	☐	☐	☐	☐	☐
I have a personal relationship with God (or Jesus) that is nourishing to me.	☐	☐	☐	☐	☐
Overall, celibacy has been a positive experience for me.	☐	☐	☐	☐	☐

Comment regarding last question: _____

_____

My greatest satisfaction as a priest today is:_____

_____

My biggest problem as a priest today is: _____

_____

The most important thing I could say about the morale
of priests is:_____

_____

Additional comments: _____

_____

My age is: ☐ Under 29 ☐ 30–39 ☐ 40–49 ☐ 50–59 ☐ 60–69 ☐ 70 and above

I am a: ☐ diocesan priest ☐ religious priest ☐ bishop ☐ married priest
   ☐ other _____

I have been ordained for:
   ☐ 1–9 years ☐ 10–19 years ☐ 20–29 years ☐ 30–39 years ☐ 40–49 years
   ☐ 50 years and above

Theologically, I am considered to be:
☐ very liberal ☐ liberal ☐ middle of the road ☐ conservative
☐ very conservative

What major theologate did you primarily attend? _____

What country were you born in? _____

I am: ☐ African American ☐ Caucasian ☐ Hispanic ☐ Asian ☐ African
☐ Native American ☐ Pacific Islander ☐ Other: _____

My height in feet and inches is: _____ My weight in pounds is about: _____

My last medical checkup was: ☐ within the year ☐ 1–2 years ☐ 3–5 years
☐ 6–10 years ☐ more than 10 years

I feel depressed: ☐ all the time ☐ most of the time ☐ occasionally ☐ seldom
☐ never

I regularly take a day off per week: ☐ all the time ☐ most of the time ☐ occasionally
☐ seldom ☐ never

I take a vacation each year: ☐ all the time ☐ most of the time ☐ occasionally
☐ seldom ☐ never

I feel lonely or isolated: ☐ all the time ☐ most of the time ☐ occasionally
☐ seldom ☐ never

I regularly read/study theological and spiritual books, articles, or tapes to stay current:
☐ all the time ☐ most of the time ☐ occasionally ☐ seldom ☐ never

My Spiritual Practices

How long ago did you last receive the Sacrament of Reconciliation?
☐ within the last month ☐ 1–3 months ☐ 4–8 months
☐ 9–12 months ☐ 1–3 years ☐ Over 3 years

How often do you pray the Liturgy of the Hours?
☐ all of it ☐ most of it ☐ a little each day ☐ some each week ☐ seldom ☐ never

My last retreat was:
☐ within the last 6 months ☐ 7–12 months ago ☐ 1–3 years ago ☐ 4–7 years ago
☐ more than 8 years ago

I currently have a spiritual director whom I see regularly: ☐ no ☐ yes

I belong to a priest support group that meets regularly: ☐ no ☐ yes

I have been on a sabbatical at some point in my priesthood: ☐ no ☐ yes
☐ no, but will go

How much do you pray privately in a day? ☐ none ☐ 1–15 minutes
☐ 16–30 minutes ☐ 31–60 minutes ☐ more than 1 hour

Appendix 2
The 2009 Priest Wellness Survey

You are invited to participate in a survey that is interested in different issues that priests have gone through during their lives, before and after ordination, and how it affects their overall wellness.

Instructions: Please read each set of questions carefully, as the responses to each set are answered in different ways. Please be open and honest in answering each question. This survey is completely voluntary and anonymous. You will not be asked to provide any personal identification. While this survey is not intended to create or cause any discomfort, if issues are raised for you that are troubling, contact a helping professional.

Informed consent: I have read and understand the instructions above and agree that, I am at least eighteen years of age, and completed this survey voluntarily: ☐ Yes ☐ No

The number of years I have been ordained is: ☐ 0–10 ☐ 11–20 ☐ 21–30
☐ 31–40 ☐ 41–50 ☐ more than 50

My age is: ☐ 25–29 ☐ 30–39 ☐ 40–49 ☐ 50–59 ☐ 60–69 ☐ over 69

My country/race/ethnicity is: ☐ (Hispanic) ☐ (From Africa) ☐ (African American)
☐ (Caucasian) ☐ (Vietnam) ☐ (Philippines) ☐ (Poland) ☐ (India)
☐ (Other)_____

I am a ☐ Diocesan Priest ☐ Religious Priest ☐ Permanent Deacon
☐ Other _____

My height is _____ inches; my weight is _____ lbs.

I take a day off per week: ☐ almost all the time ☐ usually ☐ sometimes ☐ rarely
☐ almost never

I take an annual vacation: ☐ almost all the time ☐ usually ☐ sometimes ☐ rarely
☐ almost never

I receive the Sacrament of Penance about: ☐ at least weekly ☐ monthly
☐ every three months ☐ every six months ☐ yearly ☐ less than yearly

I pray privately each day about: ☐ not daily ☐ 1–15 minutes ☐ 16–30 minutes
☐ 31–59 minutes ☐ 60 minutes or more

I make an annual retreat: ☐ almost all the time ☐ usually ☐ sometimes ☐ rarely
☐ almost never

SD=strongly disagree D=disagree N=neutral A=agree SA=strongly agree

1. Growing up, I had close friends:	SD	D	N	A	SA
2. I currently have close priest friends:	SD	D	N	A	SA
3. I did well academically in school:	SD	D	N	A	SA
4. I get emotional support from others:	SD	D	N	A	SA
5. I have consistent problems getting along with people:	SD	D	N	A	SA
6. Growing up, I suffered from depression:	SD	D	N	A	SA
7. I am thinking of leaving the priesthood:	SD	D	N	A	SA
8. I grew up in a dysfunctional family:	SD	D	N	A	SA
9. During the seminary, I made some close friends:	SD	D	N	A	SA
10. I share my problems and feelings with close friends:	SD	D	N	A	SA
11. I use people to satisfy my own needs:	SD	D	N	A	SA
12. A member of my immediate family has suffered from psychological problems:	SD	D	N	A	SA
13. From the beginning, my family has supported my vocation to the priesthood:	SD	D	N	A	SA
14. Growing up, I saw a mental health professional for some difficulties:	SD	D	N	A	SA
15. I was emotionally abused as a child (before the age of eighteen):	SD	D	N	A	SA
16. I was physically abused as a child (before the age of eighteen):	SD	D	N	A	SA
17. I have trouble managing my anger:	SD	D	N	A	SA

SD=strongly disagree D=disagree N=neutral A=agree SA=strongly agree

18. I exercise on a regular basis:	SD	D	N	A	SA
19. Obesity is a problem for me:	SD	D	N	A	SA
20. Growing up, I suffered from anxiety:	SD	D	N	A	SA
21. When I have difficulties, I work out my problems by myself:	SD	D	N	A	SA
22. I get angry when others criticize me:	SD	D	N	A	SA
23. I suffer from loneliness:	SD	D	N	A	SA
24. I know my sexual orientation, and I am at peace with it:	SD	D	N	A	SA
25. My relationships seem to have more conflict than others have:	SD	D	N	A	SA
26. I pray most or all the Liturgy of Hours daily:	SD	D	N	A	SA
27. I have a good relationship with my bishop:	SD	D	N	A	SA
28. I support my bishop's leadership:	SD	D	N	A	SA
29. Others are often envious of me:	SD	D	N	A	SA
30. Mary is an important part of my priestly life:	SD	D	N	A	SA
31. Despite its challenges, celibacy has been a grace for me personally:	SD	D	N	A	SA
32. I have a problem with my Internet usage:	SD	D	N	A	SA
33. I read theological or spiritual books/magazines regularly:	SD	D	N	A	SA
34. Priests in my diocese/religious order are supportive of each other:	SD	D	N	A	SA
35. I feel a sense of inner peace:	SD	D	N	A	SA
36. I have a good self-image:	SD	D	N	A	SA
37. I attend priest gatherings in my diocese/order as often as I can:	SD	D	N	A	SA
38. I feel that God loves me personally and directly:	SD	D	N	A	SA
39. I have difficulty feeling like I can be forgiven:	SD	D	N	A	SA

SD=strongly disagree D=disagree N=neutral A=agree SA=strongly agree

40. I believe God has called me to live a celibate life:	SD	D	N	A	SA
41. I feel a sense of closeness to God:	SD	D	N	A	SA
42. I feel thankful for my blessings:	SD	D	N	A	SA
43. I have some unhealthy ways of coping with stress (such as excessive food or alcohol):	SD	D	N	A	SA
44. I am too hard on myself:	SD	D	N	A	SA
45. I have a devotion to the Virgin Mary:	SD	D	N	A	SA
46. From time to time, I feel a joy that is a grace from God:	SD	D	N	A	SA
47. Growing up, I had difficulty coming to grips with my sexuality:	SD	D	N	A	SA
48. My special gifts are not being recognized:	SD	D	N	A	SA
49. Obedience to religious authority is an important value for me:	SD	D	N	A	SA
50. I have a relationship to God (or Jesus) that is nourishing for me:	SD	D	N	A	SA
51. I have angry outbursts which upset others:	SD	D	N	A	SA
52. Growing up, I had a good relationship with my mother:	SD	D	N	A	SA
53. Growing up, I had a good relationship with my father:	SD	D	N	A	SA
54. I feel some conflict around my sexuality:	SD	D	N	A	SA
55. I have good lay friends who are an emotional support for me personally:	SD	D	N	A	SA
56. My morale as a priest is good:	SD	D	N	A	SA
57. Overall, I am happy as a priest:	SD	D	N	A	SA

1. While in the seminary, I changed dioceses/religious orders:	Yes	No
2. My parents are divorced:	Yes	No
3. I have a learning disability:	Yes	No
4. I have failed a grade in school:	Yes	No
5. I was sexually abused before the age of eighteen:	Yes	No
6. Alcohol has interfered with my professional/ religious/ personal life:	Yes	No
7. During my priesthood, I have voluntarily sought out a counselor:	Yes	No
8. At some time in my life, someone has expressed concern about my drinking:	Yes	No
9. I have been evaluated at a residential treatment program during my priesthood:	Yes	No
10. I have gone through a residential treatment program during my priesthood:	Yes	No
11. I played sports in school:	Yes	No
12. I have diabetes:	Yes	No
13. I belong to a priest support group that meets regularly:	Yes	No
14. I have been asked to see a counselor by my diocese or religious order:	Yes	No

During the past thirty days, how much of the time did you feel:

Circle only one number for each question. Response options are as follows:
1=none of the time, 2=a little of the time, 3=some of the time, 4=most of the time,
5=all of the time

1. so sad nothing could cheer you up?	1	2	3	4	5
2. cheerful?	1	2	3	4	5
3. nervous?	1	2	3	4	5
4. in good spirits?	1	2	3	4	5
5. restless or fidgety?	1	2	3	4	5
6. extremely happy?	1	2	3	4	5
7. hopeless?	1	2	3	4	5
8. calm and peaceful?	1	2	3	4	5
9. that everything was an effort?	1	2	3	4	5
10. satisfied?	1	2	3	4	5
11. worthless?	1	2	3	4	5
12. full of life?	1	2	3	4	5

Please describe yourself on the following statements:
1=Strongly disagree, 2=Disagree, 3=Slightly disagree, 4=Neither agree nor disagree, 5=Slightly agree, 6=Agree, 7=Strongly agree

_____ In most ways my life is close to my ideal.

_____ The conditions of my life are excellent.

_____ I am satisfied with my life.

_____ So far I have gotten the important things I want in life.

_____ If I could live my life over, I would change almost nothing.

Read each one carefully and circle the number of the response that best describes:
How much that problem has distressed or bothered you during the past seven days including today. Circle only one number for each problem (0 1 2 3 4).

How much were you distressed by:

0=Not at all, 1=A little bit, 2=Moderately, 3=Quite a bit, 4=Extremely

1. Faintness or dizziness	0	1	2	3	4
2. Feeling no interest in things	0	1	2	3	4
3. Nervousness or shakiness inside	0	1	2	3	4
4. Pains in heart or chest	0	1	2	3	4
5. Feeling lonely	0	1	2	3	4
6. Feeling tense or keyed up	0	1	2	3	4
7. Nausea or upset stomach	0	1	2	3	4
8. Feeling blue	0	1	2	3	4
9. Suddenly scared for no reason	0	1	2	3	4
10. Trouble getting your breath	0	1	2	3	4
11. Feelings of worthlessness	0	1	2	3	4
12. Spells of terror or panic	0	1	2	3	4
13. Numbness or tingling in parts of your body	0	1	2	3	4
14. Feeling hopeless about the future	0	1	2	3	4
15. Feeling so restless you couldn't sit still	0	1	2	3	4
16. Feeling weak in parts of your body	0	1	2	3	4
17. Thoughts of ending your life	0	1	2	3	4
18. Feeling fearful	0	1	2	3	4

Please read each statement carefully and decide if you ever feel this way about your ministry. If you have never had this feeling, write a "0" (zero) in the space before the statement. If you have had this feeling, indicate how often you feel it by writing the number (from 1 to 6) that best describes how frequently you feel that way.

0=Never, 1=A Few times a year or less, 2=Once a month or less, 3=A few times a month, 4=Once a week, 5=A few times a week, 6=Every day

How Often:

1._____ I feel emotionally drained from my ministry.

2._____ I feel used up at the end of the day.

3._____ I feel fatigued when I get up in the morning and have to face another day of ministry.

4._____ I can easily understand how my parishioners feel about things.

5._____ I feel I treat some parishioners as if they were impersonal objects.

6._____ Working with people all day is really a strain for me.

7._____ I deal very effectively with the problems of my parishioners.

8._____ I feel burned out from my ministry.

9._____ I feel I'm positively influencing other people's lives through my ministry.

10._____ I've become more callous toward people since I took this position.

11._____ I worry that this assignment is hardening me emotionally.

12._____ I feel very energetic.

13._____ I feel frustrated by my ministry.

14._____ I feel I'm working too hard on my work.

15._____ I don't really care what happens to some parishioners.

16._____ Working with people directly puts too much stress on me.

17._____ I can easily create a relaxed atmosphere with my parishioners.

18._____ I feel exhilarated after working closely with my parishioners.

19._____ I have accomplished many worthwhile things in this assignment.

20._____ I feel like I'm at the end of my rope.

21._____ In my priesthood, I deal with emotional problems very calmly.

22._____ I feel parishioners blame me for some of their problems.

Instructions: Below are twenty statements describing people's behaviors. Please use the rating scale below to accurately describe how each statement describes you. Read each statement carefully and then circle the number to the right that best applies to you. Circle only one number for each question.

1=Very inaccurate, 2=Moderately inaccurate, 3=Neither inaccurate nor accurate, 4=Moderately accurate, 5=Very accurate

1. I often feel blue.	1	2	3	4	5
2. I rarely get irritated.	1	2	3	4	5
3. I dislike myself.	1	2	3	4	5
4. I seldom feel blue.	1	2	3	4	5
5. I am often down in the dumps.	1	2	3	4	5
6. I feel comfortable with myself.	1	2	3	4	5
7. I have frequent mood swings.	1	2	3	4	5
8. I am not easily bothered by things.	1	2	3	4	5
9. I panic easily.	1	2	3	4	5
10. I am very pleased with myself.	1	2	3	4	5
11. I feel comfortable around people.	1	2	3	4	5
12. I have little to say.	1	2	3	4	5
13. I make friends easily.	1	2	3	4	5
14. I keep in the background.	1	2	3	4	5
15. I am skilled in handling social situations.	1	2	3	4	5
16. I would describe my experiences as somewhat dull.	1	2	3	4	5
17. I am the life of the party.	1	2	3	4	5
18. I don't like to draw attention to myself.	1	2	3	4	5
19. I know how to captivate people.	1	2	3	4	5
20. I don't talk a lot.	1	2	3	4	5

I am in the (Arch) Diocese of _____.

Please write in the name of your diocese. Religious priests should write in the name of the diocese they are ministering in.

Please check to make sure you answered all the questions clearly. Thank you!

Appendix 3

2009 Survey Composite Variables

Composite variables emerged using three extraction methods: principal components analysis and two factor analyses—maximum likelihood and principal axis. These three analyses suggested that individual survey items clumped together into larger factors. By combining these individual items into larger composite variables based on these analyses, we have higher validity and reliability that the composite variables actually measure what they are purporting to measure and do so with greater psychometric accuracy.

To measure internal consistency or reliability of each of these composite variables, a Cronbach's alpha was computed. When it was lower than .70, a Spearman-Brown was also computed. The latter is often used to estimate the reliability of a longer scale when the number of items in each new variable is low, which in this case is present for all the variables. The largest new variable had only six items. The Spearman-Brown Formula estimated the reliability of the scale if it contained 40 items.[1]

As can be seen in each of these cases, the Cronbach's alpha and/or Spearman-Brown results were more than sufficient to support the formation of these new variables.

Relationship to God

"I feel that God loves me personally and directly."
"I feel a sense of closeness to God."
"I feel thankful for my blessings."

"From time to time, I feel a joy that is a grace from God."
"I have a relationship to God (or Jesus) that is nourishing for me."
Cronbach's alpha=.839

Anger Problems

"I have consistent problems getting along with people."
"I have trouble managing my anger."
"My relationships seem to have more conflict than others have."
"I have angry outbursts which upset others."
Cronbach's alpha=.744

Dysfunctional Childhood

"I grew up in a dysfunctional family."
"A member of my immediate family has suffered from psychological problems."
"I was emotionally abused as a child (before the age of eighteen)."
"I was physically abused as a child (before the age of eighteen)."
"Growing up, I had a good relationship with my mother."*
"Growing up, I had a good relationship with my father."*
Cronbach's alpha=.601
Spearman-Brown=.91

Close Friends

"Growing up I had close friends."
"I currently have close priest friends."
"I get emotional support from others."
"During the seminary, I made some close friends."
"I share my problems and feelings with close friends."
"I have good lay friends who are an emotional support for me personally."
Cronbach's alpha=.760

Relationship to the Bishop

"I have a good relationship with my bishop."
"I support my bishop's leadership."
Cronbach's alpha=.817

Devotion to Mary

"Mary is an important part of my priestly life."
"I have a devotion to the Virgin Mary."
Cronbach's alpha=.917

View of Celibacy

"Despite its challenges, celibacy has been a grace for me personally."
"I believe God has called me to live a celibate life."
Cronbach's alpha=.846

Sexual Conflicts

"I know my sexual orientation, and I am at peace with it."*
"Growing up, I had difficulty coming to grips with my sexuality."
"I feel some conflict around my sexuality."
Cronbach's alpha=.686
Spearman-Brown=.97

Obesity and Unhealthy Coping

"I exercise on a regular basis."*
"Obesity is a problem for me."
"I have some unhealthy ways of coping with stress (such as excessive food or alcohol)."
Cronbach's alpha=.582
Spearman-Brown=.95

Childhood Mental Health Problems

"Growing up, I suffered from depression."
"Growing up, I saw a mental health professional for some difficulties."
"Growing up, I suffered from anxiety."
Cronbach's=.689
Spearman-Brown=.97

Priestly Happiness and Morale

"My morale as a priest is good."
"Overall, I am happy as a priest."
Cronbach's alpha=.877

Lonely and Unappreciated

"I get angry when others criticize me."
"I suffer from loneliness."
"I am too hard on myself."
"My special gifts are not being recognized."
Cronbach's alpha=.581
Spearman-Brown=.93

Learning and School Problems

"I have a learning disability."
"I have failed a grade in school."
Cronbach's alpha=.329
Spearman-Brown=.91

Inner Peace

"I feel a sense of inner peace."
"I have a good self-image."
Cronbach's alpha=.768

Time Off

"I take a day off per week."
"I take an annual vacation."
Cronbach's alpha=.612
Spearman-Brown=.97

Prayer and the Sacrament of Penance

"I receive the Sacrament of Penance about: at least weekly, monthly, every three months, every six months, yearly, less than yearly."*
"I pray privately each day about: not daily, 1–15min, 16–30min, 31–59min, 60min, or more."
"I pray most or all the Liturgy of Hours daily."
Cronbach's alpha=.690
Spearman-Brown=.97

Alcohol Problems

"Alcohol has interfered with my professional/religious/personal life."
"At some time in my life, someone has expressed concern about my drinking."
Cronbach's alpha=.733

Residential Evaluation and/or Treatment

"I have been evaluated at a residential treatment program during my priesthood."
"I have gone through a residential treatment program during my priesthood."
Cronbach's alpha=.920

Age and Years Ordained

"My age is . . ."
"The number of years I have been ordained is . . ."
Cronbach's alpha=.914

Narcissistic Traits

"I use people to satisfy my own needs."
"Others are often envious of me."
Cronbach's alpha=.301
Spearman-Brown=.90

Note: Composite variables were formed by the simple addition of the values of all the individual items included in the composite variable. Strongly disagree=1; Disagree=2; Neutral=3; Agree=4; and Strongly agree=5. *Items with asterisks loaded negatively on the factor (or Composite Variable) and thus were coded in reverse for inclusion into the new variable.

Appendix 4

Correlations among Variables Predicting "Happiness and Morale"

Variable	1	2	3	4	5	6	7	8	9
Happiness and Morale (1)	...	.59	.53	.47	-.46	.38	-.38	-.37	.36
Inner Peace (2)		...	.55	.32	-.50	.27	-.43	-.36	.21
Relationship to God (3)			...	.36	-.33	.26	-.35	-.31	.30
View of Celibacy (4)				...	-.31	.25	-.21	-.24	.49
Lonely and Unappreciated (5)					...	-.28	.50	.40	-.23
Relationship to Bishop (6)						...	-.22	-.19	.38
Anger Problems (7)							...	.42	.37
Dysfunctional Childhood (8)								...	-.20
Obedience to Religious Authority (9)									...
Close Friends (10)									
Childhood Mental Problems (11)									
Sexual Conflicts (12)									
Priests Support Other (13)									
Difficulty Feeling Forgiven (14)									
Prayer and Sacrament of Penance (15)									
Devotion to Mary (16)									
Attends Priest Gatherings (17)									
Obesity and Coping (18)									
Family Support of Vocation (19)									
Theological Reading (20)									
Annual Retreat (21)									
Work Out Problems Alone (22)									
Narcissistic Traits (23)									

Note: All significance tests were two-tailed; * means the significance $p<.05$; NS means it is not statistically significant; all others were significant at $p<.001$.

10	11	12	13	14	15	16	17	18	19	20	21	22	23
.35	-.35	-.31	.29	-.28	.27	.27	.27	-.23	.20	.18	.16	-.11	-.10
.40	-.39	-.38	.27	-.36	.17	.21	.26	-.32	.20	.21	.10	-.09	-.10
.46	-.26	-.31	.15	-.39	.23	.32	.25	-.22	.17	.24	.12	-.12	-.12
.17	-.20	-.28	.18	-.18	.47	.47	.19	-.15	.13	.13	.19	-.06*	-.15
-.24	.43	.37	-.28	.34	-.18	-.18	-.17	.32	-.18	-.13	-.07*	.13	.29
.19	-.22	-.17	.35	-.18	.20	.21	.33	-.11	.13	.07	.17	-.07	-.07
-.30	.46	.34	-.16	.37	-.11	-.13	-.17	.26	-.18	-.12	NS	.09	.28
-.20	.59	.36	-.19	.25	-.17	-.21	-.16	.25	-.31	-.05*	NS	-.07*	.18
.14	-.16	-.23	.20	-.12	.42	.43	.20	-.13	.11	.05*	.17	-.04*	-.11
...	-.21	-.23	.19	-.24	.13	.13	.19	-.14	.21	.23	.12	-.29	NS
	...	.39	-.16	.31	-.13	-.14	-.19	.26	-.21	-.09	NS	NS	.18
		...	-.10	.31	-.20	-.21	-.12	.22	-.15	-.11	-.08	NS	.20
			...	-.09	.20	.07	.27	-.14	.15	.10	.12	-.06*	-.05*
				...	-.08	-.08	-.14	.16	-.14	-.11	-.05*	.05*	.15
					...	.51	.14	-.22	.06*	.18	.28	-.09	-.13
						...	.08	-.15	.08	.10	.10	-.04*	-.16
							...	-.08	.11	.12	.31	-.09	NS
								...	-.08	-.16	-.06*	.06*	.14
									...	.07	.04*	-.04*	NS
										...	.17	-.10	-.08
											...	-.13	NS
												...	.05*
													...

Notes

1. Summary of Findings

1. John Jay College of Criminal Justice, *The Nature and Scope of Sexual Abuse of Minors by Catholic Priests and Deacons in the United States, 1950–2002* (Washington, DC: United States Conference of Catholic Bishops, 2004), 39.

2. The *optimism bias* may also be at work here. In this phenomenon, people tend to see their own situation in a more favorable light and are likely to be overly optimistic about the success of their own plans, compared to their evaluation of others.

3. Dean R. Hoge and Jacqueline E. Wenger, *Evolving Visions of the Priesthood.* (Collegeville, MN: Liturgical Press, 2003), 25.

4. *Christus Dominus*, no. 16 and *Presbyterorum Ordinis*, no. 7, *Documents of Vatican II.*

5. Garret Condon, "Priests (mostly) Happy, Survey Says," *Hartford Courant*, January 19, 2003, http://articles.courant.com/2003-01-19/news/ 0301190010_1_catholic-priests-sociology-at-catholic-university-survey.

3. Physical Health and Self-Care

1. For ease of interpretation, Time Off was coded so that as the variable increases, the individual was more likely to take time off.

2. The standards used for the BMI were: Normal=18.5–24.99; Overweight=25–29.99; Obese=30–39.99; Morbidly Obese=40 and above.

3. Robert Longley, "Americans Getting Taller, Bigger, Fatter says CDC," About .com, http://usgovinfo.about.com/od/healthcare/a/tallbutfat.htm.

4. Nanci Hellmich, "Obesity Can Trim 10 Years off Life," *USA Today*, March 17, 2009.

4. The Psychological Wellness of Priests

1. Eugene C. Kennedy and Victor J. Heckler. *The Catholic Priest in the United States: Psychological Investigations.* (Washington, DC: United States Catholic Conference, 1972), 3.

2. Ibid.

3. Ibid., 4.

4. Thomas F. Nestor, "Intimacy and Adjustment Among Catholic Priests" (dissertation, Loyola University, 1993), 140.

5. Ibid.

6. Ibid., 136.

7. Ibid., 141.

8. Melvin C. Blanchette, "Review of Research on Psychological Factors in Priestly Morale" in *Consultation on Priests' Morale: A Review of Research*, National Federation of Priests' Councils, vol. II, no. 5 (Chicago: NFPC, 1992), 14–15.

9. Leonard R. Derogatis, *BSI-18: Administration, Scoring, and Procedures Manual* (Minneapolis, MN: NCS Pearson, Inc., 2000), 1.

10. Ibid., 6.

11. Ibid., 2.

12. Thomas F. Nestor, telephone conversation and e-mail with the author, June 2010. These numbers are not in his dissertation.

13. Nestor, "Intimacy and Adjustment Among Catholic Priests," 124.

14. John Jay College, *Nature and Scope*, 4.

15. Thomas Plante, PhD, "Six Important Points You Don't Hear about Regarding Clergy Sexual Abuse in the Catholic Church," *Do the Right Thing* (Blog), *Psychology Today*, March 24, 2010, http://www.psychologytoday.com/blog/do-the-right-thing/201003/six-important-points-you-dont-hear-about-regarding-clergy-sexual-abus.

16. Richard Cross, "Does Celibacy Contribute to Clerical Sexual Abuse?" *In Depth Analysis* (Blog), Catholic Culture.org, May 19, 2010, http://www.catholicculture.org/commentary/articles.cfm?id=442.

17. Plante, "Six."

18. John Jay College, *Nature and Scope*, 47.

19. An ANOVA was accomplished in this study to compare, on the four BSI-18 scales, those priests in the sample who were sexually abused with those who were not, and the results confirmed previous studies. Those who reported having been sexually abused as minors had statistically significant ($p<.001$) but modest increases in reported levels of anxiety, depression, somatization, and thus the overall level of psychopathology, as measured by the BSI-18. On the BSI-SOM, for the abused $T=50.78$, for the non-abused $T=48.71$. On the BSI-DEP, for the abused $T=51.46$, for the non-abused $T=48.71$. On the BSI-ANX, for the abused $T=49.60$, for the non-abused $T=47.28$. On the BSI-GSI, for the abused $T=51.94$, for the non-abused $T=48.84$.

20. On the y axis, not being sexually abused was coded as "0" and being sexually abused was coded as "1." So, as the line rises, the rate of victimization rises.

21. National Center for Victims of Crime, http://www.ncvc.org/ncvc/main.aspx?dbName=DocumentViewer&DocumentID=32360.

22. John Jay College, *Nature and Scope*, 41.

23. The conservative Scheffe post-hoc test showed the differences between those ordained 31–40 years and all of the other age groups trending toward significance from p=.07–.08. The y axis is coded in this figure and all figures of individual survey items from the 2009 survey, unless noted otherwise, as follows: Strongly disagree=1; Disagree=2; Neutral=3; Agree=4; Strongly agree=5.

Table N.1. "Growing up had difficulty with sexuality" for ordination cohorts

	Strongly disagree	Disagree	Neutral	Agree	Strongly agree
Number of years as a priest					
0–10					
n	121	135	27	59	14
%	34.0	37.9	7.6	16.6	3.9
11–20					
n	76	130	32	74	18
%	23.0	39.4	9.7	22.4	5.5
21–30					
n	62	140	44	108	18
%	16.7	37.6	11.8	29.0	4.8
31–40					
n	83	208	61	184	29
%	14.7	36.8	10.8	32.6	5.1
41–50					
n	130	200	49	119	13
%	25.4	39.1	9.6	23.3	2.5
More than 50					
n	104	130	30	64	6
%	31.1	38.9	9.0	19.2	1.8
Total					
n	576	943	243	608	98
%	23.3	38.2	9.8	24.6	4.0

24. John Jay College, *Nature and Scope*, 41.

25. John Jay College of Criminal Justice, *The Causes and Context of the Sexual Abuse of Minors by Catholic Priests in the United States, 1950–2010* (Washington, DC: United States Conference of Catholic Bishops, 2011), 36.

26.

Table N.2. Years ordained and BSI-18 anxiety; and BSI-18 depression

Number of years as a priest	BSI-18 depression	BSI-18 anxiety
0–10		
Mean	49.42	48.04
n	356	356
Standard deviation	8.363	8.507
11–20		
Mean	49.60	48.26
n	330	330
Standard deviation	8.265	8.338
21–30		
Mean	49.33	48.35
n	372	372
Standard deviation	8.299	8.492
31–40		
Mean	49.51	48.08
n	565	565
Standard deviation	8.320	8.388
41–50		
Mean	47.98	46.18
n	511	511
Standard deviation	7.318	7.746
More than 50		
Mean	47.91	46.05
n	334	334
Standard deviation	7.431	7.545
Total		
Mean	48.95	47.47
N	2468	2468
Standard deviation	8.025	8.225

27. For a similar finding of lower levels of anxiety, stress, and anger in older Americans, see Arthur A. Stone et al., "A Snapshot of the Age Distribution of Psychological Well-Being in the United States," *Proceedings of the National Academy of Sciences* 107, no. 22 (June 1, 2010), 9985–9990, http://www.pnas.org/content/107/22/9985.full.pdf+html?sid=b951ee21-8d4f-4a04-8ec0-aecf5e6431ad.

28. The *y* axis is measured by adding all of the individual items with the scoring key for each item being: Strongly disagree=1, Disagree=2, Neutral=3, Agree=4, Strongly agree=5.

29. http://ipip.ori.org/.

30. Tom Buchanan, "Online Implementation of an IPIP Five Factor Personality Inventory," version 1, January 5, 2001, http://www.docstoc.com/docs/36825859/Big-Five---Online-Implementation-of-an-IPIP-Five-Factor.

31. "Address of John Paul II to the Bishops of Brazil's Eastern Region on Their *Ad Limina* Visit," September 5, 2002, #5, http://www.vatican.va/holy_father/john_paul_ii/speeches/2002/september/documents/hf_jp-ii_spe_20020905_ad-limina-brazil_en.html.

5. Burnout and the Priesthood

1. Christina Maslach et al., *Maslach Burnout Inventory Manual*, third edition (Mountain View, CA: CPP Inc., 1996), 19. Recipients were given the MBI-HSS version, that is, the version that "was developed to measure burnout as an occupational issue for people providing human services." This is most appropriate for priests who clearly are providing human services. There is precedent for words being modified for the specific group surveyed. Thus, for example, "recipient" is changed to "student" when the inventory is given to teachers. In this case, "recipient" was changed to "parishioner," and "job" was changed to "ministry" or "priesthood" for the priests. Indeed, the manual instructs the respondent, "Because persons in a wide variety of occupations will answer this survey, it uses the term *recipients* to refer to the people for whom you provide your service, treatment, or instruction. When answering this survey please think of these people as recipients of the service you provide, even though you may use another term in your work."

Nevertheless, in order to confirm the results of this survey, another four dioceses were given the Maslach Burnout Inventory. A total of 217 priests were given this second round of surveys in 2010, and the words were left unmodified, that is, *recipient* and *job* were left in. The results were similar to the original survey. For this second survey, the means for the three scales were: Emotional Exhaustion=16.11; Depersonalization=5.67; Personal Accomplishment=37.21. These follow-on, smaller sample means are roughly similar to the original findings, thus confirming the original results.

2. Maslach, *Maslach Burnout Inventory Manual*.

3. Ibid., 5. Numerical cutoffs are provided in table I on p. 6 of Maslach's manual for the general sample as well as the subsamples.

4. Scheffe post-hoc tests showed that the oldest, those ordained more than 40 years, were significantly different from all of the younger priests on both the Emotional Exhaustion and Depersonalization scales. The very oldest priests, those ordained more than 50 years, were significantly different from priests ordained 21–40 years on the Personal Accomplishment scale.

Table N.3. Burnout scales and ordination cohorts

Number of years as a priest	Burnout-Emotional exhaustion	Burnout-Depersonalization	Burnout-Personal accomplishment
0–10			
Mean	16.00	5.14	37.01
n	355	355	355
Standard deviation	9.986	4.535	7.382
11–20			
Mean	16.38	5.05	37.49
n	328	329	329
Standard deviation	10.266	4.923	7.019
21–30			
Mean	15.90	4.64	38.56
n	372	370	371
Standard deviation	9.847	4.873	7.172
31–40			
Mean	14.70	4.21	38.14
n	562	564	563
Standard deviation	9.473	4.252	7.094
41–50			
Mean	11.14	3.29	37.70
n	510	508	508
Standard deviation	8.456	3.554	8.132
More than 50			
Mean	7.31	2.29	36.33
n	332	332	332
Standard deviation	7.181	2.915	9.401
Total			
Mean	13.56	4.07	37.62
N	2459	2458	2458
Standard deviation	9.736	4.308	7.728

5. The values were coded in reverse for ease of viewing the chart, that is, 1=5, 2=4, 4=2, and 5=1, thus Strongly agree=5 and Strongly disagree=1. The highest levels of feeling overwhelmed showed up as the highest point on the chart. Scheffe

post-hoc tests showed those ordained 10–19 years were significantly different than all of the other groups except those ordained 20–29 years.

6. Paul Perl and Bryan T. Froehle, "Priests in the United States: Satisfaction, Work Load, and Support Structures," CARA Working Paper Series No. 5 (Washington, DC: Center for Applied Research in the Apostolate, September 2002), 24.

7. Ibid., 26.

8. National Conference of Catholic Bishops Committee on Priestly Life and Ministry, *The Health of American Catholic Priests: A Report and a Study* (Washington, DC: US Catholic Conference, 1985), 65.

6. Happiness and the Priesthood

1. Condon, "Priests (mostly) Happy."

2. The Conference Board, "US Job Satisfaction at Lowest Level in Two Decades" news release, January 5, 2010.

3. Condon, "Priests (mostly) Happy."

4. Jill Darling Richardson, "Poll Analysis: Priests Say Catholic Church Faces Biggest Crisis of the Century," *Los Angeles Times*, October 20 and 21, 2002.

5. Hoge and Wenger, *Evolving Visions of the Priesthood*, 29.

6. Perl and Froehle, "Priests in the United States," 21.

7. Ibid., 1.

8. Daniel K. Mroczek and Christian M. Kolarz, "The Effect of Age on Positive and Negative Affect: A Developmental Perspective on Happiness," *Journal of Personality and Social Psychology* 75, no. 5 (1998): 1335.

9. Hoge and Wenger, *Evolving Visions of the Priesthood*, 29.

10. Perl and Froehle, "Priests in the United States," 21.

11. Michael N. Kane, "A Qualitative Survey of the Attitudes of Catholic Priests Toward Bishops and Ministry Following the Sexual Abuse Revelations of 2002," *Pastoral Psychology* 57 (2008): 191.

12. William Pavot and Ed Diener, "Review of the Satisfaction with Life Scale," *Psychological Assessment* 5, no. 2 (1993): 164–172.

13. Ibid., 167.

14. Ibid., 166.

15. Ed Diener, "Understanding Scores on the Satisfaction With Life Scale," http://www.psych.illinois.edu/~ediener/Documents/Understanding%20SWLS%20 Scores.pdf.

16. Nestor, "Intimacy and Adjustment Among Catholic Priests," 94.

17. Hoge and Wenger, *Evolving Visions of the Priesthood*, 29.

18. Ibid., 30.

19. Ibid.

20. Jeanna Bryner, "Survey Reveals Most Satisfying Jobs," Live Science, April 17, 2007, http://www.livescience.com/1431-survey-reveals-satisfying-jobs.html.

21. "Americans Hate Their Jobs More Than Ever," Live Science, February 26, 2007, http://www.livescience.com/health/070226_hate_jobs.html.

22. Perl and Froehle, "Priests in the United States," 20.

7. Factors Contributing to Priestly Happiness

1. Perl and Froehle, "Priests in the United States," 37.

2. As we shall see in later chapters, there are significant differences among the different ordination cohorts of priests. Thus, in order to make sure that years ordained was not a confounding variable, I separately ran an *MR* equation and first entered "Years Ordained" to hold for the effects of ordination cohorts. Moreover, since the relationship between happiness and years ordained is actually a U-shaped curve, I squared the variable of years ordained before it was entered. The results of the *MR* equation with this method were virtually identical to the results reported in this chapter. Thus, we have greater confidence that the results reported here are valid and not skewed by ordination cohorts.

3. Robin Lloyd, "The Keys to Happiness, and Why We Don't Use Them," Live Science, February 27, 2006, http://www.livescience.com/health/060227_happiness _keys.html.

4. Pope Paul VI, *Sacerdotalis Caelibatus*, June 24, 1967, http://www.vatican .va/holy_father/paul_vi/encyclicals/documents/hf_p-vi_enc_24061967_sacerdotalis _en.html.

5. *Presbyterorum Ordinis* no. 4, 6, 7, *The Documents of Vatican II*, http://www .vatican.va/archive/hist_councils/ii_vatican_council/documents/vat-ii _decree_19651207_presbyterorum-ordinis_en.html.

6. *Christus Dominus*, no. 16 and *Presbyterorum Ordinis*, no. 7. *Documents of Vatican II*.

7. Carmen Nobel, "Amid Recession, Americans Hate Their Jobs," Mainstreet, January 11, 2010, http://www.mainstreet.com/article/career/employment/ amid-recession-americans-hate-their-jobs.

8. Larry B. Stammer, "Most Priests Say Bishops Mishandled Abuse Issue," *Los Angeles Times*, October 20, 2002.

9. Perl and Froehle, "Priests in the United States," 49.

10. Mark M. Gray and Paul M. Perl, "Catholic Reactions to the News of Sexual Abuse Cases Involving Catholic Clergy," CARA Working Paper Series No. 8, (Washington, DC: Georgetown University, April 2006), 17, http://cara.georgetown.edu/ CARAServices/FRStats/CARA%20WorkingPaper8.pdf./

11. The *y* axis on these charts refers to the responses on the survey. Strongly agree=5; Agree=4; Neutral=3; Disagree=2; Strongly disagree=1. Scheffe post-hoc tests were conducted and the differences between priests ordained 0–40 years and priests ordained 41 years and more were statistically significant ($p<.001$).

12. Perl and Froehle, "Priests in the United States," 55.

13. The *y* axis on these charts refers to the responses on the survey. Strongly agree=5; Agree=4; Neutral=3; Disagree=2; Strongly disagree=1. The Scheffe post-hoc tests show that the difference between the priests ordained 0–30 years and those ordained over 41 years was significant ($p<.001$).

14. Stephen J. Rossetti, *Behold Your Mother: Priests Speak about Mary* (Notre Dame, IN: Ave Maria Press, 2007), 36.

15. Perl and Froehle, "Priests in the United States," 40, 43, 55.

8. Those Thinking of Leaving the Priesthood

1. Hoge and Wenger, *Evolving Visions of Priesthood*, 40.

2. Susan Pinkus, "Poll Analysis: Priests Satisfied with Their Lives," *Los Angeles Times*, October 21, 2002.

3. The *y* axis on these charts refers to the responses on the survey. Strongly agree=5; Agree=4; Neutral=3; Disagree=2; Strongly disagree=1. Scheffe post-hoc tests showed significant differences at the .05 level between those ordained 11–20 years and those ordained more than 30 years.

4. Dean R. Hoge, *The First Five Years of Priesthood* (Collegeville, MN: The Liturgical Press, 2002), 64.

5. Ibid., 33.

9. The Spiritual Lives of Priests

1. John L. Allen Jr., *The Future Church: How Ten Trends Are Revolutionizing the Catholic Church* (New York: Doubleday, 2009), 255.

2. Hans Urs von Balthasar, "Mary in the Church's Doctrine and Devotion," in *Mary: The Church as the Source*, trans. Adrian Walker (San Francisco: Ignatius Press, 1997), 117.

3. "Annual Retreat" correlated significantly with "Relationship to God" ($r=.12$) but was not entered into the *MR* equation by the statistical routine because of its high relationship with variables already in the regression model preventing it from adding significantly to the prediction. However, its importance for one's spiritual life should not be overlooked.

10. Priests and Prayer

1. Scheffe post-hoc tests showed significant differences between the groups that prayed the least each day and those that prayed the most.

11. Young Priests, Old Priests, and Those in the Middle

1. Sample sizes are as follows: for the 2004 survey: ordained 1–9 years=201; 10–19=216; 20–29=264; 30–39=282; 40–49=200; 50 years and above=78; missing data=1 for a total sample of n=1242. For the 2009 survey: ordained 0–10 years=356; 11–20=330; 21–30=372; 31–40=565; 41–50=511; over 50=334; missing data=14 for a total sample of n=2482.

2. Hoge and Wenger, *Evolving Visions of the Priesthood*, 69.

3. Ibid.

4. Ibid., 78.

5. Ibid., 59.

6. Ibid., 113.

7. In figures 11.2 and 11.3, the composite variables on the y axis are measured simply by adding the responses of all the individual items that make up the composite variable. Strongly disagree=1; Disagree=2; Neutral=3; Agree=4; Strongly agree=5. Items were coded in reverse if the wording of the item (its valence) was opposite that of other items in the scale.

8. Scheffe post-hoc tests showed those ordained 31–40 years having a statistically significant difference from all groups except those ordained 21–30 years for both variables, Devotion to Mary and Prayer and the Sacrament of Penance.

9. Allen, *The Future Church*, 56.

10. Scheffe post-hoc tests showing statistically significant differences between the newly ordained and those ordained 20–29 years, and between the newly ordained and those ordained 30–39 years.

11. These are 2004 survey statistics and thus many of the group ordained 20–29 years in 2004 would fall into the group ordained 31–40 years in the 2009 survey.

12. "Americans, Catholics React to Reports of Child Abuse by Priests" poll, CBS News/*New York Times*, May 4, 2010, http://www.cbsnews.com/htdocs/pdf/poll_catholics_050310.pdf.

13. Ibid.

14. Hoge and Wenger, *Evolving Visions of the Priesthood*, 40.

15. In this graph, the y axis is scored as follows: Strongly agree=5; Agree=4; Unsure=3; Disagree=2; Strongly disagree=1.

Appendix 3: 2009 Survey Composite Variables

1. The Spearman-Brown formula is K x Cronbach's alpha/(1 + [(K-1) x Cronbach's alpha]) where K=40/(number of items in the scale).

M sgr. Stephen J. Rossetti, a priest of the Diocese of Syracuse, served for many years at Saint Luke Institute in Silver Spring, Maryland, where he became president and CEO. He is a licensed psychologist with a doctorate in psychology from Boston College and a doctor of ministry from the Catholic University of America. He is the author of scores of articles and several books, including *Born of the Eucharist, The Joy of Priesthood*—recipient of a Catholic Press Association book award—and *When the Lion Roars*, and he is editor of *Behold Your Mother.*

Rossetti has received a Proclaim Award from the United States Conference of Catholic Bishops as well as a Lifetime Service Award from the Theological College of the Catholic University of America. In 2010, he received the Touchstone Award from the National Federation of Priests' Councils for a lifetime of work with priests. He lectures to priests and religious internationally on priestly spirituality and wellness issues and serves as clinical associate professor of pastoral studies at the Catholic University of America.